Paddle

A LONG WAY AROUND IRELAND

Jasper w~ 2011

Sort Of
BOOKS

Paddle

A LONG WAY AROUND IRELAND

JASPER WINN

PADDLE by JASPER WINN

Published in 2011 by
Sort Of Books
PO Box 18678, London NW3 2FL
www.sortof.co.uk

Distributed by
Profile Books
3a Exmouth House, Pine Street,
London EC1R OJH
in all territories excluding the United States and Canada

10 9 8 7 6 5 4 3 2

Typeset in Iowan Old Style (10/14) to a design by Henry Iles

Printed in the UK by Clays Ltd, St Ives plc
on Forest Stewardship Council (mixed sources) certified paper.
336pp

A catalogue record for this book is available from the British
Library.
ISBN 978-0-95600-388-1

To my father – closer than we knew

Contents

Part Three

Part One

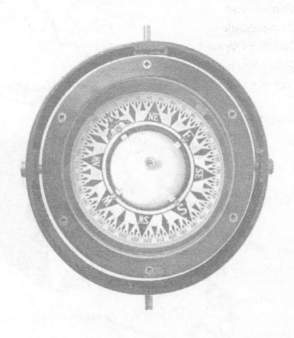

CHAPTER ONE

A Gut Feeling

THE GREY, SWILLING WAVES that I'm paddling through are, what? – a foot high? – two feet? – six feet? Or, maybe, they're just uppity ripples and better measured in inches? Even here, right in amongst the waves, I realise that I don't really have a clue as to how big they are – and abstracts like feet and inches and miles per hour, and their metric equivalents, and even the more nautical fathoms, knots and Beaufort speeds, are not much help in getting a grip on confusions of water and air.

Wet stuff, especially when it's moving around and being frothed up by a stiff breeze, as it very nearly always is in Irish seas, can feel very big. And many times it is. Other times, you take a look and think it's on the benign side, not worth taking seriously, and discover too late how wrong you are. Like jostling a small, mild-looking guy at a bar by mistake, and finding him full of close-wound anger and quick with his balled-up fists. Then – at a bar or at sea – there's the shock of sudden blows and struggling and being thrown round and fighting back and coming out the far end with heart racing, wondering how you could have missed all the signs, and how lucky not to have got badly hurt.

Right now – day one of my kayak trip around Ireland – the waves are looking and feeling, well, quite big. And the sky doesn't look so great, either. Everything I see in an arc southwards from the west back to the east is either sea or sky. Even the coast far to the north is no more than a thin, dark haze squeezed between more water and air. Everything in my long vision is monochrome grey. Close up there are splashes of bright, plasticky yellow, blue, orange and scarlet; the kayak, my buoyancy aid, the sleeves of my cagoule and the paddle blades.

And if I don't have the measure of the waves, then I have even less idea of the size of the smooth Atlantic rollers rising under the kayak and lifting it slowly up and up and then slowly dropping it again. The waves are sharp little peaks knocked up by the local winds here and now. But the swell is a powerful heaving. A storm shadow rippling across the ocean from some long-past hurricane off the coast of the Americas that pushed millions of tonnes of water up into towering hills and then left their subsiding energy to oscillate through subsequent days and across thousands of miles. And as it travelled, the swell has picked up the earth's own resonance from its out-of-kilter orbiting, and from the pull of the moon. Here, in the Celtic Sea, just off the coast of West Cork, where the sea bed is shallowing from thousands of feet to a few hundred, the rollers are running out of depth and so lifting even higher to corrugate the surface of the zinc-coloured ocean. Inshore, against the dark suggestion of the cliffs, I can see them running aground, but under me the rollers are silent. There is only the odd sharp splash sound as wave peaks of similar bulk and height smack into each other. Or into the kayak. It's all just so much more stuff that I can't measure.

The wind, though? Well now, that's definitely blowing a force three. Unless, those are real white-caps and not just scummy foam streaks coming off the tops of the waves (the waves that I don't know the height of), then it's somewhere around a four, maybe gusting five. Of course, if only I was closer to the land – which would be about two miles distant, I suppose – then I could do some Beaufort Scale checks to see if the leaves are barely shivering on the trees, or smoke is being whisked sideways from chimneys, or escaped hats are bowling down streets.

I keep paddling. The kayak stretches fore and aft of me, so it's like sitting up in a yellow coffin. The feel of its hard plastic under my arse, as well as the heft of the paddle loom as I dig the blades in one side after another, are the only solids amongst these shifting, immeasurable elements.

I'm still trying to make sense of my surroundings. Most of the waves muscling in on me look, I now decide, about the height of a coffee table. The bigger ones, every now and again breaking over the bow, are pitched about the height of a kitchen table, while occasionally one rises as high as a fairly substantial breakfast counter. The swells, meantime,

I chart at the height of plump sofas, with their white surf flapping over the heavy waters like linen loose-covers.

Calibrating the seas in terms of furniture and upholstery helps them seem familiar. It makes the waters seem domestic and indoorsy, like paddling through an IKEA catalogue, rather than the threatening reality of cold and wet. I'm wrong about this, of course, but reassuringly wrong. Kayaking amongst these furniture-sized blocks of water I picture myself as a drunk making his way across a large room booby-trapped with dancing armchairs, scuttling three-piece suites, wobbly occasional tables, scattered bolsters and ruckled carpets. I'm likely to fall at any moment but, with a drunk's confidence, I'm pretty sure I can make it from, say, the door to the drinks cabinet with no more than the odd lurch. In terms of what I'm doing now that means paddling from the Stags Rocks, which I'm just passing to seaward, and then onwards some twelve miles further west to reach Roaringwater Bay – around which there are, appropriately enough, a number of drinks cabinets, so to speak. MacCarthy's. Bushes. The Jolly Roger. Caseys. The Algiers Inn.

Hello! He-llo! How are you? Lovely day, isn't it? A bull grey seal is flopped out on a narrow ledge on the Stags Rocks, high above the splash of waves. He raises himself into a 'U' shape, his head peering down at me, the furled bunching of his tail flippers twitching skywards.

Don't mind me. Just passing through. No, no, no, don't get up, please, please, don't bother, really ... I greet him politely, aloud, glad of the company, feeling a little less alone to find him so at home out here, a couple of miles offshore.

The seal, exuding bad temper and bad breath, gets up anyway and undulates heavily across and down the sharp blades of rock, putting me in mind of a plump slug. He

4

tumbles into the water with a surprisingly light splash and disappears. His head pushes up through the waves beyond the rim of rocks, stiff whiskers bristling. He gives me an irritated look. I provide him with a gruff, disgruntled deep baritone voice to answer me in.

Sod off, you yellow weirdo ... I'll come over and tear your nasty pointy little head off and stuff your stupid red flippers up your arse.

Barely into the trip and I've started talking to seals. As a seal. Talking to myself, in other words – and not in my own voice. Nor uttering what I would have thought of as my own sentiments, either.

●━━━━●

It is early June and I've set off to kayak the whole way around Ireland. Ahead lie a thousand miles of these furniture-sized seas. A month and a half of paddling, perhaps. Two months? Or, depending on the weather, maybe even longer. A lot of talking to myself, anyway.

Ireland is only the world's twentieth biggest island. Far smaller than Greenland, New Guinea, Borneo or Madagascar; smaller by half than the mainland of Britain. But twentieth place is still a fair ranking. Ireland is many times bigger than any of the Mediterranean islands – Crete, Cyprus, Malta, Sicily, Corsica – or even the two-country, Caribbean bulk of Hispaniola. Bigger, too, than Sri Lanka, which is roomy enough to accommodate herds of wild elephants.

Which means that kayaking around it, on your own, is a serious undertaking. So serious, in fact, that nobody had thought to do so until Tim Daly paddled himself into the record books in 1979. And, since then, you can count the solo kayakers on your fingers. Most people with any sense go in teams. Not that sense is always foremost in this particular pursuit. Take Sean Morley, who decided that his route must go outside all of the inhabited offshore islands of Ireland – meaning he had to loop out around Tory, Rathlin, Lambay and all the Arans, as well as Inishvickillane, the last inhabited of the Blaskets. Or Tetsuya Nogawa from Japan, who not only spoke no English when he arrived in Ireland in 2000 but navigated the coastline using a road map.

All of which, I reflect, is encouraging. But on the other hand ... one doesn't know so much about those paddlers who set off to 'go round Ireland' and then give up. Those kayakers whose frail hull of dreamy optimism crashes into a sharp, pointy rock of realism when faced with the cold and the wet and relentless grinding. I sense that I'm thinking about giving up a little too much for comfort on day one. That I have some gut feeling I'm not going to make it. That it would take just one too-big wave, or even the sobering realisation of just how vast the sea is, to send me pulling for shore and walking away from the whole daft idea.

And the reason I am thinking this is that I have already failed to kayak around Ireland. Failed rather miserably.

It had been a year ago, to the week, that the two of us – myself and my partner Elisabeth – had set off, paddling out to sea from the very same bay that I had left just a few hours ago. And I had been in the same kayak then that I'm in now – a plastic Necky Narpa. Mine was coloured the dull, glazed yellow of a burger-bar mustard dispenser; Elisabeth's a matching red, like ketchup. A pair of recycled, squeezy condiment bottles, bobbing companionably along.

Back then we'd trained together for the trip, paddling out almost daily in wind, rain and frost through the early months of the year. We'd practised all of the safety manoeuvres – 'T' and 'X' rescues, rafting-up, wet entries, towing, assisted rolls – that we might use to save each other. Skills depending on two people paddling together that mean little now that I'm solo. We'd bought a VHF radio and flares, and a tent and a complicated petrol stove. Elisabeth had referred to the camping part of the trip as 'cam-ping,' pronouncing it with a gleefully emphatic note as if we were off to a summer-long Mardi Gras festival on a tropical beach.

Neither of us had huge kayak experience but, given luck with the winds and weather, I felt we had every chance of getting a fair distance around the south and up the west coasts. And maybe, if the weather was exceptionally good, a reasonable hope of making it right around Ireland. But getting around wasn't that important, we'd told each other. It was to be a fun trip. Elisabeth had declared that we'd stop if it became clear we'd overestimated our abilities or underestimated the risks, or if there was unremitting rain and winds, or the trip became miserable. I had gone along with this manifesto, though deep down I'd made other vows. That if Elisabeth wanted to stop, then I'd keep going alone – whatever the risks, however awful the weather.

I didn't mention this to Elisabeth because it was 'our' trip we were embarking on. But I should have been more honest. I should have owned up that, for close on three decades, the idea of kayaking around Ireland had been a touchstone for me, its plans blueprinted and rehearsed in my imagination many, many times, and new details added whenever I found myself looking out from a cliff path over an unfamiliar bay. It was a reverie to return to whenever I was landlocked or urbanised or had spent too long abroad. Because beyond any physical adventure it had become an idea of calibrating my 'Irishness', testing if this country where I'd been raised by English parents – albeit with a dash of Irish ancestry – was indeed my home. Just like the sea's swell and its waves, I had been born in one place and brought up in another – and at times the passage had seemed a choppy one. But here was a chance to both explore and bind myself to my adoptive country. And it wasn't a chance I was going to lightly abandon.

●——●

Elizabeth knew a lot of this, of course, but not the extent of my determination to continue, come what may. Which in retrospect was fortunate. For it was entirely down to me that our circumnavigation came to an end only four days after we had started.

The trip had started with much promise. For the first two days, the weather was fine and we made good progress, camping out on remote beaches with bottles of wine and ambitious meals and laughter, finding ourselves oddly at ease with the swells and seas. Then, pinned down on shore for a couple of nights, whilst we waited for high winds to drop so we could round the Mizen Head, I woke at midnight with an odd feeling in my gut. By dawn I was in sweat-popping agony. Mid-morning I was in hospital, unconscious, with a sign reading 'NIL BY MOUTH' over my bed-head and a nexus of tubes and pipes, catheters and IVs running into and out of different parts of my body.

The diagnosis was gallstones. I must have had them for years, it seemed, and ignored the symptoms whilst they were merely uncomfortable. But then the gall gravel had shaken loose and turned my bile ducts and pancreas and other bits of internal plumbing into a dangerously infected tangle. That sounds oddly routine and could have been so, but there was a problem when the first-line antibiotics failed to work. A rather more serious problem when the second-line antibiotics didn't perform, either.

The doctor was chatty but not reassuring: 'To be honest, your stones are a bit worse than we'd like to see. There's quite a problem in the way they've inflamed everything around them, and because they're not responding to the drugs, well, actually that's not so good ... But don't worry; we will find an antibiotic that works and then that'll ease things. The pain is pretty bad, right now, though, is it?'

I nodded despairingly. I couldn't speak.

'Haven't had gallstones myself, I'm glad to say. In medical school we were told it was like a combination of childbirth and a heart attack, which sounds bad enough already ... and you've a few complications on top of that.'

I fell in and out of consciousness. Joint-locking rigours convulsed my body, leaving me shivering and juddering; then came wild temperature swings, where first the sweat ran from my skin in a steady, continuous hot flow, then I would feel frozen ice granules within my flesh. And there was fear, too. Fear of not living for much longer. Or, worse, feeling like I wasn't going to live for much longer, but actually living for far longer than I could bear.

When I did drift back into lucidity, it was invariably far into the night, jolting awake alone and even more fearful. My co-patients were all elderly men, laid low by falls, or failed plumbing or senility. They filled the gloom with a sound-collage of coughs, farts, mumbles and sighs. I had the life-sapping feeling of being on an interminable intercontinental flight, going the wrong way across time zones to a destination I didn't want to arrive at.

After two weeks I left the hospital – no longer a round-Ireland kayaker but an invalid, bent and frail, barely able to walk a hundred yards even with a stick, nor to hold a thought steady in my mind for more than a few minutes. It was as if I'd caught chronic elderliness from the men in my ward. And hanging over it all was that, while a final course of drip-feed antibiotics had pulled me off the danger list, I still needed an operation to have the gall-sac removed.

The waiting list was long, throwing me into six months' of limbo, advised never to be more than a few hours from a good hospital. I started on walks across the hills that grew longer until I'd walked myself back to some kind of fitness. Then a few hours in an operating theatre undid it all. It was spring before I was pronounced fit by the surgeon. Though, fit for what? Not for kayaking round Ireland, that was for sure. I hadn't even played a part in retrieving our kayaks, which for weeks lay abandoned in a field on the Mizen Head, before Elisabeth had them brought back to our starting point on the quay in Castletownshend.

And yet I couldn't shake off the idea of the trip. It began to take shape again as a kind of rebirth, after the days of fear. And as the spring edged towards summer, my misguided, silent manifesto from the year before – to keep going alone if necessary, whatever the risks, however awful the weather – still had to be made good. Only, this time, there wasn't much of a choice about the going-alone part. Elisabeth and I were no longer together, so I would be going solo.

CHAPTER TWO

Out of My Depth

T HERE'S A GOOD REASON why most round-Ireland kayakists paddle in teams, or at least pairs. It means that if they capsize they have a decent chance of getting helped back into their kayak, and if in trouble they can raft-up to rest or be towed to safe haven. Solo paddlers, by contrast, are entirely reliant on their own skill, decision-making and courage. Kayaking out at sea, unaccompanied, in poor conditions, is quite a risk.

As noted, I have quite a few other things against me as I launch again in mid-June from Castletownshend, chief among which is a lack of fitness and training. It seems hard to credit the lunacy, but this new attempt to paddle solo around Ireland is actually the *first time* I've been out at sea in a kayak since I went into hospital, almost a year ago. Not only am I unfit, but whatever kayaking ability I had is forgotten and unpractised.

Perhaps equally serious, I don't know an awful lot about sea kayaking. The longest I've been at sea with a kayak previously is a week in Croatia. But that was on day jaunts in the Med – in summer and with friends. Ireland is a harsher assignment with its untrustworthy seas.

My other kayak trips have all basically avoided the sea. The toughest was a trip down at the very southern tip of Patagonia, a trip that took us along freezing rivers and lakes to reach the shattering of icebergs that had fallen from the snout of the Serrano glacier. With the cold, and the danger from the shifting bulks of ice, that had been mildly danger-ous. But I'd been with people who knew what to do – and we stopped when we reached the sea, after floating around for an hour or two amid the cool toothpaste blues.

The other big trips were in a much more distant past. As a teenager, I spent a summer paddling out of Dublin in a fibreglass kayak along a flow chart of canals and rivers that carried me across the country, through the south of England and down the length of France. I had become hooked on kayaking, thinking of myself as a paddle-propelled Kerouac-esque beat-hobo, searching for sartori by going 'On the River'. However, my silences stemmed less from Zen wisdom than from very bad French, and – more pertinent to this trip – when it came to crossing the Irish Sea and the Channel, I had taken ferries.

Then, several years after that – so in the mid-1980s, before the tumbling down of the Berlin Wall – I had propelled, with two friends, a couple of Pouch *Faltboots*, bought from a department store in Ulm, down the two thousand kilometres length of the Danube, from its Black Forest source to its Black Sea delta. Our naïve conceit was that we were on international waters and that we had the right of free passage, but this didn't stop a Romanian soldier in olive-drab pyjama-like uniform from screaming at us to stop, and then firing shots in front of our bows as we kept padding, hurriedly, towards the Bulgarian shore. That trip taught me a lot about absurd politics, state police, the general goodness of human nature and surviving home-distilled spirits. But again there was no sea involved – apart from arriving at one, then stopping.

I comfort myself with thoughts of a man called Paul Caffyn, who paddled nine and a half thousand miles around Australia. Alone. I've only got a ninth of that distance to cover. Which I decide means that I only need to be one ninth as fit, one ninth as dogged, one ninth as skilful and only about ten times as lucky.

I do, though, rather wish that I had nine times less kit to load into the kayak. Whilst preparing equipment, there had been so many items on so many lists that at one point I'd made a list of the lists to keep track of them, which I headed *Listing Heavily to Port*. It became the frontispiece of a sheaf of papers itemising kayaking gear, safety tackle, clothing, food, camping paraphernalia, cooking utensils, cameras and numerous amusements. I realised the folly of it earlier this morning, trying to pack a car-sized load into a kayak. Eager to leave, I'd started unloading kit at the high-water mark. The water fell further and further down the beach, like an hourglass, and still I couldn't get all the stuff into the hold.

The problem was that I hadn't properly allowed myself to decide if I was off on an expedition or going on a jaunt, just seeing how things went. Whether I was a competent Ernest Shackleton figure victualling himself for months of deprivation, or a Jerome K. Jerome type who only needed a dog and a banjo to be happy?

A give-away that I had lost sense and perspective lay in the list I'd made for books, which was headed 'Ship's library'. The 'library' had a large waterproof bag to itself that bulged with Melville's *Moby Dick*, Celtic nature poetry, field guides to flowers, birds, weather and stars, an Irish dictionary and *The Oxford History of Ireland*, as well as a block of novels swept up from second-hand shelves as a defence against the boredom of being pinned down in my tent.

And books weren't the half of it. I had spent the previous months dreaming up situations that could only be resolved by, for example, a bunch of cable-ties, a sheet of waterproof nylon, a thick-nibbed permanent marker and a jar of Vaseline. And then, as if they were essential talismans for success, or at least a substitute for my lack of real seamanship, I'd felt compelled to go out and buy exactly those things. And many, many other things as well.

In the most unlikely of shops – a chemist, a garden centre, a garage – I'd seen supplies and items that I needed: Norwegian fisherman's hand unguent; a sea-fishing line with spare feathered hooks; a folding corkscrew; a length of one-inch hose; twelve slim notebooks with charcoal-grey covers and rich cream-coloured pages; waterproof binoculars; a digital Dictaphone; three tin-whistles in the key of D, C and a particularly shrill one in F; a blue-and-white-striped woollen hat for cold weather; a kepi-style cap for sunny weather; a pack of different length bungee cords. Oh, and an underwater housing for my camera that would protect it to forty metres of depth and therefore far past the point at which I would already have drowned.

In an actual specialist sea-kayak centre, and in a ships' chandlers, I'd filled counters with more legitimate purchases: flares; Imray charts; waterproof tape; a paddle-float; roll-top waterproof bags; a map case; a deck compass, a long-john wetsuit; and lengths of rope in different diameters. Then there was the 'Wardrobe List'. Warm clothes in case it was cold. Dry ones in case it was wet. Cool ones in the hope that it was going to be a long, hot summer. And into the same bag I stuffed shirts and trousers that would allow me to go ashore disguised as someone who wasn't paddling around Ireland.

Standing on the beach this first morning of the trip – Friday 9th June – forcing stuff into the holds of my canoe, I curse all this folly. If I don't launch soon, I will miss the favourable tide running westwards to Baltimore and will be struggling against the current. As with pretty much everything else to do with the trip, I decide things will sort themselves out once I got going. So I fix the two left-over bags onto the decks, fore and aft of the cockpit, rather pleased that the impulse buy of bungee cords has been justified so early on. I pull on my paddling clothes, bundle my shore clothing into a bag behind the seat, and inch by inch drag the hugely heavy kayak down to the water's edge.

I know this first stretch of coast pretty well. I paddle down Castlehaven Bay from the spit of gravel at Reen, past the village of Castletownshend, where Elisabeth and I had lived together for nearly a year, and where – almost exactly twelve months ago – we left from to kayak around Ireland ... or, as it turned out, just a bit up the coast.

Other boats are on the water already: the two small potting boats that fish out of the bay, a couple of yachts and, swinging from a buoy, an *Ette* – one of a local class of small, Edwardian sailing boats. In the summer there is still an Edwardian air to the big houses and holiday homes filled with families who have been coming here for years, and in some cases generations. This is where Somerville and Ross lived and wrote the *Adventures of an Irish RM* books, about the bemused English and shouty, tweedy Anglo-Irish aristos, and the moral virtues of having a good seat over jumps. Edith Somerville proclaimed: 'I would put in a plea that the parish of Castlehaven may be kept as a national reserve for idlers and artists and idealists.' She and her sisters had done their best to that end, combining a penchant for lounging around on the seashore in the nude with a practical interest in the new art of photography.

Leaving for the second time in a kayak, I feel some claim of my own to idealist and idler, but try to focus on the task ahead and think myself into nautical mode. So at the end of the bay, I say to myself, I'll turn starboard, along a heading running roughly south-west-west, on an initial course of around 235°. Coming out into the open sea, looking back over my left shoulder I can see Skiddy Island behind me and, beyond it, the bulking of High and Low Islands, and, very far to the east, Galley Head. It seems impossibly optimistic to believe that, if I just keep Ireland on my right – er, starboard – and paddle a lot, that in several weeks' time I will come upon the Galley, and then High and Low and finally Skiddy again on the home strait. Actually, it feels more like an article of faith, like being a medieval navigator trusting that the world is really round and that I won't paddle off the edge into the unknown.

If there is an unknown edge, though, it is a long way from here. An hour after paddling out from Reen, I am still in familiar waters. On this stretch of coast, I'd sat afloat and motionless watching an otter playing in the waves on an early March morning when I'd had to knock frost crystals off the kayak's hull before my dawn launch. Here, from right under where I'm paddling now, I'd pulled up tens of mackerel one summer evening whilst floating on a glass-flat, gold-flecked sea. Some of them, I muse, are still in Elisabeth's deep-freeze, neatly gutted and bagged.

Paddling between Flea and Horse islands, I spy two kayaks pulled up on the shingle of Horse and next to them a pair of naked pink bodies lying out in the weak sun like hermit crabs out of their shells. The pairs of bodies and kayaks give me a pang of loneliness. Several miles ahead, far offshore beyond the high cliffs of Scullane Point, off Toe Head, I catch sight of the Stags Rocks, a wall and towers of crenellated rock rising up from the rough waters. The wind comes and goes, chill in the gusts, warm in the calms, when I smell the sun-heated nylon of my new cagoule.

Halfway across Scullane Bay, just here where I am now, Elisabeth and I had been kayaking back late one afternoon on one of our practice runs. As we paddled abreast, I'd been shocked to see an enormous, smooth black rounded hump suddenly roll up from the water only a few metres beyond her kayak. A minke whale spun slowly through the water as if the revolving rim of a tyre of some monstrous undersea vehicle, rising and rising till as high as her head.

The memory of the whale's size and how it dropped back under the sea emphasises how precariously I'm balanced atop an element that is not welcoming. The enormity of the trip is beginning to sink in, just as the enormity of what lies below nags at my mind. The conditions, the waves, the wind right now are not bad at all; for many sea-kayakers, anyone who actually knew what they were doing, this would be a lovely day for a paddle-stroll. But I feel oddly out of my depth and all at sea, and only one or two other metaphors away from Shit Creek.

It takes nearly two hours of paddling to get past the Stags – where I conversed with the seal. A further hour and I'm further offshore in a kayak, alone, than I've ever been before. The distant coast is too far away to see any detail finer than cliffs, hills or possibly woods. It's much, much further than I could hope to swim if things go wrong.

I'm far out to sea because, counter-intuitively, following the shortest route around Ireland's circumference means being away from the land for long periods. If even the idea of a 'shortest route' sounds puzzling in the context of circling something, then have a squint at a map of Ireland. The country looks, arguably, like a very shaggy teddy bear sitting somewhat awkwardly with his limbs thrust out into the Atlantic, and head twisted round to look over his shoulder towards Scotland. To the west and north, the bear's shag-furred arms, legs, toes and fingers, as well as ears, chin and nose, form deep bights, long peninsulas, prominent forelands and all kinds of other geographic innings and outings and, thus, distance. By contrast, his back and arse, to the east and south-east, are almost smooth.

If I was to follow every contour of the coastline – paddling into each cove, up to the mouth of all the rivers and along both shores of inlet after inlet and promontory after promontory – then I'd end up covering the 'official'

Irish coastline length of around 3,500 miles. But that's an abstract figure based on a sensible scale interval. Increase the fineness of the measurement, so it follows all the twists of the shoreline. and you could end up with a distance three times that amount. Paddlers, like me, who want to round Ireland's coastline in less than a year, bring the distance down to the achievable thousand-mile mark by cutting across from headland to headland, across the mouths of coves, and between the tips of peninsulas.

So going around Ireland means, in fact, avoiding Ireland as much as possible. A lot of the trip is going to be spent a couple or five or maybe ten miles out at sea. What I'm experiencing along the coast of West Cork on my first afternoon of kayaking around Ireland – the immensity, the all-aroundness of the sea that I'm 'walking' across paddle stroke by paddle stroke – is going to be much of my world for the coming summer.

I've another nine hundred and ninety-four miles to go.

For a remote corner of Europe, the Celtic Sea has seen an astonishing number of wrecks. I've already passed over the corpse of the 300-metres-long *Kowloon Bridge*, an ore-carrier sunk in a storm in 1986, when it ran onto the Stags to become one of the world's biggest wrecks. Off the tip of Sheep's Head lies the shattered body of the Air India plane *Kanishka*, a 747 blown up the summer before that by Sikh separatists, killing all 329 people aboard.

There is a scuttled U-boat, too, which must be some-where close by – a hundred and fifty feet or so below me. I know about it because my father was fascinated by salvage.

Many of the machines he invented were designed for working undersea: an unmanned submarine like a submerged flying saucer, and a six-wheeled, remote-controlled underwater vehicle with an arm like a crane that could roll along the sea bed. There had been talk about using these to explore the wrecks littering the coast hereabouts.

These submersibles never got beyond a prototype, but there were other of my father's machines that did make it to production. One promising 'robot' worked underwater and could clean the hulls of even the biggest ocean-going ships within a few hours, saving shipping companies the cost of dry-docking their fleets. This and other inventions made him money. But the family economy was boom and bust; everything he made was reinvested into the research and development of more robotics and remote-controlled vehicles. In times of plenty my father bought old machinery; an ever-growing collection of rusted steamships, unwanted cinema organs, ancient cars and beautiful wood and canvas twin-engine planes from the 1940s.

It was during a prolonged bust period, in the bad weather of winter, when he took off to fly one of these *Miles Gemini* planes to a friend's airfield, only a few miles away, where he could hangar it and restore it to full air-worthiness. News of the crash reached me where I was staying in a cottage in the Black Forest. I was twenty-three. There was just enough time to return to his funeral in rural West Cork.

I'm feeling hungry. And tired. And, truth be told, bored. The waves are beginning to look very similar to each other. I've already eaten the two biscuits and an apple that I'd tucked under the deck netting in front of the cockpit. It'll take another hour or so of repetitive paddle strokes to reach the Kedges and then another half an hour to get right inside Roaringwater Bay.

A realisation of just how much time I'm going to spend shovelling water behind me, in doing the equivalent of hundreds of sit-ups and twist crunches every hour if I want to get round Ireland, begins to sink in. Bloody miles ... and miles ... and miles. If I take, what, roughly ... let's see, fifty strokes a minute, then that's fifty by sixty, um ... hang fire ... five sixes, uh, thirty, plus a couple of noughts, so that's ... three ... three thousand odd strokes an hour, and I'm doing, somewhere around four miles an hour ... say four, no, let's say three miles an hour with breaks and stuff ... so that's a thousand strokes a mile – nice round figure, very handy – which over a thousand miles is ... uh, yuh, a thousand thousand, um, so one and six noughts which is six, no, hang on, one, it's ... what ...? A million ... a MILLION strokes?

My mind is working on several different levels now. Most of my conscious brain is doing the mental arithmetic and talking out loud to itself. But I'm also thinking about, or at least conscious of, the feel of paddling and the balance of the kayak under me and adjusting my weight as I cross the uneven patterning of waves. And, somewhere deep down, the earlier thoughts of wrecks and sunk shipping and the downed plane have released dark imaginings of the many silent drowned who lie below. I have tensed up, maybe with a fear of drowning, maybe from keeping the fives and sixes and noughts ordered in my mind.

There's a sudden, enormous, crashing splash just behind my shoulder, right next to the kayak, spraying me with water. I'll never know what has surfaced so close, and what, in a panic, has immediately thrown its weight back down into the depths. A seal? A fish? A porpoise? Another minke whale? But the shock, my own moment of panic, makes me jump and throw myself to one side in the kayak. The kayak begins to roll out from under me. Off-centred, I'm like a cyclist sliding sideways on loose gravel, canted over at an impossible angle, only nanoseconds from falling, and slapping down on the road. Except out here I will first fall onto the surface of the water and then I'll fall right through it, to hang upside down gasping for breath, cold seas rushing in under my clothing.

The worst scenario for a solitary sea-kayaker is to capsize in open water in big seas far from land and to then come out of the kayak. This is easy to do. It's what I'm about to do. What I'm actually doing. Once out in the water amongst waves, the chance of re-entering the craft will be low, and then hypothermia leading to drowning becomes a distinct possibility.

So, paramount amongst sea-kayaking skills is the Eskimo roll – righting a capsized kayak from upside down by using a paddle stroke from under the water to pop oneself upright again. The waterproof, neoprene spray-skirt that stretches tight across the space between the paddler's waist and the rim of the cockpit will keep the water from flooding the kayak, so a successful roll means no more than a few seconds swirling around beneath the surface, coming right way up again with a wet head and then continuing paddling.

I've practised rolling in the past. But that's all it was: practice. I'd take a deep breath, and purposefully flip the kayak over, so there was no surprise in finding myself upside down. Easy, then, to push the paddle up to the surface and bend forward and get the blade flat on the water, and then give a big, twisting heave as I uncoiled my body backwards, levering myself off the surface whilst hip-flicking the kayak round, and rotating myself upright again. And if it went wrong and the roll failed and I had to come out of the cockpit in a 'wet exit', well, being a practice meant that I was in a few feet of water, only a short swim from the shore.

A wet exit out here, where the water is hundreds of feet deep under me, and the shore is miles away, would be very bad indeed. Of course I might be able to climb back into the kayak using the paddle float – it's somewhere on the back deck tangled up with all the other crap I tied on at the last minute. But it's unlikely. There is, realistically, only a limited chance that my VHF radio will be able to transmit a signal from water level amongst these rising seas. My flares may or may not be seen.

Once I'm out of the kayak I will be cold and wet. I'm not wearing my wetsuit; that too is stuffed in the forward bag, with the flares, for use in 'bad' weather. Today is meant to be an easy paddle, through known waters, in good weather. In shorts and fleece and jacket I've been warm whilst paddling, but once in the June sea, bare-legged and waterlogged, my body temperature is going to fall quickly. I may have twenty minutes, perhaps half an hour, when I can still function mentally and physically. Twenty minutes with fingers losing feeling, in which time I'll have to get the paddle float out, fix it onto the paddle and then lock everything together so I can try and climb back in. I've done this before, but that was a practice exercise, too. I've been stupid in many ways today. If I go over, there's every chance that all of the day's small stupidities are going to get rolled together into one big ball of colossal idiocy.

Solo paddlers talk about a 'bombproof' Eskimo roll as their primary safety skill: the 'guaranteed' ability to swing oneself back to the surface, upright and ready to keep paddling, within seconds of a capsize, no matter how strong the winds or how chaotic the waves. A 'bombproof' roll is what separates the capable kayaker from a floating fool.

Now it seems that I'm about to test the coefficient of my idiocy. I make a last desperate hip-flick, trying to jack-knife my body sideways to pull the kayak back under me again before it goes fully over. It's a desperate, last-ditch move. But I'm saved by a wave that drops away, from under the kayak at just the right moment, so that as it falls it spins back towards the upright. I've got the paddle blade free of the water, too, and I slap it down flat on the surface to push myself fully upright. I catch my balance. I might be an idiot, but I am an idiot afloat. Pure luck.

I sit in the cockpit, heart thumping, looking around at a world that is still mostly air and the right way up, and not all water and upside down as I'd expected. *HA! WOAAAAAH! Oh, ho-ho-ho! huh, huh! Oh, man, that was close. Shiiiii-yt. CLOSE! Too close. Close, close, close.*

Deep down I know I don't have a bombproof roll. Maybe, on a good day, a 'firecrackerproof roll'. Today might have been a good day. Maybe not.

CHAPTER THREE

A Landfall a Day

ONE OF THE SIMPLEST DEFINITIONS of successful sea-kayaking – of all seafaring, if you think about it – lies in the knack of making exactly one landfall for each time you head out to sea. Get that simple binary pairing right and there's the happy proof that one hasn't slipped beneath the waves or otherwise been lost offshore somewhere. Dying on land rather than drowning at sea is a mark of a lucky sailor, I'd have thought. So, arrivals are a good thing for Jolly Jack Tars and paddlers alike. Leaving Reen Spit was the first launch of my voyage. Coming into Roaringwater Bay is my first arrival.

My course beyond the Stags brings me slowly closer and closer to land and to the Kedges, a row of separated, rocky islands like a gum of sharpened teeth chewing their way through a quarter-mile slab of sea. There are three or four blocky molars with walls high enough to support tiers of ledges with colonies of nesting shags and other seabirds, then jagged canine-like pyramids and, furthest from the land, Kedge Island itself, a huge, single, buck-toothed incisor a hundred feet high.

I'm following the cliffed shore, threading between the molars in a swirling and luminous aquamarine surge. The churning and grinding where the rocks and the land meet the water have minced and masticated the long swells and big waves of the open sea into a soup of smaller, rougher shreds of chop and foam. I'm deludedly reassured by the closeness of land as the current speeds me between Sherkin Island and Beacon Point. I sit back and stretch, recurving my spine from its hunched-over crouch, breaking the knots out of my biceps and wrists, easing my knees, shrugging and rotating my shoulders. If I was on a bicycle I would be freewheeling.

In the past I've climbed to the two white radar domes that sit like a pair of teed-up golf balls on the summit of Mount Gabriel on the Mizen Peninsula far to the north-west. From there, four hundred metres above sea level, I could look down on Carbery's Hundred Isles, scattered across the bay, like drab-coloured leaves gathered up in a grey apron. Some ten thousand years ago, at the end of the last great ice age, the waters rose here, submerging hills to make islands. In some complex way – which, thinking about it at sea; I find hard to figure – as the ice melted across Europe those lands further to the north previously weighed down by ice-sheets 'rebounded' by a greater distance than the meltwater raised the sea level. Non-glaciated or lightly iced land areas, on the other hand, and this southern Atlantic corner of Ireland must have been one of them, were inundated by a hundred foot rise in the waters and, at the same time, due to some continental plate flexing, actually sank. The Atlantic Seaboard was suddenly – that's suddenly in geological terms – thrown over, pulling whole valleys and mountains under the seas.

Ten thousand years ago, I reflect, my current vantage point would have been that of a raven on the wing threading its way between the highest of peaks – now islands – riding updraughts (today's currents and tides) off the slopes, far above the ground. Looking down through the waters, I imagine the kelp-forested chasms far below me.

Out to sea there's the last bastion of Ireland's land, the Fastnet Rock, Ireland's most southerly point, eight miles offshore, the final and logical expression of a straight line of reefs and islands running south-west from the mainland, that undulate over and under the sea's fabricky surface like a child's first thick, uneven attempt at stitches. The islands are, in order, Innisbeg, Ringarogy, Spanish, Sherkin and Cape Clear, and then a long gap of open sea – two or three missed stitches? – before the Fastnet Rock and its slender sixty feet of lighthouse.

Folklore has it that once a year at a particular dawn the Fastnet island, ship-shaped as if under bare masts, sails away to sea before coming back to anchor again. See this happen and they say you'll never drown at sea, or – I can't now remember which – you'll be lost on your next voyage.

Probably the latter. The Fastnet is usually symbolic of gloom. In Irish it's *An Charraig Aonair*, 'rock of solitude'. The current name, 'Fastnet', is thought to be a corruption of the *Norse Hvastann-ey* – 'sharp tooth island' (it seems

I wasn't the first to be struck by the dental metaphor of rocks). For famine-fleers and economic emigrants taking passage for the United States, leaving from Cork Harbour, the Fastnet was their last view of Ireland, and became, in allowable sentimentality, 'Ireland's Teardrop'.

Still being carried along by the flood tide, I round the buttress of rock under Beacon Point. The white-painted conical marker showing the entrance to Baltimore harbour is above me. There are small figures gathered around it; one points at me far below and another in a bright-yellow jacket waves. On the Imray chart the beacon is tagged WH.TR (50), but the Irish linguistic genius for renaming public works and monuments demands alternatives. In Dublin's city centre, the bronze statue depicting Molly Malone wheeling her wheelbarrow of cockles and mussels is either the 'Tart with the Cart' or the 'Trollop with the Scallop'. James Joyce, looking Chaplinesque with hat and cane, has been dubbed 'The Prick with the Stick'. Here, in the country there's less ribaldry and more learning in the demotic names for landmarks. The dazzling, salt-white cone of Baltimore's beacon is known locally as Lot's Wife.

I paddle across in the calm of my first around-Ireland evening to Sherkin Island. Over the years I've spent winter weeks and summer days on the island, writing by day, playing music by night in the Jolly Roger, enjoying the no-hurries, no-worries, moon-pulled, tide-tabled time-table of the island. 'Sherkin beats working,' the islanders claimed, as if this was some kind of economic truism on a par with the theories of John Locke and Maynard Keynes. In the warm summers, late dusks flared into early dawns with little intervening buffer of darkness between them.

I moor the kayak to the pontoon, as if tying up a horse in a western town, and stiff-legged from four hours bent into an 'L' shape, draped in sweat, with sea-damp shorts and T-shirt, make my way to the bar.

Outside the Jolly, sitting at one of the bench-and-table combinations there's a girl in a long, rose-pink, empire-line dress. She could be a character in a Jane Austen television adaptation, if you ignored the half-smoked cigarette. Inside the bar, everybody's in similar finery. There are flashes of silks and flounces of bows and expensive shoes, and suit jackets and ties and magazine-picture hairstyles. But it's quiet. And everyone is sitting down.

I realise, at that point, that I'm still wearing my buoyancy aid, which is looped round with the lanyards attached to a knife, whistle, strobe light and all the other kayak safety stuff. I feel like the party guest who's misread 'formal dress' as 'fancy dress'. But, still, this is a public bar. In fact it used to be my local. I've been in here sometimes wetter and quite often less dressed than I am now. And as a winter islander, too, not just a soft summer-incomer.

'You're here for the wedding, are you?'

The voice belongs to a big man standing behind me, dressed casually, and with the physique of a team sports man. 'It Takes Hard Wood and Balls of Leather', I read across his chest, so he must be a hurler. Which makes him a hard case. Ireland's traditional sport, hurling, has teams of players cracking a small, hard ball around the pitch using ash clubs. It's like hockey but played at head-height. Or, as popular shorthand has it, hurling's a good stick-fight interrupted by a ball.

'Am I here for the wedding?' Things are making sense now. 'No, no. I just paddled in for a drink. Good wedding?'

'Fab'lus, boy. Two days an' an all-nighter last night. There's hardly anyone's slept since Thursday night – maybe longer, some of them. And they're getting geared up to go again, I'd say.' As if on cue, the girl in the pink dress has come in and squeezed onto a bench seat against the wall. A breath of fresh smoke seems to have revived her.

It's been a long time since I was on Sherkin, but amid the Jane Austen extras I'm beginning to recognise a few faces. A man with an Iggy Pop mop of strawy hair gets up and puts a chair in front of the upright piano in one corner. He raises the lid and, without looking at the keyboard, indeed rather throwing his head back so as to look up over the piano top with its piles of abandoned glasses, hammers into a striding boogie-woogie. The music starts like an engine catching at the first turn of an ignition key. Of course, Chicken. And then a woman with red hair, sitting with her back to me, has begun singing. 'Tanned and tall and young and lovely ...'

Again, it's familiar. The first time I came out to the island in the '80s, with a bunch of musician friends, we'd played here several nights. I still have a photo: Rob on mandola, Dave and myself on guitars, and me singing with ... Josephine, that's it. She was good then – her voice a wonder of phrasing and tone that sent shivers through the bar – and she is even better now, caressing the Girl from Ipanema.

When Josephine finishes, there's a muted murmur of voices. A few 'good on yous', 'well done yourselfs' and 'loverrlys'. Then Chicken begins on 'Ain't Misbehavin'. He gets through the first verse. I take over on the second. We've sung this together before at some point, years ago. I may have gatecrashed a private wedding as a kind of modern-dress Ancient Mariner but people look over, mostly genially, as if I'm a novelty singing telegram that some wag has ordered from the mainland. The Albatross-a-gram, maybe. In league with the Chicken.

Josephine recognises me, or my voice. This is something I hope is going to happen a lot on this trip. Knowing people. Meeting friends, or friends of friends. After the song, whilst Chicken motors out 'Willin', Josephine tells me it's her daughter's wedding. This seems unlikely. But then so does what I'm doing.

She asks me what I'm up to. Good question. I pause for a moment, find I don't want to declare the whole kayak around Ireland plans just yet. 'Sort of a holiday, usual craic,' I tell her. 'A few days round the bay, see how it goes, and then I just dropped in for a drink and look what I find.'

Chicken is still playing 'Willin''. I sing a verse. Have another glass of wine. I feel happy now I know what I'm doing. Not with the music, but with the kayaking. I'm just paddling around a bit for fun, a holiday. Which sounds doable. Which, in fact, sounds fine.

●━━━━●

I go down to the kayak to pull out some shore-worthy clothes, and a harmonica or two. But once down on the pontoon I feel tired. And drunk. Suddenly I want to find some place to set up camp and sleep. More, there's now a double kayak tied next to mine and I know who it belongs to: Jim Kennedy, who has paddled over from Baltimore with his wife, Maria.

I don't want to run into Jim tonight and, if I did, I'd tell him the same story as Josephine – that I'm just paddling around Roaringwater Bay. For Jim is the most able kayaker I know. An Olympic contender, an endurance champion, a winner of the punishing non-stop 128-mile Devizes to Westminster canoe marathon, and an expert sea-kayaker. I've paddled with him a bit over the past few years, when he's led groups around Castlehaven. In fact, pretty much all the kayak technique and sea-paddling knowledge I have, I probably learnt from him. And I'm pretty sure he knows something I don't know, which is whether I stand a chance of going solo around Ireland. This is something I don't want to ask him. Mainly because I don't want to know the answer.

Which sets me to thinking about self-confidence – and just where I fit on the spectrum between, say, Ernest Shackleton (experience-backed, courageous) and Donald Crowhurst (self-deluding dreamer).

Shackleton was a childhood hero to me. The man who faced impossible odds and triumphed; who in the long, long darknesses of the Antarctic winter put on comic theatrical productions, and when he lost his ship led his men off across some of the harshest and roughest seas in the world in what was basically a rowing boat; and got the lot of them to safety. But Crowhurst also caught my boyish imagination. He was an amateur sailor who entered the Golden Globe single-handed yacht race round the world in 1969, then lost the courage to leave the Atlantic for the wilder waters of the Southern Ocean (seas that Shackleton had crossed in an open boat). Instead, he sailed around the mid-Atlantic for several months, falsifying his logs to conjure up a record of a course around the world, in the hope of being able to slip in unnoticed at the tail end of the finishers. If the race had gone well, it could have worked, and he would have saved face. But as more and more front-runners dropped out, Crowhurst realised that he was going to 'win' by default, meaning his voyage would come under intense scrutiny and the deception discovered. His boat was eventually found adrift. Inside the cabin were the double set of books logging both his real and the fictive voyage, along with searing cine footage, self-shot as he shored up his confidence in wild, bragging conversations with himself.

At this point, towards the end of day one of my trip around Ireland, I feel – perilously – closer to Crowhurst. I really have no clue if I'll be able to keep going, paddle stroke after paddle stroke – a million of them, if my maths is anywhere near right – when I'm cold, wet, tired and scared. And I could be in danger, because I'm not brave enough to give up. I do know that I'm already talking to myself. So that's an ominous tick in the Crowhurst box.

But I first have the night to get sorted. Climbing into a kayak as darkness falls, to head off to find a landing place somewhere along a coast I can't see clearly, and a little too drunk to walk straight, maybe isn't very smart. Though as I slip down into the cockpit and stretch the spray-deck over the coaming and pick up my paddle and push off without too much rocking and swaying, I let the alcohol award me a swoosh on the inventory of Shackletonian self-belief.

I splosh along in the dark, eyes adjusting to the gloom, enough at least to see the line between land and water. It's a falling tide now, but the waters are still high on the rocks. The splash of each paddle stroke and the bow splattering through the small waves sounds loud. I'm tired, and when I see a lowish stretch of land at the landward head of Sherkin I pull in and play a torch – in a Shackleton touch I'd remembered to find my torch before leaving the pontoon – just above the high-water mark. It seems like a place to camp.

It takes an hour to unload the kayak, laboriously pulling out each of the waterproof bags and the endless bits of loose kit and scrambling up the rock. To get the kayak up to the camp I have to lift and swing its considerable weight up onto my shoulder and then climb up the rocks with it grinding into my collarbone. I manage this feat of balance just fine. I'm not as drunk as I'd thought. Or maybe I am, because it takes another half an hour to put up the tent.

I'd bought a second-hand Saunders Jetpacker just before leaving, and now I'm confused by a piggle-stick tangle of poles, odd bits of metal, two billowing duvet covers of fabric and hanks of unattached guy lines. I keep in mind that the primary idea of shelter is to protect one against the prevailing elements. The sky is clear and starry. With few elements looking to prevail, in the end I just prop one of the bits of fabric over a rough 'A' of poles, and pull the most fragile of my kit and my sleeping bag and mat under it. I fall asleep listening to the sound of curlews along the shore and the sudden piping of a roused oystercatcher and little splashes and gurgles as the tide falls away and down the rocks.

An hour later, I wake suddenly, with the urgent thought that I've left my paddle down on the rocks where I landed. Oh, sod it. I pull myself out of my warm bag and, naked and barefooted, pick my way across thistles and down the rocks. Luckily the tide was still going out, so it's where I'd laid it down. Still, a Crowhurstian moment. Or perhaps just a bit of Jerome K. Jerome-ish slapstick.

❮━━●━━❯

I wake looking up into the loose green parachute of nylon over my face. It's illuminated from outside like a stained-glass window. The air inside the not-tent is still and hot. Outside, the sun is beating down. I crawl out onto the grass. I feel wonderful. Even the amateurism of my camp – spread around the kayak there are a scattering of bags and pouches and plastic boxes, and my kayaking clothes lying in a damp heap – doesn't dampen my spirits.

Breakfast ... I'm very hungry now ... coffee, oh yes, coffee ... and then a big fry – bacon, eggs, black pudding, the lot, everything.

I clatter round my kit-bags, finding the stove, the pan, a water bottle, the petrol bottle, and after a lot of searching a lighter. Later, with coffee in a mug beside me, I lie out in the hot sun. I have a wonderful feeling about this trip. This is what it'll be – bars and music and wine and swift paddles across purple seas to island campsites and big breakfasts.

I unfold my small map of the whole of Ireland from the chart case. In my mind I count the previous day's distance as half a day, so double it to make a 'day' and then walk off 'days' around the whole coastline with my fingers. I make optimistic jumps across wide bays, and assume that I'll be paddling a full 'day' every day, at the same rate in glorious summer weather. Then I jot down some figures.

Six weeks ... maybe seven, I suppose, if I lose a few days here and there ... bad weather, whatever ... but I'll be getting fitter so should be able to increase the distance, so that's, somewhere around six weeks as a bogey time ... meaning, back and finished by early August – might even go round faster than that ... five weeks? Five weeks! I could be finished and away to Spain by mid-August ... lovely, lovely.

But it turns out I do far less than a 'day' that day. Just enough to get me to the small raised beach of East Skeam island, a single knight's move away from Sherkin on the chessboard of the bay's islands.

Not that it's a bad day. There's little untoward as I cross the old pirate waters of Roaringwater Bay, reflecting on its heyday in the first twenty years of the seventeenth century, when it was a free port for Atlantic privateers, and a stronghold of the O'Driscoll clan. Piracy of that age was outlawed on paper but too strong a part of the economy to be eradicated. Pirates were occasionally punished after showcase trials – a popular outcome had them hung and left to rot in cages suspended above quays. But there was a tacit complicity by British officialdom so long as plundering was confined to ships belonging to the Spanish or other recent enemies.

The need to bring booty ashore safely and then 'launder' it onto the open market created the need for free ports on remote coasts near to the open sea. Baltimore was one such pirate harbour and must have been, even without the sun and palm trees, a Hollywood pirate template. Buccaneers on shore leave would have hefted pouches heavy with doubloons, pieces of eight, talers, dinars, sovereigns, silver marks and crowns – carousing money that the O'Driscolls and other shore-hugging Irish clans could only have dreamt of with their more austere economies of banditry.

They would have been a cosmopolitan mix – British, Irish, French, Norwegians, Basques, Dutch, Moors, Galicians, Cretans and Mulattos – dressed, draped and wrapped in a mix of luxury fabrics snatched from looted trunks bound for the colonies. Clothing would have been accessorised by such plundered oddities as knee-high riding boots, bangles and earrings, baldricks and belts and buckles, hats and plumes and scarves, lace and linens. Arguments would have been settled with scavenged flintlock pistols, magnesium-veined damask blades, cutlasses, rapiers, eastern kris, Solingen-steel daggers and Scandinavian swords.

As I paddle around Sherkin, I look back across the bay at the village of Baltimore, rising up the hill in tiers. There's a familiar feeling in imagining the trawlers on its quay as pirate ships. And then I recall that I have experienced something not unlike a pirate scene, only a couple of decades ago, at Castletown Bearhaven, two peninsulas west. Forecasts of storm-force autumn winds had brought in tens of French, Spanish, Russian and Irish fishing boats and they sat eight and nine abreast off every quay wall. Hundreds of fishermen, rich in those boom fishing years, filled the bars with a Babel of different languages. There was laughing, drinking, bursts of song, quick-flared brawls, bodies slumped over counters. Many fishermen had made drunken impulse purchases in the clothes shops and knick-knack stores and all wore unlikely hats and caps. There were late-night dances and out-of-town girls come to trawl the bounty or make quick snatchings at romance.

Then, of a day, the weather settled and the harbour emptied of boats, their crews jumping and stumbling and falling aboard even as the mooring ropes were untied and thick diesel fumes choked the harbour. Peace and silence fell over the town. There was a counting of damage and money. I watched as a solitary Gallego sailor raised his head – topped by a new, bright, checked-tweed golfing cap – in McCarthy's Bar, shook himself from a stupor, looked around and then out the door at the emptied quays, realised he'd been abandoned, and ordered another drink.

Perhaps because I'd not covered much distance, hesitant to approach the Mizen, my first test of potentially troublesome water, I make my landing at East Skeam in what could almost pass for an accomplished fashion. It takes less than an hour to unpack the kayak and get everything, including my paddle, above the tide line. It only takes fifteen minutes to get the tent up and stretched neatly over the poles and guyed out. I tie the paddles and the two halves of the spare paddles from the back deck into a tripod and hang my kayaking clothes on them to dry and air. I light the stove and simmer rice and chopped onion together and then stir a tin of tuna and another of sweetcorn into my single pot. Dusk falls as I eat, so it's already late. I mean to lie awake and listen to the Irish shipping forecast but instead fall asleep.

But the day looks clear in all directions when I awaken. Blue sky. The air already warming. The stove boils water for coffee and porridge. The tent skin is still wet with dew. As are my kayaking clothes, which I forgot to bring into the tent the night before and which are going to have to dry on my body as I wear them. I realise that any comforts to be enjoyed on this trip are going to be rooted in mundane good housekeeping habits. And I resign myself to the idea that much of the trip is going to be spent packing and unpacking stuff. But, in fact, the reality of this voyage is that I am almost free of 'stuff'. I feel the exciting potential of this, as I have in the past when I've put a few things into a rucksack and just walked away for a few days, or weeks, or months. Sure, I have a bit of surplus gear, but I could hardly go seafaring with less kit unless I stripped off and swam round Ireland's coastline.

The day is heating up already. A hot sun in the azure sky. It's like a remembered summer's day from my boy years on this same coast. The water sparkles invitingly. Swimming around Ireland might be pleasant. Instead I slip into the cockpit, pick up the paddle and push off, paddling a straight line towards the Mizen, still ten and more nautical miles away down at the end of Roaringwater Bay. As I go further and further out into open waters, all the landscape that is not sea seems two-dimensional, like a slapdash theatre backdrop when the action is going to take place downstage.

Coming into the small walled harbour of Crookhaven I imagine it as Llaregub from *Under Milk Wood*. It's the very essence of harbour: a grey breakwater and a door-sized entrance into the mini-haven, a sandbox-sized beach of yellow sand that dries out at low tide. As I float in to land, I can look down under the kayak on crabs scuttling amidst bright seaweeds and anemones in lollipop colours. There's a jolly tub of a rowing boat moored on a long rope. Above my head I can see figures sitting on the quay walls with glasses in their hands. I beach on the sand and climb the stone steps up to shore level and walk across to a bar, O'Sullivan's.

Ireland's most southerly point, the blunt maul of the Mizen, just to the west, is infamous for its harsh seas. The point cleaves the incoming Atlantic currents and rollers like a wedge being driven through knotty wood, tearing and splintering the waters apart with brutal force. Traversing the Mizen seems like some arcane rite of passage, like rounding the Horn might be for real sailors. I need local advice.

'Ah, God, it can be very messy around d'Mizen, alright. You'd want to be careful. Get it right, like, d'ya know. There'd be fierce currents off the head ... at any old stage of the tide, and if you got a blow of wind then, Jaysus, the waves would get very raggeddy ... but sure you'd only expect that.'

My new friend isn't a fisherman, he tells me, but he does 'a bit of fishing, like'. Which sounds like he's probably a fisherman. He knows the waters around the Mizen well.

'Oh, that's your can-oo, is it, the yellow yoke down there in the harbour? Jayz, t'is small enough, so! Well, you'll want to be in close to the head, very close in if you're in a small boat and you'd be right to go an hour or more ahead of the slack water and then just past the entrance to Barley Cove, to the west, you'll see a rock and if the sea is breaking over that, then turn back, because it'll be far worse round the head and then it'll be too late to turn against the current ...' (unaware, he's slowly swaying the half-empty pint glass in his hand so the lager swills up its side) '... but if it looks alright, you'd want to go on as the tide turns, d'yoo see, and then the seas might calm for a bit and you'd row on then, nice and handy like.' He takes a sup of his now-calming pint. 'If you're going tomorrow, you'd want to be out around seven, I'd suppose, to catch it right but sure it might be shite by tomorrow.'

A beach just beyond Crookhaven is where Elisabeth and I had camped waiting for good weather the previous year. Before my exploding gall bladder had finished the voyage for us. Getting around the Mizen, back then, had seemed a worrying challenge, a point where we might lose our nerve, or see sense and just paddle around West Cork for a few weeks. Now, faced alone, the Mizen seems even more ominous. Since leaving Castlehaven three days earlier, I have merely been recreating the previous summer's trip. The Mizen is where I have to break free.

After I'd come out of hospital, in some pathetic invalid (and how apt that word seemed) activity, Elisabeth and I had driven over one afternoon to look down on the sea from the tip of the Mizen Head. There had been lizards amongst the sun-warmed rocks and the white flowers of sea campion juddering in the breeze. We'd crossed the suspension bridge to the lighthouse and from its high vantage point looked out on the Atlantic.

Even on a hot summer's day, and though diminished by altitude, the waves looked big, and the swells huge, but it wasn't until a trawler had chugged round from the east and nosed into the confused waters off the head that suddenly there was a scale to the seas below. The boat rocked from side to side, throwing up huge gouts of spray as its bow rose up and then fell forwards, butting hard into the waves. The biggest swells almost obscured the hull altogether, leaving visible just the tips of the spars and the roof of the cabin with its white barrel of liferaft.

It's an image I don't really want to recall.

CHAPTER FOUR

Mizen in Action

I CAMP ON THE FAMILIAR BEACH just short of Brow Head. To seaward the Fastnet light flashes over and over, behind me now, to the east, no longer ahead. It's hard to sleep as the light rotates its beam twelve times each minute – four and a bit seconds of darkness followed by 0.14 of a second of diffused light – glowing through the green walls of the tent. So, in the early hours, wide awake, I switch on the radio.

What kind of a mad coincidence is it that, straight up, there is an interview with a survivor of the infamous 1979 Fastnet Race? I know the history of this but I'm all ears, hearing first-hand detail. The summer race – a 600-mile loop from Cowes around the Fastnet Rock and back to

Plymouth – had 303 yachts at sea, most already racing hard out in the Western Approaches, when winds began to freshen, quickly turned to gales and then to storm force. The seas were reported as 'mountainous', which in these waters is not always hyperbole; in 1881 a storm had sent seas high enough to smash the Fastnet's lantern glass, on a thirty-metre tower built on the highest part of the rock. Even the replacement lighthouse, assembled over five years at the turn of the century, and using more than two thousand keyed blocks of solid Cornish granite to raise the light to nearly fifty metres above sea level, can still disappear in surges of spray and wind-driven waves.

In that one terrible day of the 1979 Fastnet Race, twenty-four yachts were abandoned and five sunk; fifteen sailors died as lifeboats, coasters, helicopters and naval ships struggled to pick up survivors and tow in stricken ships. Some 136 people were rescued in what was claimed as the biggest sea rescue since Dunkirk.

On the radio I'm listening to Nick Ward, who back then was one of the youngest sailors crewing in the race. He's describing how he was left alone on the crippled *Grimalkin* after the rest of the crew took to the liferaft. The yacht ran before the storm in huge seas – the same summer seas I can hear breaking on the beach and into which I will have to launch myself to go round the Mizen. Ward talks of how he struggled out of the cabin and into the topsy-turvy cockpit where he waited for rescue, with a dead crew member tied into the other corner of the well.

It's a terrifying account. But it gives me grim comfort. There's no Eskimo roll in a yacht. And at least in my kayak, if things go wrong, there will be no dead fellow crew man to sit vigil with in the darkness as there was on the *Grimalkin*.

Ward had felt abandoned by his fellow crew. His voice is bitter, still, all these years later.

I fall in and out of sleep for the rest of the night until the shipping forecast at five twenty. The sky is light, but grey, when I stick my head out of the tent and look across the beach to the sea. There is a dirty drizzle and a strong breeze. The waves have small white caps. But the BBC shipping forecast for areas Fastnet, Irish Sea and Shannon is less pessimistic than the weather looks. There is a high out in the Atlantic, the wind is from the south, a force five now but due to drop, visibility is poor at this moment but should improve. There's no severe weather in any of the surrounding sea areas. For these waters it's a good forecast.

Wriggling out of my sleeping bag and into damp clothes, I have a strange, disconnected feeling. My sense of time has shrunk to little more than the moment. In fact, it seems I've begun acting in discrete blocks of time – twenty minutes each, even five. Coffee. Pack. Launch. As I snap the spray-deck around the coaming, I feel the cold of the wind, yet without being cold myself. It's still very early in the morning but there are a few seagulls in the air. This, I think, is a good sign. I pull offshore a few hundred yards and find a rhythm in the frequency of the swell.

The waves are bigger than they had looked from the shore. The mist and drizzle is blowing sideways, the Fastnet is obscured though I can hear the faint dull drone of its fog horn every twenty-five seconds or so. It is almost meditative, clearing my head of thought. The movement of the kayak, too. The paddle strokes are automatic. I'm in the zone that comes when – what – when one is committed to something, when one is flooded by and then drained of adrenalin, when one has too little sleep and food and too much coffee? Were I thinking, I'd probably think of this as the 'moment of truth' that comes when there is no spare brain capacity for worrying.

I've been paddling already for three-quarters of an hour and passed Brow Head and reached the mouth of Barley Cove, last land shelter before the Mizen. I keep going.

I'm trying to find some kind of harmony with the waves and the wind, to relax into the paddling and enjoy the balance needed to keep an unstable pairing of man and plastic box upright. My mind is absolutely right not to think beyond this. Thinking would be a disaster right now, I start to think. Then stop. I'll end up worrying and then get scared and then tense. And being tense won't work with the sliding and swivelling and shimmying over the waves.

I see the rock the fisherman had talked of. It's smaller than I'd imagined and the waves breaking against and, occasionally, over this dark hump of stone are big – too big for 'furniture'. I can see the lighthouse on the tip of the Mizen far ahead and high above me, atop the soaring black wall of cliff. I paddle close in under the headland to look for more sheltered water. The waves have become unruly and arhythmic, but my paddle strokes somehow match them.

What's happening here coming into the Mizen – to anthropomorphise the hydrodynamics – is that the water is confused. Driven by the swell and the wind, swept unopposed across the thousands of miles of open ocean that lie to the south-west, the energy in the sea is hitting land for the first time, and each molecule of water has to decide where to go, either up the west coast of Ireland or out along the south coast and into the Irish Sea. Water, it seems, isn't that good at making decisions, and leadership from the currents, tides and eddies is far from absolute. So right here, at the very tip of the headland, a lot of the water stops flowing and just jumps up and down angrily like a roused mob. It seems keen to attack something foreign and alien. Like me and the kayak.

Now I'm paddling over standing waves. These are big slapping gouts of water that just fly up into the air without going anywhere. If I'm on top when it shoots upwards, I'm like one of those ping-pong balls sent aloft on a spout of water in a fairground shooting gallery. If I'm on the side of a wave when it erupts, then I'm one of the bobbling yellow plastic ducks. If I'm in between standing waves, then everything disappears from view except two enclosing walls of water – a long greyish-blue corridor with no doors or windows to escape through.

The random dynamics are added to by the waters bouncing off the flat face of the cliff and veering back into the oncoming waves and swells. These reflected waves are called – it's one of the few technical sea-kayaking terms I know – clapotis. Probably I only remember it because it sounds to me like a terrible mix of venereal disease and bad breath. Clapotis is like getting a bucket of water and stirring it around with a big stick until the surface is falling over on itself and sloshing up the sides. And I'm left trying to stay afloat in that bucket.

The actual sound of the wind and the waters is white noise. I don't consciously hear the hissing and roaring and whistling, but they drown out all other sounds, so that seagulls showering off the cliffs and into the air open their beaks to cry but seem silent.

We're going to crack this ... I'm on the way. I try talking aloud, but being barely able to hear my own voice drains my confidence rather than bolsters it, and I shut up.

I'm under the Mizen lighthouse now. Tucked into a dead-end cove bitten back into the cliff on a scatter of tide-exposed, bed-sized seaweedy rocks, there's a seal laid out like a plump happy slug on a cabbage leaf. I've rounded the Mizen, I suddenly realise. I've turned a corner. Vanquished a fear. The waves, now I'm past the actual point of the headland, are still big but we're back in familiar living-space – dining-room-table height – and they've reordered themselves. On this side of the head all the waters have agreed that westward is the way to go, and so have fallen into an even, ordered marching gait. They rise up under me and bear me along.

There's a long but steady paddle parallel to the cliffs leading to Three Castle Head. Then an open sea crossing across Dunmanus Bay to Sheep's Head. A short streak of black rolls out of the water just on the edge of my vision. Staring at the spot I see only white caps and turquoise, but then as my eyes wander I see it again, a harbour porpoise bounding up from behind the waves like a black cat jumping through snowdrifts. It's the first I've ever seen. A reward, I feel, for having reached these new waters, for having rounded the Mizen. I'm no longer kayaking around a bit. Now I'm paddling round Ireland for real.

I land on Sheep's Head at a small quay near Foilavaun Point and pull the kayak up the slip in the lee of a steep bank of rock. There are fields of thick grass above me hedged by brambles. The land feels more solid than it did when I pushed out to sea only a few hours ago. That's another reward – this hyper-reality – for the daftness of what I'm doing. I'm hungry and tired and feel wrung out. But also elated and a bit mad. *Mizen in action* – I try out. *The Mizen Link. Per-mizen to land.*

In my triumph I'm amusing myself hugely. I cook up two packets of vegetable soup and mix in crumbled oat biscuits and a tin of tuna. Still dressed in my wetsuit and cagoule, soothed by the lap of water, warmed by the sun, lulled by the distant crying of seagulls, I slip in and out of slumber and then fall deeply asleep, thrown back across the rocks like a drowned man cast ashore by the tide.

When I wake up, I am befuddled by the sun and sleep and nervous exhaustion. I then look around and I snort a short laugh: *Oh, somebody is not going to be happy ... somebody has been a fool.* I'm looking at someone's kayak bobbing a hundred yards or so offshore, caught by the wind and serenely sailing out to sea. In my sleep-confused mind I assume that somebody – clearly an amateur – further up the headland has failed to drag their kayak far enough onshore on a rising tide. I feel the virtuous sense of being able to render a service coming over me. I'll just paddle out and tow it back in, and at least it'll be on land then, and whoever lost it will be able to find it.

And then the realisation kicks in that it's my own kayak floating away and getting pushed further and further offshore by a breeze that is now coming from the north-east. It had been relaunched by the spring tide that is now lapping at the top of the quay and threatening to take off the rest of my gear as well. I run along the rocks and prepare to dive in. Then realise that what has so far only been stupidity is on the cusp of becoming tragedy. To swim out to the kayak would mean reaching it, of course, but then I'd be left hanging off its side and without a paddle, unable to climb in nor to bring it back to the shore. I would then have drifted out to sea, blown by the strengthening wind, heading westwards from one of the remotest stretches of coastline in Europe. Brilliant.

Running up and down the quay I swear non-stop. I am now fully awake, though, and thinking smarter. At the top of the slip I'd noted a heavy tub of a rowing boat. It is far too heavy to move alone, I discover, as I tug at its bow. But then in the shag of grass and brambles behind it I spot an orange plastic sit-on kayak. My shouts are now jubilant. I lug it down to the water, swing on my buoyancy aid, grab the paddles, flail my way out and round up my escaping kayak. Back onshore with everything higher up the quay, sheltered behind a storm wall, with the sun behind dark clouds I lie down in the grass and fall asleep again in a fine drizzle. *Mizen in action*, indeed.

Sheep's Head is the smallest of five headlands that make up the south-west corner of Ireland. After the ordeal of the Mizen, I decide to spend a night away from the sea, staying with Kate, a friend since childhood days in West Cork, and Holly, my goddaughter. Since reaching her late teens, Holly has unleashed a wonderful bluesy singing voice and I've been able to do some godfatherly good by playing guitar with her when we meet up. Tonight is no exception, and between talk and glasses of wine and a huge supper we sing swing songs and jazz standards and then rousing ballads till late.

I oversleep, missing the favourable tide next morning, but don't really care. By the time I launch, the sun has broken through and I set out into aquamarine seas in a glow of warmth. An extra two hours' paddling seems a pleasure rather than penance. This is the summer weather in which I'd imagined myself rounding Ireland.

Far ahead I notice that the clouds over the Beara Peninsula are bunching up. As I get closer it's only because I know the area well that I can make out the entrance, behind Berehaven Island, that leads into Castletownbere – the port those storm-bound fishing fleets had turned into a pirate free port. Then I'd spent the duration in MacCarthy's Bar, the one with the handy and compliant nun in the doorway on the cover of Pete McCarthy's book *McCarthy's Bar*.

Time and weather plays tricks. One minute, or so it seems, the coast is a long dark streak of distant cliffs and rising hills, and the next I can clearly see the white marker on the south end of Berehaven, and flashes of red fuchsia along the lanes, and farmhouses and the patchwork of fields rising up the slopes. At the small bay of Cahermore I land and set up camp on a patch of grass. There's a distant road and some houses to the left and a large field already mown to a fuzz from an early cut of hay.

The clouds have kept their distance, for the time being at least, and I strip to a pair of swimming togs and lay everything out in the sun to dry; the wetsuit and the spray-deck are quickly frosted with a rime of salt crystals evaporated from the sea damp. My sleeping bag plumps up in the heat. With a mug of coffee in hand, I set off beachcombing. Amongst the supermarket bags, and timbers and plastic bottles, fishing floats, single shoes and rubber work gloves, I find a small plastic, mustard-coloured duck. With a cable-tie cinched around its neck I fix it to the mooring line at the bow of my kayak; the bath toy seems an appropriate figurehead. It is the first talisman on what will become a string of totems.

When I wake at dawn, the tent skin is cracking above me amid a pelleting of raindrops. Outside it's grey and there's a sharp wind blowing, and waves – chest-of-drawers-high – exploding against the cliffs. I doze until the shipping forecast. Neither Fastnet nor Shannon, it seems, are expecting particularly poor weather, but that's according to a woman sitting in a warm studio in the heart of Broadcasting House in the centre of London. On Cahermore it looks like a shite day. I eat a cold breakfast of oats and milk powder and a dribble of honey mixed with cold water, and drink tepid tea made from the previous night's Thermos flask. This willingness to enjoy a less than gourmet experience allows me the luxury of breakfast in bed.

I launch through the surf, waves running over the top of the kayak. It's not their height that's the problem but the wind which is blowing the waves at an angle of forty-five degrees across the swell, turning the surface into a cross-hatching of texture so that the kayak twists and rolls under me. A couple of hours and I'll be on the far side of the headland, past Dursey island, and able to land in Allihies. But the seas out here are bigger, far bigger, than I'd like. There is a driving rain that needles my eyes when I look over my shoulder, and my resolve is ebbing away. The unbroken line of cliff-face where the land meets the water offers no escape and so provides both the fear that makes me want to stop and the reason I have to keep going. I'm like a mouse scampering along the edge of a high black skirting board with no hole to dive into. Except, then I see a small – mouse-sized – chasm, running as a narrow, deep bite back into the rocks.

I paddle cautiously towards the inlet's entrance. The swell picks the kayak up like flotsam, indeed like the other flotsam – logs, a booming empty forty-five-gallon drum, rafts of seaweed – that rush past me heading inshore. I have to paddle backwards hard to keep from being dragged along by the churning water. Some of the waves are breaking in great rushes of surf. I have lost my nerve here, too. I don't want to keep going along the coast, and now I don't have the guts to dive into what looks like a maelstrom of foam, spray and big blocks of water crashing against the rocks at the back of the tiny bay. But then I notice sets of waves running more smoothly into the right-hand corner. The sluicing rain makes it almost impossible to see anything clearly, but there seems to be a quay? And, perhaps, what looks like a boat moored in a pool of what must be calm – calmer – water. I'd prefer a short burst of high risk now, than a longer period of lower – slightly lower – risk over the coming hours. I want to be onshore. And quickly.

I get my wish. Launching myself into the huge mounds of water driving inwards, I'm picked up by the waves. The kayak becomes a toboggan rushing as if downhill through powder snow, bouncing over aquatic moguls, skidding and slewing but incredibly staying upright. In the far corner, protected by a rock buttress – thank Christ – the sea quite miraculously calms. The moored boat barely bobs in a creek of water behind a high quay. I come to a halt looking down through the rain-spattered surface at seaweed fronds two and three metres down in crystal-clear waters, just swaying in the current.

It takes me a long time to pull the kayak up the almost vertical slope of the slip, using a rope as a handhold, as if climbing a rockface whilst pulling a dead body behind me. The rain has become even heavier, and there's no let-up in sight. I'm soaked and cold, on a remote quay at the end of an unpaved boreen, without even a few square metres of flat ground to put up the tent. And no shelter of any kind in sight. The adrenalin rush of the paddle in, and the relief of landing, turns to frustration and misery. *Sod it! I've had it. Enough's a bloody 'nough. This is just stupid, stupid, STU-PID ... shit weather, bastard seas, sodding stupid idea, the whole thing.*

I keep up a steady mumble, and the odd shout, of self- and general loathing as I peel off my wetsuit and bundle it and nearly everything else back into the kayak which I lay in a ditch, itself running with water. *If anyone wants it they can have it, the whole lot ... it's there for grabs ... first person ... whoever ... whatever ... I'm gone.*

And then I abandon the kayak and nearly everything else. Some dryish clothes, camera, wallet and a few other odds and ends I seal into a dry-sack and heft onto my shoulder. Within seconds the jeans and light shirt I've pulled on are plastered to my body, but half an hour of walking – a mere thirty minutes of not being a round-Ireland kayaker – restores good humour. Then the rain eases to a light drizzle before stopping altogether and fuchsia flowers appear in a shimmering cloud of scarlet in the hedgerows. The bars of Allihies are only six miles' walk across the headland.

I dry and warm as I walk. Cheerful now, and logical, I decide that I'll give up the kayak trip at this point. I've covered a respectable distance; in fact, have done pretty much what I'd told people I'd do and had a pleasing paddle jaunt around West Cork. I'm glad that I have told very few people I was going the whole way round Ireland. It was time to abandon that idea. And, in a rush of clarity, I conceive a plan. Instead of paddling, I'll continue on foot. I'll walk on. A long walk, perhaps right around the coast of Ireland. Yes, that's it. I'll take the tent and the stove out of the boat, get a pair of walking boots and set off. It'll be the same kind of trip but without the daft kayaking, which is patently dangerous for someone like myself, constantly at the very edge of his ability and far too dependent on luck.

I've made the right decision. I'll start walking around Ireland tomorrow. So with hope in my heart I walk into O'Neill's, where I order a steak and salad and a pint of Murphy's. My new plan of becoming a walker with solid land under my feet, able to sit out inclement weather in bars, is looking even better when the afternoon returns to bucketing, wind-driven rain that runs along the road in streams. I order another pint and write a long, rambling, self-justifying journal entry and look at maps and plan my promenade around Ireland. Then I have another Murphy's.

There are whole families in the bar, sheltering from the downpour. Bored children suck down Day-Glo drinks and hoover up crisps, kicking at the bench uprights. I look around to see if there is anyone I might know. I spent time here a decade or so ago, hanging out with a posse of artists and rural Buddhists and neo-gypsies. But I draw a blank. It's been a long time.

A girl with a heavy rucksack comes staggering in through the door. She is pretty, in a doused-hair-plastered-across-her-face kind of way. Or perhaps she is pretty because she seems to have walked through a time-warp portal from my past – carrying a backpack, walking long distances in foreign countries, with perceptions of everything gloriously skewed by romance, and books and songs and wishes and optimism. And above all by youth. I'll bet my next pint – currently standing under the tap waiting for its final top-up – that rucksack girl is German and is walking hill tracks to find stone circles. She's probably philosophical about the rain, maybe even thinks it adds a further layer of Celtic mysticism to her travels. She's looking around expectantly for her next adventure.

I need someone to talk to. So I fold up my maps, and head to the bar to pick up my pint. I've been here long enough that I only have to catch the barman's eye and nod to have him start the slow draw of the next pint, and he only has to nod at me when – seven or eight minutes later – it's ready to pick up. We've been nodding back and forth at each other a fair bit this wet afternoon. The German girl has swung her pack down beside a bench, and she's shrugging and tunnelling herself out of a poncho that's pooling water onto the floor. I'll say hello on the way back to my table, I tell myself.

But going towards the bar I first swing to the back of the lounge to the *fir* – the gents. A sleeking-down of the hair is in order, amongst other things. I swing round from the urinal to the sinks and – Jesus Christ ... the ... oh, for feck's sake. I am, according to the mirror, the survivor of some unspecified but horrific wilderness drama. Probably the sole survivor. I have a mangy stubble across chin and jowl; a broad slash of wind- and sunburn across my cheeks that stops abruptly where my hat-brim has shaded my eyes; and my hair is tangled and algae-coloured as if I'm wearing a sloth's pelt as a wig. What strikes me most, however, is how old I look. It's my eyes: deep-set in reddened wrinkles and dark rings, as if the last few weeks have piled years on me. I feel as though I've stepped across a fault line running through my forty-sixth year, and now that I'm on the other side it's been busily widening, forming an uncrossable chasm. I screw up my eyes to blur the reflection of my face ,but I still don't like it and I'm not sure I can expect anyone else to like it either.

Back at the bar I pick up my pint. The German, now drying charmingly into Pre-Raphaelite serenity, sits at her table a little away. Our eyes meet for a moment, but I've become oddly self-conscious and can barely hold my head up when I pass the drinks' worth of money across the counter. I'm remembering being in bars when I was younger and watching as older men – bored barmen or self-deluded rakes – sidled up to young women to try their luck. Was that how people would see me now? Was that how I saw myself? And, come right down to it, wasn't kayaking around Ireland a younger man's adventure?

I down my drink and step out into the dark, wet night. The rain is still hosing down. Having abandoned the kayak and its contents in the ditch, I imagine it floating on rising waters, and shooting as on a flume down the road, across the quay and on out to sea without me. Resigned, I squelch into the hostel next door and ask for a bed. Then, sitting on the bottom tier of a narrow, unwelcoming bunk, I hear a tinny, double beep from my mobile phone. A text message. A few words thumbed out from the north of Sweden have sent love and a simple, confident hope that I've had a good day's paddling. Someone else's belief in what I am doing and a trust that everything is okay sees off my self-pity.

Moments pass. I swivel round to lie down, ready to sleep, and realise that I've fallen back into thinking that I am going to keep paddling around Ireland after all. The walk will have to wait.

⚬━━⚬

At five in the morning there is sparkling sunshine. It takes me only minutes to break camp in the empty dorm and set off to walk the six miles back to the kayak, which I now rather hope hasn't been washed out to sea. As I walk over the hills, the Atlantic, reflecting the low sun, has all the silvers, blues and dazzling light flashes of a shattered mirror. A blackbird singing from a hedgerow remains in earshot for a long time.

Gravity and a rope borrowed from on top of a pile of lobster pots help me ease the packed kayak down the almost vertical slip. The swell out at sea is still big, but the quartering waves have flattened, the wind is only a breeze and the sunlit sea looks almost benign. I paddle efficiently, ticking off the heads and islands as I pass, noting a greater number of animal names than usual: I round Crow Head, venture inside Cat Rock and outside Crow Island. Further out to sea there are Calf, Heifer, Cow and Bull islands. And when I get through Dursey Sound I'll be heading off Cod's Head across from Lamb Head, and on towards Horse Island, Hog's Head and Pig's Rocks. The last of this menagerie of islands, heads and rocks run over the border into Kerry. From then on, rather than English zoology, the names of geographical points become composites of Irish words; *carrigs, duns, knocks, mores, gorts, fadas* – rocks, forts, hills, big, fields, long – and the like.

Dursey Island, at the head of the Beara, has high cliffs and poor landings for boats. It's joined to the mainland by the umbilical of a cable car, just big enough to take a handful of people, or two men and a cow. As I approach the narrowest part of the sound, where the waters are compressed and pushed together, I see the small silvery box juddering forward along the wire high above the water. The passengers waiting for the next crossing, on the landward side, are not looking at the cable car, though, but rather down into the sound where the water is troubled. Within the currents, shoals of sprats or small mackerel are milling up to the surface and skittering along the water's skin. But it's a large triangle of fin that the people above are craning over to watch. A basking shark is circling slowly and ponderously along the edge of the fastest current. At one point his tail fin comes clear of the water, and measuring the distance between the two fins the fish is probably somewhere around eighteen feet in length.

The basking shark is competing with the sprats for tiny organisms – zooplankton and phytoplankton – dancing like dust motes in this wash-cycle of water. You'd think that evolution would have taught basking sharks to just compound the interest on their energy investment and suck up the fish that have already sucked up the microorganisms, but being semi-prehistoric and the second largest species of fish in the world, they haven't got where they are today by making rash and hurried change.

Paddling in amongst the dancing shoals of tiny fish and towards the slowly waving fin, I'm adding to the joyous anticipation of the viewers on the hillside. Unless they know about basking sharks, what they'll be seeing is some eejit in a bit of yellow plastic paddling blissfully towards a very, very large shark. From above, through the clear water, they can probably see the full extent of its size and bulk, and so will know that it's longer than my kayak. I can imagine the horror movie playing in their minds, along with the *dun dun, dun dun, dun dun, dun dun, dun dun, dundun dundundundun hum* soundtrack from *Jaws*.

The shark and I whirl past each other on the speeding, gyrating current, as if I'm in the fast lane on a motorway and the shark is a leviathan truck rumbling along on the hard shoulder. Basking shark, I reflect, bitterly, are one of the reasons I'm out on the waters today, and going around Ireland this summer. Folklore has it that sightings of basking shark early in the year are a sign of settled weather. Back in May's sunny, calm days, when I was still deciding whether the trip was a go or not, large shoals of baskers had welled up to the surface along the coasts of Cork and Kerry, day after day, a surefire sign of long hot months to come. That belief was one of the few positives that had propelled me to take to the circumnavigation this year rather than waiting and training for another twelve months. But now, after a week of squalls and rain and cold, looking at this lone weather forecaster rolling through the chilly waters under a greying sky, I am struck by the absurdity of trusting climatic prediction to fish with a prehistoric brain the size of an avocado. I feel like having a few words with this inept, finned meteorologist who has conned me out of a lazy, hot summer – *Oi! You! Over here – now!*

CHAPTER 5

Winn, as in Penguin

ICROSS THE FRONTIER LINE between Cork and the Kingdom of Kerry in late afternoon, cutting across the middle of the wide bay, which on maps and charts is designated as the Kenmare River. That's a 'river' as much as Ben Nevis is a hillock. As the locals will tell you, with a resentment that is still apparent, the whole roiling area of sea I'm kayaking across was designated a 'river' in the 1700s by Lord Landsdowne so that his estate could extend its riparian rights far out to sea.

Not that I can get too Marxist and uppity about this, or not around here, anyway. On the other side of the Iveragh Peninsula, a remote ancestor of mine built Winn's Folly, a mock-Germanic castle, towards the end of the nineteenth

60

century. I once stayed with friends not far from the folly's ruins and out drinking in local bars was told to go easy mentioning my surname: 'He was hated, that man Winn, sure didn't he feck everybody off their land back in the time, no wonder they burnt down his auld folly given the chance.' In some way – a not un-Irish way – I felt the bad Winn might have been balanced out by a relative on my mother's Irish side: an O'Farrell who was, according to family legend, shot by the British for refusing to paint his name in English, rather than Irish, on his carriers' carts.

'Winn, as in pen-guin,' I'd say to people when I did talk about my paternal surname. Wynn, or Wynne or Gwynne and all the other variant spellings were from the Welsh word for 'white'. Thus my mention of pen-guin – 'white head' – which is a linguistic legacy of Welsh seafarers. But I'm not Welsh and neither is my father. Instead I am almost Irish, or not-Irish, by dint of two names spelt or misspelt; through living here for most of forty years; and because I have Irish blood. However, under 'birthplace' my Irish passport used to announce *sasanach*, which means 'English' – indeed 'Saxon' – in Irish.

None of which makes my degree of 'Irishness' clear. I'm not Anglo-Irish but certainly not pure, tribal or clan Gaelic either. Nor am I exactly a *blow-in*, as the Irish call recent foreign settlers. Nor an economic migrant, or *new Irish*, as the euphemism was for the incomers who came to find jobs, *craic* and prosperity, or sometimes asylum, in Ireland's boom years. This is a confusion of identity and belonging that has pursued me since my teenage years, when an uncertain Irish nationality was given unwelcome focus by Bloody Sunday and 'the Troubles'. And it had no obvious answer, then, any more than now.

I was born in England. When I was eight, I and my younger sister had been sent off to separate boarding schools. When we came home for the first Christmas holidays, it wasn't to our house in Gloucestershire. Instead we crossed to Dublin on a ferry that heaved across a rough sea through the night, and smelt of rust, strong tea and cattle shit. We drove south in sheeting rain along mud-slicked roads, behind slow lorries hauling knobbly loads of sugar beet. As my sister and I remember it, this was when we were first told that Ireland was now home.

The move had come about quickly. In the late 1960s the British Government was threatening to stop the 'brain drain' by prohibiting key engineers and scientists from leaving Britain. At the same time the Irish Government was keen to attract incomer businesses and small industries, especially to their rural areas. My father joined the dots.

There was more, I'm sure, behind my parents' sudden decision to move to Ireland, though the idea of freedom to do exactly what he wanted was always high on my father's list of priorities. As was his compulsion to invent or reinvent both machines and his life. I don't think that Ireland was in itself important to him. But for my mother it was a sort of homecoming. She had spent long holidays as a child on an estate in Limerick amongst horses and dogs, and her O'Farrell grandmother provided the necessary Irish heritage, under the nation's 'Ireland for the Irish' rules, for my parents to buy some farm land and the roofless shell of a medieval hilltop castle within sight of the sea.

So, while we were out of the way, the contents of my father's workshops and laboratories, and our family life, were relocated: lathes, chemicals, horses, furniture, dogs, stores, testing equipment and my own guinea pigs all moved. I found my parrot already settled in, burbling happily as we clattered into our new home, a small cottage in the shadow of the hulking castle ruin, in whose yards and stables and outbuildings we discovered our piano, saddles, boxes of clothes, crates of books and the rest of our 'English' life.

Within a week I'd pushed my explorations of this new world far beyond the woods and fields of our own land to disappear with the dogs into the December-dark forestry, to wade across swollen streams or to trespass across surrounding farms. After Gloucestershire this landscape seemed wild, full of adventures, foreign. I was excited, too, by the exoticism of not being able to understand the speed, nor tones, nor many of the words spoken by the local men clearing ivy, erecting scaffolding, stone-walling, carpentering beams and frames around our castle building site.

I settled in quickly and felt at home in Ireland. Indeed, it took me years to grow a sense of unease at being part of a complex history not of my making but which I couldn't escape. And as I became more and more aware of being English-Irish, a foreign-local, insider-stranger, I was forged into a strange alloy. My accent was default English but my syntax and vocabulary and enthusiasm for words were all Irish. I spent unusually long periods by myself, too, an independence caused, or forged, by the way I was being brought up. At ten years old I left school for good. I had hated boarding school with a fierce misery, and left two of them mid-term, the last after sinking my teeth into the headmaster's hand before sprinting off into the night. Back at home, subject to the most informal regime of 'home schooling', I lost myself in books and guitar playing, roamed the coast birdwatching, rode horses and made plans for adventure and travels.

I made my first trip away from home at sixteen, fired by reading about Jack Kerouac and Woody Guthrie. With a guitar I could barely play, forty old Irish punts and a sleeping bag, I hitched and busked through France and Spain for several months. At last I'd found the place I belonged – travelling – being at home anywhere. And I discovered the person I was, too – the easy stranger. My life took on elliptical orbits around and through Ireland. Ireland was 'home' when I was away, but then so it seemed was Spain, Eastern Europe, Morocco and, as my orbits around Ireland grew wider, the Sahara, Iran, Australia – anywhere there were horses, guitars, fun.

In this perhaps I was truly Irish. I may have been travelling for my own reasons through the late-1970s, 1980s and on into the 1990s, but then so were all my Irish friends. We went abroad to work, for the *craic*, because there wasn't enough to hold us at home. But in the boom years of the twenty-first century, much of the Irish diaspora had come back to start businesses, invest in property, to share in the good times. Few, I supposed, had come back with the intention of spending several months being wet, cold and frightened each day whilst labouring away at paddling and then squatting in a damp tent each night.

Yet this is exactly what I'm in the process of doing. Right now, out here at sea, I'm close to Ireland, but not too close. That probably means something.

All the way along this Kerry stretch I'm in sight of the Skellig Islands, as I had been in sight of the Fastnet on the West Cork coastline. The two Skelligs lie on the horizon –

one a little like a basking shark fin, the other lower, like a child's drawing of a ship's hull with a squat funnel, the two pointed at each other as if on a collision course.

These islands – with the monastery of Skellig Michael, redolent of Ireland's golden age of saints and scholars – are iconic for anyone travelling around the Irish coast. Seven miles offshore, they formed the nucleus of Irish monastic life from the sixth century until the twelfth – a golden age here, set apart from 'dark age' Britain. And the austerity of those stone oratories and beehive huts and monks' cells clinging to the scoured cone of rock, has perhaps even more resonance if you're the kind of person who voluntarily submits to a month or two of being swilled by Atlantic waves and sleeping in a flimsy tent. Kayaking around Ireland is arguably quite a monkish activity.

Paddling past the islands, you cannot avoid contemplating the self-contained medieval world of the monastery on Skellig Michael, nor the teeming avian metropolis of Little Skellig with its twenty thousand breeding gannets. I feel peculiarly at home out at sea, or camped on a remote island or headland, sharing my world with the birds, fishes and mammals. Birds, particularly, make sense of the world of water and weather I am navigating through, just as they did for the Celtic contemporaries of the Skellig monks of a millennium before. One of the books I've brought along on this trip is an anthology of medieval Celtic verse – poems with haiku-precise observations of goldfinches on a thistle head, frost on a hazel catkin or the bellowing of stags across the mountains, or the glide of a gull along the cliffs.

That night I make my camp at the entrance to Portmagee Channel, across from Valentia Island. I've made a fair distance, around the seaward side of the Ring of Kerry, and feel relaxed, as if at last I've settled into the rhythm of the trip. Beachcombing I find a small flattened oval of smoothed driftwood and draw the sea view towards the Skelligs on it with an ink pen, and a few days later stick a stamp on its reverse, write an address and send it to Erika, my text-friend in Sweden.

From the head of the Iveragh to the head of the Dingle Peninsula is fourteen miles. There's reasonable weather predicted to start with, but later in the day it's set to deteriorate. The long-range forecast is continued bad weather for the foreseeable future. I don't want to get stuck on this side of Dingle Bay for days camping in rain – if foul days are coming, I'd rather be in Dingle, with a bed and bars. The shipping forecast is given a surreal immediacy as one of the coastal weather stations quoted is Valentia, just across the channel from me. It's as if I'm within hailing distance of the weather gods themselves. It doesn't help me make an informed decision, though. Fourteen miles, I tell myself, is five hours or so of paddling, given a neutral current. I weigh up the charts and tide tables. I still can't decide. Finally I do what worked so well for the Mizen – simply head out to sea.

Once round Valentia Island and looking across at the Dingle Peninsula, it seems obvious I should go on. There's a watery sun, little wind, moderate waves, a big but even swell. Far, far ahead I can see the low bulks of the Blasket Islands – Ireland's most westerly point. I feel myself drawn across the sea. It's remarkable how quickly the land drops away behind me. Glancing back after half an hour, it looks as though I'm as far off Valentia as I am from Dingle. The land ahead of me is obviously racing closer with every paddle stroke. It's going to take far less than five hours. Three, I'd guess. The trip is just fun, good-humoured.

I spot a rod fishing boat far out where the bottom deepens, a few miles offshore, and sneak up on it, paddling quietly up behind the five men arranged in a row along the lee rail. They're all plump and dressed in primary-coloured cagoules like a quintet of garden gnomes on holiday. 'Hello,' I suddenly pipe up. 'Lovely day. Any luck?' They all do double-takes. Three of them stare wildly around but mostly up into the sky; one automatically reaches for his mobile phone; another, the skipper perhaps, starts moving towards the dog house and radio. Then they spot me almost out of sight behind their hull. They're not particularly amused.

The seabirds are better company. A fulmar sweeps by, tipping a wing to swing sideways round and glide in towards me. I feel a particular affinity with *Fulmarus glacialis* – to the point that I have named my kayak *An Fulmaire*. The Irish word mimics the English, as fulmars were latecomers to Ireland, first breeding on the island's coast as recently as 1911. Like me, they are outsiders – though I would expect most locals, even fishermen, imagine the fulmars natives. Unlike the mobs of swaggering gulls and squabbles of razorbills and the ancient tribes of cormorants, fulmars never gang up. Instead, they fly alone and nest in discreet pairs, barely in view of the next pair along their exposed cliff ledges. They have an endearing habit of flying out of their way to pass close to the kayak, seeming to make eye contact, friendly and curious. It's become a talisman act for me to call out a short greeting to each one as it dips in and passes – a 'Hi!' or 'Hullo!' or 'How's it going?'

There's a necessary fault in the fulmar, of course, to balance its perfections. When they come in close I can see that each bird's nasal tubes drip constantly. As a true pelagic species – making landfall only to breed – fulmars must drink saltwater, and the excess salinity is excreted in a run of thin, clear snot that balls on the tip of their beak before dropping off. It's like seeing a lithe, tanned, blonde cheerleader chewing tobacco and spitting.

An hour's paddling later, far further out at sea, there are only shearwaters and gannets left to greet.

When kayaking for any real distance offshore, one's safety net lies in being able to paddle faster than the changing currents for long, long periods. A safe paddler is one who can keep their craft going along at close to its maximum speed for six hours or so at a time. Unlike a runner, who can just fall back to a jog or a walk or a standstill if they've overestimated their ability or underestimated the distance, a paddler has to keep moving against the current however tired. Stop or slow for too long and, even if you set off with the current in your favour, it will turn and you'll end up going backwards or sideways. And the longer one spends on the water, the greater the danger that the weather will turn – invariably for the worse.

In the shipping forecast 'imminent' means within six hours, 'soon' from six to twelve hours, and 'later' is generally beyond that. The dawn forecast had been for high winds 'soon'. I'd waited for the tide to turn in my favour before setting out, and now, a few hours out from Valentia, it's already past twelve. The winds are strengthening.

I paddle on. A further hour later, Valentia looks very far away behind me. But the Dingle Peninsula doesn't look any closer. I stop to check the chart. 'Barrack Rock', marked to the west of my course, apparently 'Breaks in Gales'. And beyond, much further out at sea than my course will take me, there's the 'Wild Bank', marked on the chart with several sets of paired wavy lines to indicate habitually troubled seas. Just knowing about them makes me feel uneasy.

I spot a sudden dark roll of a body up through the waves – a minke whale, most likely. First I stare at where it sounded and then throw my eyes out of focus so they cover more area in less detail, but nothing registers. Minkes usually only make one surfacing and then disappear. But it's given me a scale for the waves, which I realise are much bigger now. Forget furniture – I'm measuring sea states by comparison with Cetaceans, now: minke, pilot, sperm or blue. A few waves are tumbling, tumbling over into white foam on their crests. I check the large-dial watch I keep buckled upside down to my buoyancy aid on my chest so I can read it by looking down. *Shit!* I say aloud. *I've been out here paddling for five hours already and I'm not getting any closer.*

My earlier hubris seems laughable. I've lost the positive tide, and I'm starting to worry that I'm not paddling fast enough to make headway against the current that has set down the bay and is heading out to sea. The weather is getting very dirty, too. The gannets, which only half an hour ago were overhead in great wheeling flocks, have cleared from the skies. The odd one shoots past, flying in a straight line back towards the Skelligs. The sky has darkened. Looking back the land is a dark, low shape, whilst looking ahead is a similarly diminished and very distant line of dark, indistinct just-solidity. There's a lot of darkness around.

Looking down the bay, some thirty miles inland, the Slieve Mish Mountains are a low undulation often totally eclipsed by a horizon of water.

I don't know whether to keep going or turn back. I've got to the point where I'm equally far from anywhere. Except, that is, from the open sea. Actually, by all sane measurements I'm already out on the open sea. America is becoming a landfall possibility to consider.

I've been paddling very, very slowly, I realise, and break into a flurry of hard, fast actions. My heart rate rises as the kayak surges forward, rocking and yawing on the waves as I dig the blades in and pull back on them, opening holes in the sea's surface so the water floods into them again as if I'm mixing concrete. Within a few minutes I've exhausted myself, chest heaving for breath. I've shown all the physical symptoms of panic. Now my mind's threatening to supply the clinical detail.

I calm down, rest my paddles and have another look at the chart, do some more calculations. I'm back to my usual problem with water and weather – getting a perspective. I don't know how far I still have to go. Nor how fast the current is going, and in what direction exactly. I don't know how much strength I have left.

I bend to my paddle again, stroking out for the land. For another hour nothing changes; the land is still the low, dirty mix of colours run into each other like a landscape painter's wipe-rag laid along the horizon. I'm paddling at a rate – albeit barely a jog – that I'm confident I can keep going at. I have stopped thinking and am just counting my strokes, numbering them off like telling beads. I could do this forever, like a goldfish endlessly swimming around its tiny globe-bowl of a world. But it's unlikely that I'm actually making much or any headway across the water's currents as they move contrary-wise under me, as if my personal goldfish bowl that I'm so busy paddling around in has been put on a train that is slowly but surely heading somewhere the goldfish doesn't want to go.

Then, blankly staring at the unchanging thin line of land ahead, I imagine an actual something – no more than a faint pixillation on what I know to be the side of Mount Eagle. This faint dot fades in and out of vision for the next ten minutes or so. Then it is there all the time. There's another pixel of less lighter colour to one side. Relief. They're houses. Many, many paddle strokes later and I can guess at squares within the squares. A hint of windows, suggested only because I know that houses have windows. The day has become darker still, there are sudden gusts of wind from out of the black clouds, and the sea still feels as if it's racing against me. But as I paddle on, a house comes into focus. I can count the windows, see the door and a tiny blue blur that must – surely – be a car in the front. I'm only several miles offshore now. I can see three ribbons of colour demarcating the coast line: white surf where the sea hits the cliffs, the black cliffs and then the scrubby umbers, and greens of the individual fields above.

I'm so close now, but fighting a sped-up tide that is sweeping out of Ventry Bay – and along and offshore from the cliffs. I have to increase my pace to avoid standing still. Crawling like some insect across a huge floor. Detail comes faster and faster. A shower of white confetti blowing across the face of the cliffs: seagulls. The car noiselessly moving off and down a track, in and out of view behind hedges.

There's a boat in the mouth of Ventry Bay, stationary whilst two people fish; twenty or twenty-five foot of tubby hull with a small doghouse steerage cabin. Watching it rising up and rolling and corkscrewing on the waves, and pitching forwards down the swell, I'm close enough to catch a view of its propeller and its rudder at the apex of one steep yaw, the one turning and the other flapping in the air. I could just paddle across to them and ask, demand, beg to be rescued. I laugh at the idea. I'm safe – and through my own muscle power and grit. I've as good as made it.

There's another twenty minutes against the tide to get into Ventry Harbour, and drive the kayak up onto the slip. I've been seven hours without a break. I'm like an old man getting out of a tight, deep bath, staggering as I step onto the concrete. I can look out of the harbour mouth under the smudged sky, across a pewter-coloured mass of water and very, very, very far away see a thin smudge running along the horizon. I've paddled from there. Crossing this bay, from head to head, is one of the longest open-water stretches on the trip, and barely a week out from the start I've done it.

Deep down something in me nags. What if I hadn't made it? If I couldn't have kept going? What then? Would I still be out at sea right now, being pulled over the Wild Banks, past the Blaskets, out into the Atlantic? Or capsized, and helpless, still heading seawards. That's a thought that stays in my subconscious. But consciously I'm packing up my gear and heading to Dingle town for a celebratory drink.

CHAPTER 6

Dangling in Dingle

THE RAINBOW HOSTEL is a mile or so outside Dingle town. In my room I pull off the wetsuit. Thrown down, its black silhouette sprawls at my feet like a discarded shadow. Standing naked, I see myself in the full-length mirror: prune-wrinkled skin, hair thick with salt. The tight water-seals on my cagoule and wetsuit have left harsh red circles around wrists and ankles, giving the impression that I am some ill-favoured galley slave released from manacles for a few days' shore leave. I pull on an assortment of slightly damp clothes from the dry-bag and head through the lashing rain into Dingle town.

The Irish-speaking Dingle Peninsula has a remoteness and a slightly detached relationship with the rest of the country. I pass a placard for the local newspaper headed 'DINGLE LEFT DANGLING', which turns out to refer to a longstanding and rather peculiar spat over the region's road signs. As a Gaeltacht area, one where Irish is proudly spoken as a first language, Dingle found itself subject to a recent government edict directing that all town names and road signs should be in Irish. Dingle, though long in common usage, is actually the Anglicised version of its true Irish name, An Daingean Uí Chúis. But the locals fear that taking 'Dingle' off the signs may literally take it off the map, to the extent that foreign tourists won't know how to find the place, won't even be able to Google it. And, even if they could spell it, they'll still find it impossible to pronounce. Which is true enough. Try saying 'An Daingean Uí Chúis' aloud and, if you're not an Irish speaker, you'll make an over-long mouthful out of Daingean and then come up with a sneezy sound for 'Uí Chúis'. All of which is wrong.

Tourism is important in Dingle. The perfectly normal lives that most Dinglers live – as farmers, teachers, builders, shopkeepers and the like – are concealed behind a visitor-pleasing, euro-earning front of timelessness and happy eccentricities. And on a fine day the peninsula still has all the dazzling Technicolor green fields, white beaches and turquoise seas that so prettied up *Ryan's Daughter* when it was filmed here. It's a combination that attracts musicians, artists, poets, drunks, wits and mystics – often playing more than one part at a time – because there is, truly, a different feel to the town and the country around.

The natural world can seem surreal here. In 1984, a young bottlenose dolphin turned up in Dingle Bay and played happily for a year or so with swimmers and surfers close to the beach at Inch Strand. Then, when people began arriving from all over the world to frolic with him, Fungi, as he'd become known, perhaps cutting a lucrative deal with local boatmen, took himself off to the middle of Dingle Harbour, where he could only be approached close-up by taking a boat trip out from the town.

The dolphin's contribution to increasing tourist numbers and the town's income over twenty years would be hard to quantify. But as I walk into Dingle along the harbour road there are plenty of indications of the Fungi-effect. I'm passed by the small red van of the Dingle Harbour Commissioners, its logo a leaping, golden dolphin. A nearby gift shop is signed by a painted portrait – textbook correct – of a swimming bottlenose. Another emporium features a whole pod of full-sized wooden dolphins leaping out of the blue surface of its two-storey wall. A third, a fourth and a fifth shop have windows filled with ceramic, glass and plastic representations of dolphins in various likely and unlikely jumping and swimming poses. So does a chemist's further up the road. There are CDs of whale song – to be honest, the more musically talented of the Cetacean family – and dolphin-inspired New-Age human-music for sale, and in the square by the harbour is a large, grinning bronze Fungi sculpture, polished to gold on its fin and nose tip by many passing hands. It seems a lot of responsibility for a now elderly and portly *Tursiops Truncaitus*.

Fungi's age (dolphins rarely live beyond twenty-five) weighs on my mind as I turned up the hill into Green Street, where I go into a shop for a drink. The shop-bar is another Dingle institution and arguably far more useful than a performing dolphin. A shop-bar, or bar-shop, is exactly what it says it is. Traditionally they sold groceries as well as drink. Nowadays, though, the one I've chosen, Foxy

John's, sells bicycle accessories and hardware. Curran's nearby has hats heaped on the shelves behind the beer taps on the counter. And then there's Dick Mack's, where I head next, stepping over Dolly Parton's handprints cast into the pavement cement at the door.

Dick Mack's was once a leather workshop as well as a bar, and decorative punches and boxes of grommets, eyelets, needles and buckles still fill the shelves, above the old cutting board. But these days this is a bar, pretty much pure and simple, and in a town famed for traditional music, and talk, it's an essential stop. The talk can be almost as good as the music: well-rehearsed, set-piece talking sometimes; other times, discussions extemporised like jazz, or argumentative soloists duelling on a theme. Like traditional music, talk mostly starts with a few well-known tunes – weather, politics – then, once people are roughly in the same key, away they go, adding grace notes and jokes and digs and flights of fancy. As I walk into Dick Mack's the talk is well started; on wet summer days, things begin early.

A local man holds three shaven-headed Welsh sport fisherman in thrall: '... a German sprat, right, that's what you need for bass, and you'll cut off one of the t'ree hooks, right, just leave the other two, and you'll want a big weight, a pound at least, and a strong line. Then head down to the strand when there's a big sea, on the new moon at low tide, right on the turn – that's the only time, do you understand – and when a big wave is going back out run down to the water's edge and feck that weight out as far as you can, put a mighty swing on it, and then run like Christ back up the beach ...'

Another local is lecturing a quartet of Italian yacht sailors on the subject of local weather: 'Well, to be honest now, it is shite today ... but, ah, on a good day, with the sun out, there's nowhere like here ... white sand beaches, and blue sky and the blue sea ... oh, it's fab'lus, you know ... It's like being in the Caribbean.' 'And on a bad week,' someone butts in, 'it's like being in the bloody Kerry-bbean.' The sailors, in yellow oilskins, look bemused, take long draws from their pints, smile happily anyway.

With my arse propped on the cutting-counter, I fall into talk about the weather with a long-haired man with the lined, ruddy face of someone who divides his time fairly between being at sea and being in bars.

'Here's something you might know, now,' I say. 'How did Fungi get his name?'

My new pal looks closely at my lower face. 'The old dolphin? You're almost the answer to that yourself.'

I looked blank.

'Your excuse for a beard ... the smigeen and bum fluff.'

It's true. I can't grow a beard. The hair goes as far as it's going to go in the first week. 'But what's a beard got to do with dolphins?' I submit.

'Well, that's exactly why the Dingle dolphin has the name he has. Because there was a fisherman back years ago now, and he was trying to grow a beard, and he wasn't getting on too well ... T'was like mould on cheese, a sad old excuse for facial ornamentation. So, anyway, people took to calling him Fungus, in a friendly way, like, and it happened he was one of the first fellas that took an interest in the dolphin and so Fungus was always coming back in from the bay with stories of the creature having done this and that, and having hopped right over his boat and tap-danced and the rest. He was always talking about the bloody dolphin. So after a while people took to calling the dolphin Fungus's dolphin, and then they cut the fella out of the deal altogether and just gave the dolphin his own name. And there he is, still: Fungi the Wonder Fish.'

The conversation *craics* on, with others joining in, working out how to keep the dolphin alive, or create some kind of body double as insurance for when the fateful day arrives. And then the musicians start coming in and small intimate groups hold the snugs at either end of the bar to themselves. People bend close to listen to them. An hour or so slips by. Somebody starts up, unaccompanied, 'The Fields of Athenry', and other voices join in. A guitar comes round to me and I try a John Prine song you'd never get away with in a traditional session and Sonny Boy Williamson's 'Help Me'. There's more talk as I pass the guitar along. Then the guitarists are gone, on to play a paying gig. So, it'll be more talk, then. And shouting.

Words are lost in the din of competing voices, choking roars of laughter. Listening not to words but accents, I decipher Californian, Queenslander, Upstate New York, Parisian, Dutch, German, Dubliner, Corkonian. Pints of stout are passed over people's heads to the back of the room. There's a smell of cigarette smoke as the smokers come in from the yard; of malt from the pints; the damp dog of wet coats. The smell of warmth on a miserable night. Huddles of intimate conversation, tight flirtings, attempts at sober talk in the back rooms and corridors. Then, last rounds.

I set off back to the hostel along the soaked road, as sharp gusts of wind souse the hedges with slashes of rain. The grey of the morning is starting across the bay to the east. In my room the piles of damp kayak kit are heaped in a corner. Charts and maps and rolls of film are piled on the table. The weather has made it sensible to not continue for a while – I've realised that it's going to be more than a few days before the winds settle – and I'm happy to do that, or not do that, or to do that, not that that I'm ... I fall into a deep sleep.

Within a few days, in the happily confused but comfortable way I'd fallen into sleep, listening to the rain, that first night in the Rainbow, I fell into a haphazard and dreamlike routine. A wintry routine. Up late, my walk over the hill into the town for a cafe breakfast showing the bay filled with metal-grey sea, its waves jagged by violently gusting winds, rain chucking down. Hours in the warm internet cafe.

From the comfort of a computer terminal I discover there are others paddling around Ireland this summer. Three Irish men – Tony O'Mahoney, Derek Lyons and Brian Fahy – had set off from Dungarvan on the 27th of May and are blasting around as a team, and, having reached the slightly more sheltered east coast, are nearly home. A little after the trio had started, two Americans, Marcus DeMuth and Sam Crowley, had also launched, a few days apart, both leaving from Dublin, each paddling solo.

From reading their blogs it is obvious that there is a very different feel to being a foreigner going around Ireland, alone. The local lads write of restaurants, pubs, jokes, the results of hurling games, and are buoyed up by family and friends meeting up with them along the coast. The Americans talk of iron ration parcels being sent ahead, the weather so much worse than expected, and of the remoteness of parts of the coast. One of them is driven on by an approaching return flight to New York that leaves no time for dawdling, and is taking huge risks on the gale-lashed west coast to keep to his schedule. His postings are a record of big-wind, heavy-sea paddling days, and reading between the lines it became obvious that even his experience was allowing him very little safety margin. The other American, Sam Crowley, is still behind me, camped out in Black Ball Bay on the Beara Peninsula, pinned down by the weather.

Sam has my mobile number and we talk a number times to bemoan the relentless winds. I try not to sound too happy about our different circumstances. Sam has been sheltering in his tent for most of the time that I've been in Dingle. I feel glad to have anticipated the bad weather and made the push to get across the bay to roofs and bars rather than crouching beneath a flapping and cracking and leaking carapace of nylon on a beach for the week, and then the ten days, and then more time, that I'm dangling in Dingle.

One day, in need of quiet contemplation, I go across from Dick Mack's and into St Mary's Convent, where the chapel is filled by rainbow pools of light falling through Harry Clarke's stained-glass work. Even if Clarke's commissions were ecclesiastical, his fantastical characters owe much to the fairies, goblins and princesses of his contemporaries Beardsley and Rackham. They are crowded with twirled shells, bright sea anemones, bursts of flowers, elf-cherubs and Kate Moss-faced Madonnas. His Mary Magdalenes are the just-older sisters of jazz-age flappers, while his saints and Magi resemble beatific-faced hippies and stoners in what seem like richly brocaded kaftans and loon pants.

It reminds me of the psychedelic album covers of 1970s rock bands more than any other religious art. But there is an air of pathos about the convent. It is whispered to me that there are just three nuns remaining in the cloisters, all elderly. A figure given greater poignancy when I learn that over the same year some 228 nuns had died in Ireland, whilst only two had been ordained, with the outlook for the priesthood only slightly less pessimistic, with 160 late-lamented priests being replaced by a mere nine new recruits. Ireland's youth seemingly have other vocations, like working as bar staff or playing music.

And indeed it is the music across Dingle that makes my wait for better weather more than bearable, with each passing day offering more opportunities for a guitar-plucker and less for a round-Ireland kayaker. It is something I've done for long periods of my life, playing music. Back in the late 1970s and 1980s, I'd travelled Europe playing streets, cafes, clubs and festivals. For a brief period I'd had a successful act called Cowboys, Chickens & Jesus, when I played songs about just those three subjects. I fancied myself a troubadour and played just about every country from Morocco to the oil towns of the north of Norway, even heading behind the Iron Curtain to bring rock and roll and songs about chickens to the oppressed masses. But being a musician is an odd business. When I was playing music for a living, for enough money to eat, drink and travel, I came to realise that I just wasn't quite good enough, and unlikely to be lucky enough, to ever get off the small gigs circuit, or much beyond playing harmonica with pick-up blues bands or performing novelty songs in unlikely countries. Then, when I gave up and just sat in on sessions and played parties or got pushed on stage to blow a bit of harp as a guest musician, I'd find people wondering why I didn't turn pro.

Those days all come back to me as I migrate through Dingle's music bars. One night it is Jimmy Crowley, pamphleteer, professional Corkonian, balladeer and sea-shanty-er. And another it is local piper Eoin Duignan, who'd composed 'Lumina', a suite on the theme of Harry Clarke's

Dingle windows. And in O'Flaherty's there is a nightly session. And it is all for free. Which is just as well, for after two weeks hiding from the weather I begin to think of my summer as an hourglass, with a fine sand of euro notes sifting down from my wallet into the cash registers of Dingle's pubs, bookshops and cafes. Bad weather is possibly even more lucrative than a dolphin to the local economy.

●——●

But there is no change. The rain is ceaseless. Someone tells me that in Valentia the full July's worth of rain had fallen on the first day of the month. But it is the wind that was stopping me leaving. On average Ireland gets two high wind days in each of the summer months. But this year, after I'd arrived in Dingle, there were twelve days in a row when 'small craft warnings' were issued by the coastguard. An SCW means winds of force six or above. How wrong can a basking shark be, I wondered.

And so another night in O'Flaherty's. I watch the musicians settling themselves to play, arranging plectrums and pucks of rosin and drinks around 'their' table. Traditions in Irish music are all you'd expect in an art form that very deliberately calls itself 'traditional', and one that has six thousand or so (often quite closely related) tunes to draw upon. A whole night of jigs and reels played with fierce dedication can be much like witnessing a bunch of serious-minded folk solving cryptic crosswords rewritten as tempo and melody, or listening to mathematicians clicking and fingering abacuses as they work their way through strings of calculations.

In the purest of sessions there are no ballads. No boisterous story songs, however much the listeners might want accounts of lives ruined by whiskey and jolly plough-boys leaving their fields for war and bunches of thyme standing as metaphors for virginity. In a proper west of Ireland session, singing is the unaccompanied *sean-nos*, a style oddly akin to the yoiking of Sami reindeer herders, or the keening of Tuareg in the desert. Here on the Atlantic coast it's seemingly the sea and rocks that are given human voice. *Sean-nos* songs are haunting. And if you know Irish, they are often funny, touching and clever. But there are no rousy nonsense diddly dee, torra-lora, wacky-ma-diddly choruses that even Spanish, German or Slovak speakers can learn the first time they hear them and be ready to join in the next time the singalong comes around.

Instruments, too, are divided strictly into traditional and non-traditional. As a rule of thumb, if you stick with anything that could be made out of native Irish wood and/or the various parts of a goat or a greyhound, you are on safe ground as 'authentic'. So the bodhran is the most Irish of instruments – a hoop of ash wood skinned with goat or, ideally, lime-cured gazehound skin. And close behind it is the wooden flute, especially one with a bit of goat- or, even better, greyhound-bone ornamentation. Then come the uilleann pipe, a complex mix of leather wind-bag, wooden melody pipe and long dangling chanters, played by strapping the bag under an arm and pumping your elbow (*uilleann* in Irish) whilst fingering and chanting away.

The purists are doubtful when it comes to any stringed instrument apart from the Irish harp. There is little mention of guitars, zithers, mandolins and double basses in the annals of the past, so suspicion hangs over the lot of them. And over the pluckers who strum and pick them, too. Though the banjo, having a vellum sounding-skin that could be goat or running dog rather than cow, seems mostly okay. And the doubled-stringed mandola, or the Greek bouzouki, has earned its place in the pantheon of Irish 'correct' instruments, too, perhaps because it sounds like a harp that can play rock and roll chords.

Mind you, just when one begins to think that the pantheon of 'traditional' Irish instrumentation has either to sound pleasing or be made of dead dog, up pops the accordion. In recognition of its complex mechanics the players of accordions are referred to as 'drivers', as if they are steering the bulk and weight of a heavy goods vehicle through the delicate and crowded traffic of a session. The joke is that when you go to heaven, Saint Peter shakes your hand and welcomes you in and hands you a harp, whilst if you go to hell the Devil greets you by saying, 'Welcome to Hell, here's your accordion.'

Every session instrument has its attendant jokes. A gentleman is defined as a man who owns a banjo ... but doesn't play it. The best way to play a bodhran, proper musicians claim, is with a penknife blade. The bodhran was often seen as a session-wrecker – cheap to buy, seemingly easy to play and, in the hands of a deluded, thick-skinned eejit with a bit of stamina, capable of being beaten all night in useless thuddery. I've heard the bodhran being called the 'Irish frisbee' by one fiddler in Dingle, who'd demonstrated its aerodynamics by whirling it with a deft wrist-flick out of the nearest window into the dark.

There are no jokes about the uilleann pipes, though, because piping is an art. Everyone knows that it takes twenty-one years to be any good on the pipes. The second seven years would be spent learning, and the seven years after that goes in practice. And if you asked how a piper spends the first period of his apprenticeship, you'll be told:

'The first seven years? Sure, that would be getting any noise out of the bastards, at all at all.'

Fergus O'Flaherty runs a tight session. Nodding people in to play. Starting tunes at the right tempo. His bar is always packed in the summer, and there's often a chance for newcomer musicians to take out a fiddle and finger along, silently as is the apprentice tradition until confident of the tune, its changes, and the direction that the collective will of the ensemble might take it. Over three decades of odd visits to the bar, I've got away with playing a harmonica piece a handful of times. And I might have played a truncated piece of ragtime on a borrowed guitar once, but Fergus is quick to spot tracks running away from the main road of tradition and to stop people heading down them.

Tonight it's tunes. Alison comes in and unboxes her guitar and sings an Irish song. Fergus is on banjo. There's an accordion. Customers are crowded in. The silence around the musicians is total but the noise rises in levels the further back one goes, creating the effect of an aural amphitheatre of tiered sound with the players at its concentrated focal point. I sip my Murphy's slowly, using the closed lid of the piano for a table to rest the glass on. It looks like it hasn't been opened in twenty years. It might even be locked. It's not really a traditional instrument.

In the newspapers and on the TV news, I get to see what I'm missing out at sea whilst land-lubbered in Dingle. The biggest drug smuggling attempt in Ireland to date has gone almost comically wrong. An overladen rigid inflatable boat transferring 1,500 kilos of cocaine from the mother ship to a remote beach on the Mizen Peninsula has been trashed in big waves and high winds, turning some €440 million worth of baled-up drugs into flotsam. Navy cutters, Garda dive teams and fishery patrol boats have been called in to try and round up the drugs before beachcombers pick them up.

It's *Whisky Galore* updated for the new millennium, though this remote coastline has always been used for smuggling. When I was a boy the headline news might be of a seizure of guns from the USA or Libya, intercepted as they were spirited ashore from shadowy boats, bound for the Troubles in the north. As a teenager I'd been warned off by a local man, 'friendly, like', when my early morning rambles along the coast began taking me too often to a series of small concealed coves. But peace and economic boom had made drugs more profitable than firearms.

The press hire helicopters to get film and photographs of the Mizen and the weather that has scuppered the smugglers and is hampering the clean-up operation. 'You want to know what it was like kayaking around the Mizen?' I ask anyone who will listen when the evening news comes on. 'Well, that's pretty much the way it was.' I nod at the screen showing huge waves breaking against the rocks. Now that I've been off the water for a while, I'm full of bravado.

And so to another night in Dick Mack's, another late-night session, the crowd, having thinned out, packing back in again till there's standing room only with an in-rush of restaurant workers. I recognise Tríona and Mila from the Into The Blue fish restaurant amongst them and they're keen to dance. I play 'Route 66' with Andy's guitar and harmonica rack, watch the girls gyrating in the small circle cleared between the two counters. Then Andy takes the guitar back, cracking and wailing Dylan's 'It's Alright, Ma' and straight on into 'Maggie's Farm' and then a bunch of tongue-twisting Cornish ballads and some verbally challenging patter songs. Rob, his big musician friend, sings as well, first carefully putting down his Fantini, diamanté-studded accordion between his legs. For a big man he plays with a rare and relaxed delicacy, less 'driver' and more pilot as he loops and spins and soars arpeggios and ornamentations and lilting runs and swirling melodies above our heavy thudding rhythms. He sings in Cornish, or dialect, or whatever it is. Different enough, anyway, to disconcert the few remaining tourists who have lost track of which country they're in.

Much later, in the early hours, in the rain, I'm out on the country road walking back through the dark to the Rainbow, where I'm still staying, humming contentedly to myself. The wind is high, of course. I've been doing this, or something very like it, every night for two weeks and more. Kayaking around Ireland has become an abstract. As in some ways Ireland itself has become an abstract. I check the weather each day. And my wallet. On a few days within the past fortnight it would have been possible to pack, push off and continue, but the longer forecast was always for a return to high winds and it was easy to persuade myself that heading off for a day's paddling to be pinned down on some rain-soaked and gale-blasted headland or island for three or four days wasn't worth the shot and powder.

At one point, I'd gone to Dublin. Erika was flying in from Sweden the next day. When I'd started paddling, a month ago, we'd planned to spend these few days kayaking together along whichever bit of coast I'd got to by now. I'd confidently imagined it would have been somewhere around Connemara, at this point. Maybe further. Instead, with the weather settled into bad, we stayed in Dublin revelling in the great indoors. Civilisation, I pointed out, as I pitched the idea of remaining in the city rather than heading off to do hearty, wet outdoor stuff, did one thing really well. Roofs. Everywhere we went seemed to have one. Art galleries. Bars. Restaurants. Friends' houses. And all the shops. Roofs! I felt really smug that we weren't sitting under my dripping scrap of nylon tentage or even in damp and drafty Dick Mack's, but were benefactors of all these capital city roof opportunities. There was more seascape footage on the news of the big seas that had scuppered the drugs drop, and the press were able to hang more 'worst summer in living memory' stories on the drama of a children's dinghy race that got blown out by a sudden squall in Dun Laoghaire. Any time I wondered why I wasn't out paddling, there was a headline, a news item or the weather forecast to exonerate my failure.

Failure. Erika knew that, rather than actually kayaking around Ireland, I'd spent two weeks drinking and playing guitar in Dingle. She might have thought that I could have done very much the same in Sweden, and with her. But she didn't say it. As if she had guessed that, for all my bluster and stories, my resolve was weak, and knew that my giving up was even more of a risk than going on.

Parting was the catalyst for going back to sea. True, the weather had got a little better, but mainly I'd got a lot more determined. It was time to leave Dingle. The kayak was still on the quay where I'd left it, piled up against a holed river canoe, an outdated windsurfer and the split hull of a racing dinghy. It was beginning to fur with algae and didn't look so very out of place in this bedraggled company.

So, with a sense of dejà vu, and faded memories of fear, I stuff everything into the damp, musty-smelling compartments, shrug and wiggle my way into wetsuit and cagoule and launch myself from the quay. Dingle Harbour would be an impressively big bay, if only there wasn't already an even bigger Dingle Bay outside; more than enough for a self-chosen dolphin aquarium. As I dip and pull the paddles through the water and head the two miles out to the harbour mouth, I keep an eye out for Fungi.

I note two figures on Black Point, under the tower, looking across the sea and pointing beyond me, where the harbour narrows into a throat and the current picks up. Suddenly a dark shape on the surface comes straight towards me, a black ball of forehead and, behind that, a thick slab of fin with a curl of white foam at its bow. Fungi drops down out of sight again thirty or forty yards away.

Floating on the surface, scanning the waves around me, I feel like a small boat waiting for a stalking U-boat to make its move. This image is heightened by a feeling of having talked a little too much behind Fungi's back, and not always in the kindest of ways, about the whole Fungi phenomenon. So, what I'm thinking now as I wait for him to surface again is that I'm going to look very, very silly if dolphins are as smart and blessed with supernatural communication skills as some people claim and, like one of those fat wrestlers heaving themselves off the corner ropes, he decides to belly-flop down on top of his detractor.

Instead, several minutes later he rolls up parallel to me and I catch a glimpse of his small eye regarding me. Then he is gone. Two Fungi-watching boats are piling out from the port, rails lined with camera-brandishing tourists. I bob around to see what happens next. Which is precisely nothing.

Fungi has now disappeared totally, perhaps to build up the anticipation of the coming dolphin-huggers, or perhaps to check the small print in his appearance contract.

The boats plough up and down the harbour for a while, then start powering up next to each other, leaving a narrow gap between them filled with a high, curling double bow wave as they race along. Not suddenly at all, but slowly, a dark shape appears in the foam until Fungi has lumbered up onto the wave and is riding along on its momentum. It's as if the dolphin is a retired yet still game pro-surfer, hanging ten for old times' sake as a favour to his fans, or perhaps an elderly Edwardian captain of industry being pushed down an esplanade in a bathchair, whilst awed onlookers touch their forelocks and, in these more celebrity-focused times, the shutter buttons on their digital cameras.

Out in the bay, I am pushed along myself by a favourable march of waves following the current down the long miles of cliff and coast and on towards Slea Head. As I paddle, I mull over where my spiteful attitude towards the benignly performing bottlenose came from. What could I find upsetting in a rather rumpled middle-aged chap, who'd once been a bit of a show off and in his younger days given to revelling in his physicality by jumping over boats, spy-hopping and the like, and who'd ended up hanging out in Dingle for far longer than anyone might have expected and was still given to showing off, given half the chance, despite being not quite so svelte as he once was? I dig the paddles in, pull away from the Dingle and, now lighthearted, head south-west-west at full pace towards the Blasket Islands.

CHAPTER 7

Blaskets and Baskers

T HE BLASKETS are the most westerly isles off a western island. The next westness of any note is America. There are five main islands, with the Great Blasket by far the biggest, and they were only finally abandoned by their human populations in the 1950s, ending several millennia of semi-detached life and culture. Their main art form was storytelling. In the early part of the twentieth century this archipelago of less than two hundred people produced a slew of good, published writers, read in both their original Irish and in English translation. Proportionally, it made the literary ghettoes of Hampstead and Cambridge look illiterate by comparison. Peig Sayers' *Peig* is still a familiar text to Irish schoolchildren today, as is the 'The Islandman' – *An tOileánach* – by Tomás Ó Criomhtháin. My own favourite is Maurice O'Sullivan's *Twenty Years A-Growing*, an account of cliff climbs, hunting seals in deep sea caves, big storms and handy seamanship in the islands' skin-covered currachs. These robust rim-of-Ireland stories were steeped in an authentic Celtic reality that even Yeats could only strive toward recreating.

When the Blaskets were inhabited year-round, the islanders' contact with the mainland was across the infamous Blasket Sound. I'd been warned of rough and boisterous currents that pushed their way through the channels and straits between Slea Head and Dunmore Head on the one side and the islands on the other. I expected big waves thrown up by sharp winds coming off Mount Eagle, and breaking crests where the sea depth shallowed and dropped at random and the waters were sliced and diced by the rocks and undersea reefs.

What I get is more enigmatic and disconcerting. Rounding Slea Head the wind drops and the water flattens but doesn't still. It is as if different densities of liquids are mixing together – oils, spirits and gels – so that strange ripples and movements cross the surface. One moment the kayak sinks down deeper and deeper into lighter, airy water; the next it rises as if being pushed up by a shaft of treacle. As I paddle, whirlpools, vortexes and slipstreams grip the kayak and twitch it off course, or pull it suddenly to one side or the other, or stop it dead. I'd been in a mild earthquake in Mexico once, and the way the ground that should have been substantial moved slightly under me then felt similar to the way the water is moving under the kayak now. It feels as if the water might suddenly not have enough specific gravity to hold me up – as if I'm trying to paddle on top of fog or some swirling gas.

Unnerved, I make camp in a narrow rock fold in the small island of Beginish, out in the sound facing the beach on the Great Blasket island. It is my own island, shared only with terns, gulls and a flock of sheep. I fall asleep looking through the door of my tent at faint lights across the water that recreate the atmosphere of a Blasket island alive and populated, though I know it is just summer visitors.

Passing the wide mouth of Smerwick Bay next day, I'm reminded of a story I'd read about a Spanish galleon on the run, caught in an autumn storm, that navigated its way along this coast and then through the Blasket Sound under full sail. At least two other armada ships have been less lucky in the sound. The name Smerwick, though, recalls earlier sailors. On the east coast of Ireland a number of towns and loughs – Wexford, Wicklow, Howth, Strangford – have names of Viking origin. Here on the south and west coast, the few Norse names are attached to seamarks and islands like the Blaskets and Dursey. Smerwick is another of those names, suggesting this was a coastline of touch-and-go landings for Vikings on their way round to the Shannon River, or on raiding parties.

Here on the head, the naming of places often recalls the peninsula's famed saint, and Ireland's premier explorer, Brendan (or Brandon) the Navigator. To the north-east of me, Mount Brandon, Ireland's second highest mountain at 3123 feet, rises on the horizon – is, in fact, the horizon. I'd been told that if you can see a hat of cloud on Brandon then the weather would be good, but today's voluminous turban of cloud and mist seems unpromising. Under that cloud on the very peak is the *Teampaillin Breanainn*, Brendan's Oratory, from where the saint could have looked down on Brandon Bay, Brandon Head and Brandon Point and Brandon village with its Brandon pub. But it was the saint's westward gaze that proved important. In 535 AD, after forty days of fasting and prayer in his oratory, Brendan set off with a crew of monks in a boat made of leather to sail to pre-Colombian America. The voyage was recounted in a medieval manuscript called the *Navigatio Sancti Brendani Abbatis*, which claimed that Saint Brendan took seven years going by way of the Isle of Sheep, the Paradise of Birds, the Isle of Smiths, the Land of Crystal Pillars, then through the Region of Fogs to reach the Promised Land. And then returned.

Suppositions that the story of the voyage must be either allegorical or chronicling a much more local trip – perhaps as far as Scotland – were challenged when explorer Tim Severin and a crew of four recreated the journey in a boat of ox-hides sewn over a light, flexible skeleton of ash wood tied together with thongs. The team set off in May 1976 and reached America the following year after wintering in Iceland. The voyage revealed many of the details in the manuscript, including the route, to have been not only possible but plausible. The Isle of Sheep could have been the Shetlands, and the team identifed other waymarks as the Faroes, Iceland (its smoking volcanoes and geysers like a gigantic forge), Greenland (its icebergs recalled crystal), the fogs on the Great Banks and finally America itself.

Despite the number of pessimistic experts and nay-saying bystanders, when Tim Severin set off on his journey he and his crew could be sure that their leather covered wooden framed boat was seaworthy. The *Saint Brendan* was merely a bigger version of the currachs still found on the Atlantic coast of Ireland. The design had survived precisely because of its lightness and flexibility, allowing it to move with the sea and bob atop big swells and waves and ride out storms. And, once landed, a crew could turn the hull over and carry the boat on their shoulders only their legs visible, looking like a black beetle scuttling to shelter above the shore line; essential on a coast with few safe harbours or mooring places.

I paddle my variant on the skin boat into Brandon Creek, and as I land it begins to bucket down. I have to stop here, though, for as a teenager I'd stood on this slip of land to watch Severin's boat being launched. In the *National Geographic* article I'm in the photo, back to the camera, wearing my father's fawn coat with a 1970s mop of hair.

My connections with the Brendan voyage had all been peripheral but they added up: Tim Severin lived in Courtmacsherry near to where I was brought up in County Cork; my father had made some last-minute adaptations to the simple cooker that the expedition was taking; and I had become apprentice as a teenager to John O'Connell, the harness-maker who had overseen the stitching of the heavy oak-tanned hides with rolled flax threads that made up the *Saint Brendan*'s hull. John was the nearest I'd had to a teacher since the abrupt end of my schooldays, and his calm, patient manner was as far removed as you could get from the bluffly sadistic or disconcertingly boyish behaviour of my English prep school masters.

My parents had experimented for a short period by sending me to a school in the centre of Ireland, on the shores of Lough Derg, that seemed reassuringly unlike the one I'd left in England. It housed just twenty pupils, ranging in age from nine (me) to eighteen, who took the same lessons together in the dining room of the old lakeside house. There was a non-uniform of jeans and jumpers, ludicrous informality, and endless eccentricities that sprang from the 'Boss', as we called the ex-Naval Commander owner.

The oddities extended into the practicalities of everyday school life. If the two smallest of us went in the boot and the eldest boys hitch-hiked ahead, the whole school could be transported for outings using only the Boss's Mark 2 Jaguar. St George's had horses and boats, appalling food and a dangerous sense of anarchy. The half-understood vices that I sensed in the school, as well as – to give my unease a physical definition – being regularly picked up by my ears like a small rabbit, turned me against it. I left in the middle of the night, amid some drama, biting the headmaster after he attempted to prevent me phoning my parents, and then taking refuge in the shrubbery.

I was confident my father would welcome me, for he had recently appeared on Irish television, questioning the value of exams and qualifications and extolling the practical skills and life experience he looked for in those who came to work in his business. Pursuing these arguments with the single-mindedness that dread brings, I pushed him, and my mother, to agree to call time on formal schooling. Instead, I trained falcons to hunt, rode horses, shot rabbits, lit campfires, and skulked off into the woods or down to the coast from dawn till dusk to watch birds. I filled my room with a tawny owl, a merlin, two parakeets, a blue-fronted Amazon parrot and a vivarium of lizards. I learnt to strum a guitar, to write and to draw. Dead animals and birds that I found were skinned and cured with an alchemist's brew of dangerous chemicals and then mounted in some of the least convincing taxidermy since the invention of the teddy bear.

My sister and I were enrolled on a correspondence course, and my mother was forced to add school-ma'm to her list of jobs. But lessons became more and more haphazard until the home-schooling experiment finally ended up in my mother diligently teaching Latin, Spanish, maths and the rest of the curriculum to ... well, to herself ... whilst we were off doing more interesting things. As my parents were doing up a medieval castle, I learnt about woodwork, stone-laying and other hand-tool skills from the men working on the restoration. At various times we had cattle, sheep and pigs, and always horses. There were the annual rounds of haymaking, garden tilling, calving and pig killing. Scything and axeing were frequent jobs. I was becoming perfectly fitted for a fulfilling life lived in any of the preceding five hundred years, and still across large swathes of the globe, but not specifically useful to the era and region I was born into.

My apprenticeship as a harness-maker capitalised on the world of horses, some ability with my hands and a need to learn how to work. John O'Connell was a master craftsman. Under his tuition I learnt to plough-cut, skive, crease, prick, race and ornament leather. Everything we made was handsewn. A pair of carriage traces might be eight foot long, with a double row of stitching, at eight or even ten stitches to the inch, going round their edge. The seven thousand or so stitches in a pair of traces might take two and a half days of non-stop hand-sewing. And John was meticulous; a missed stitch, or a knot on the underside that

I'd overlooked and he'd shake his head slowly, smile and pass me the half-moon knife. 'Rip it! Rip it! Rip it all back.'

Learning to be an occasional perfectionist against my natural tendency, and finding fulfilment in the Zen-like need to concentrate without thinking when doing something so repetitive stood me in some kind of stead. It surely forms the basis of my current ability to paddle contentedly for hours each day, adjusting my stroke in the water by feel, letting time flow past, the same move over and over until, unaware of how much time has passed, I find that some progress has been made.

As I set up camp in the rain, I think of the Brendan Voyage and John and his workshop. The weather had provided all too many 'Rip it! Rip it!' moments on my trip so far. Times when I'd lost momentum or been held up by bad weather. I resolve to match my old master's advice a little more, as I pitch my tent high above the quay on a narrow patch of wet grass and mud, next to a sign showing a stick figure being overshadowed by a curling black triangle and reading DANGEROUS WAVES: People Have Lost Their Lives Here.'

It was too wet to start the stove and cook anything and, though early in the evening, the day was already dark, like a winter's afternoon. I climbed into my sleeping bag.

'Jasper! Jasper?'

The voice was outside the tent. Befuddled I wonder what friend could have found me. Then I wake properly and realise that I've been lapped by Sam Crowley, the American kayaker whom I've talked to by phone but never met. While I'd been in Dingle and Dublin, indulging in music and drinking, he'd been pinned down in his tent in a small bay back on the Beara Peninsula. But, now, he's caught me up. 'Dr Sam Crowley, I presume,' I call, ducking out into the drizzle.

Sam has the full Hemingway beard and, dripping wet, looks like some Viking hero of the seas. He's just made a very long paddle in poor weather from Valentia, across Dingle Bay and through the Blaskets. And he's worked out that a tent and a plastic kayak on this bit of coastline can only be me. I help him up with his kayak, a proper, fibreglass expedition sea craft. And his kit, all neatly packed in a disconcertingly professional way. It contrasts with the mismatched dry-bags piled around my camp, and particularly with the supermarket shopping bag I store my food in. But then again, our relative skill apart, Sam necessarily considers himself on an expedition around a foreign country, while I am simply on a jaunt at home.

I know that there is a pub only a few miles inland at Ballyroe and our meeting seems worth celebrating. So off we go on a splashy walk to find heaped plates of fish and chips and pints and whiskeys and talk into the night. The talk is all paddle lore: the best times to catch the tides and currents, whether to radio check-in with the coastguard or not, how our craft are performing. For the same amount of energy expended, Sam's kayak can go a knot – a nautical mile an hour – faster than *An Fulmaire*. It is as if he is galloping around the coast on a fine thoroughbred horse while I am trotting in his wake on a donkey. But even without this differential we are both solo paddlers and, glad as we are to have met, there is unspoken understanding that we'll both be paddling on alone.

I am first off in the morning. In a fresh breeze and big waves I turn towards Brandon Head. The cliffs are dark with huge fallen slabs slipping into the sea, the inshore chop grey and greasy. The effect is of paddling along in a giant sink full of dirty water, with piles of food-encrusted plates and cups toppling down from a draining board. The fresh breeze is behind me, though, and shreds up the clouds and opens up the sky into blue. In a shaft of sunlight I see two fins, the first about the size of shovel blade, waving in the swell. A small blue shark, less than two metres long, gives a convulsive wiggle and scythes its longer, narrower tail fin and drives down out of sight. Over on the cliffs the curves and edges of its fins are echoed in the orange down-turned bills and splayed finger-feathered wings of a gang of choughs tumbling down the rockface, their chiming 'chack' calls like hitting two flint stones together – an ideal sound for carrying through the windy air of the western coast.

I've rounded Brandon Head and I'm heading across a chord of Brandon Bay's half-circle, so that the shore curves away from me and I'm going further out to sea with each stroke. There's a big smooth swell, well over my head, but almost no waves. I'm up high on a ridge of water one moment with a view around in all directions, and then cast down into a valley of turquoise waters. Carried aloft onto a peak, I look inshore across a couple of miles of sea and spot something big and black amongst the waves. A fin. My heart jolts. As I rise up again on the next swell, I then see two huge fins, parallel to each other and then another further off. And now there's one only a few metres away rising up like a surfacing submarine's conning tower.

Basking sharks. Suddenly I'm amongst a whole shoal of baskers, rising to the surface and slowly, powerfully, swimming in circles around me. 'Shoal' seems the wrong word. A herd, maybe. Seeing only their backs and fins it's like being in amongst a herd of elephants grazing amongst tall grass. I'm awed. I know that they are toothless, benign, plankton filterers. But then again they're huge. Their scientific name, *Cetorhinus maximus*, suggests that a basker might be largish; in reality that means up to nine and a half metres in length and four tonnes in weight. But the scale is hard to grasp as one heads directly towards the kayak, its fin tip swaying high above the hull. Tensed, I see the fin touch the hull of the kayak before sliding gently down into the water. The kayak hardly moves. It's like being hit in slow-motion by a huge silk fan.

Looking down into the water I see that the head of the basker, ending in its comically pointed and snub nose, is already far beyond the other side of the kayak. Now I've seen the full iceberg-proportioned undersea bulk of the fish under the peak of its fin, I don't think of them as elephants any more. It's more as if I've been cast back into some marine Jurassic Park.

In this first sun of many days the basking shark are active. There might be as many as six or seven spread across the sea's surface, rising and sinking, turning back and forth to hoover up the thick clouds of phytoplankton drawn by heat and light from the depths. They are stately and slow, so I am shocked when ahead of me I see a sudden eruption of water as one shark, suddenly frisky, breaches. In some defiance of natural laws and gravity it has heaved its massive bulk clear of the water and for a moment is hanging in the air. Almost immediately another shark throws itself clear of the water. I'm in the midst of a brontosaurus stampede with three-tonne fish flying through the air.

Looking back over my shoulder for more sharks, I see a tiny shape bob over the crest of a wave. It is Sam's head. He disappears down behind the moving waters. Most of the time we are invisible to each other. But if the swells we are riding coincide and thrust us both up at the same time, and we are looking in the right direction, we can see each other, and shout our wonderment, like kids riding carousel horses on a merry-go-round.

Later that evening we set up our tents at the end of the headland of low machair-grassed dunes that lie between Brandon Bay and Tralee Bay, and walk up to the bar at Fahamore. Sam and I look at the few minutes of video I'd shot amongst the sharks. At one point I'd taken my camera in its waterproof casing – good down to forty metres, remember – and had filmed the fin and tail of one basker coming towards me, the two triangles following roughly the same line but waving to either side and one far behind the other. And then, as the fish came head-on to my kayak, I'd plunged the camera under the surface guessing at where the basker might be as it passed.

On the screen there was a flaring of light and then a complete moment of darkness as the camera's sensors tried to catch up with the sudden difference between the intensity of the sun and the gloom of the water. Then one could see the yellow hull of kayak at one side, distorted and plasticky. And coming out of the gloom something submarine and big, a black shape, and a black hole, and bars of white that made no sense. Until suddenly it resolved into the great gaping maw of the shark's mouth. The camera was pointing straight into the huge ribbed cavern that filters tens of tonnes of water – an Olympic-sized swimming pool's worth – every hour. It is like one of those immense Russian transporter planes that you can take a truck into through a front-opening door. The kayak could fit in the shark without touching the sides.

We replayed the piece of video over and over. 'God, it's big!' 'Huge ... and when that one breached, right out of the water ... amazing ... how many people have ever seen that?'

Our excitement attracts the barman, who leans in over our shoulders to peer at the tiny screen. 'Holy God! That's your canoe, yuh? And what's that thing ... it's a killer whale, is it? That a killer whale, huh? A whah? A basking shark? Would you look at the size of it ... Jeez Christ. A shark. That's worse. A shark and the size of it. Hey, Séamy, c'mon look at this ... that was out in the bay there, was it? You won't catch me out in the water any more ... not with those bastards around.'

CHAPTER 8

Colonic Variables

ARLY IN THE MORNING, amongst promises of a day of high winds, the weather forecaster is talking of cyclonic variables. 'More colonic variables,' I shout across to Sam where he is cooking breakfast under the fly sheet of his tent.

'Colonic variables?' he asks. 'What's that?'

'Medical term for shitty weather. I don't know if you're going to chance paddling. I know that I'm not.'

It is the wind – not rain – that is the problem when kayaking: the former is danger, the latter only discomfort. But discomfort when pinned down on land has its own hazards. There's only so much semi-lying in a sodden tent rereading week-old newspaper articles and listening to radio presenters bewailing the worst summer weather in memory that one can do before drinking seems the best way to pass the time. I used to tell foreign friends that Irish pubs were dotted around the country according to a mathematical formula based on the frequency of rain, so one was always within reach of shelter, entertainment and a hot whiskey. In this summer's weather, on the remoter lengths of coast there seems to be a shortfall in the pub network. So I've come up with a new formula: the further one has to walk or paddle to find a bar, and the wetter one gets getting there, the longer one has to stay inside drinking to justify the trip. All that time holed up in Dingle had perhaps been an extreme expression of Jasper's First Law of Compensatory Dipsomania.

Today is an opportunity for a top-up lesson. So I slosh my way the couple of miles back to Fahamore and settle into the pub again. I position myself under an Edwardian cabinet full of stuffed sea birds and drink slow pints and write through the day. The barman from the night before treats me as a character now: the man who's paddled with sharks.

Next day, Sam is up and on the water first, pulling out to sea towards Kerry Head. Fitter, more experienced and with his sleeker, faster kayak, he and I don't expect to meet up again. He'd lapped me. I loaded up my kayak amongst the beached currachs that, here, were used only as tenders to the bigger crab boats moored out in the bay. The currachs had been skinned in glass fibre to make them tougher, if less seaworthy; leather first, then canvas, now fibreglass – an evolutionary course towards my own yellow plastic kayak. There was a litter of spider-crab claws and carapaces in the shallows, and in the heating sun a rich chowdery smell came off the water.

I find myself contented to be at sea again, watching the dull, drink-fugged land drop away behind me. I plan a straight-line course to Kerry Head – a route that will take me four and five miles offshore – and launch into a day of dreaming and paddling, sewing neat, even stitches across the water. I reach Kerry Head far sooner than I'd expected and look across the wide mouth of the Shannon River, with almost ten miles to cross to reach Loop Head: a distance that, again, fell easily astern. How different from my long haul across Dingle Bay. The lighthouse here, on top of its hundred feet of cliff, getting clearer and clearer before I came in so close to its base that it is obscured by the lip of the land.

The sea gets lumpy as the current surges round the headland and a few paddle strokes take me from a smooth swell into breaking waves and great surges of surf. A sharp wind has blown up and the afternoon turned grey. Much as at the Mizen, the incoming swell and matrix of competing currents divide and there is the same mayhem here where the waters rent themselves apart or crash into each other. Suddenly I am amid the largest waves that I've come across so far, the waters rearing as high as cabinet fridge-freezers before toppling over in roaring surges of foam. I take as many paddle strokes to stay balanced as to move forward. With the black cliff faces, the leaden clouds, the grey waters and the white surf, my world has grown cold and mono-chrome and – whether turning back or pressing on – there is no landing within miles.

A large crabbing boat rolls and surges towards me – a strangely cheering sight. Out at sea these fishing boats give me a grounding and perspective. My adventure is someone else's working-day life. This is reassuring, even when, like now, the large boat's wild pitching, and the gouts of spray breaking on its bow and sousing backwards over the decks, shows just how big the seas are. There is a movement in the wheelhouse of the boat and a figure steps out of the door to wave. The deck crew sorting ropes at the stern, muffled in yellow oilskins and sou'westers do the same, straightening themselves to look and then raising an arm each. I'm not entirely alone.

The cliffs beyond the head are formed of horizontal strati. The lowest, softest layers of rock have been reamed out by the sea-making deep, squared-off caves. The swell driving into them explodes back in the dark with muffled but loud percussions like distant artillery. Higher up there are step after step of ledges providing ghettoes, project housing, airy penthouses and semi-detached terraces for gulls, kittiwakes, guillemots, shags and razorbills. As I pass, thousands of heads peer down at me.

I camp that night just short of Ross Bay, setting up my tent above a narrow beach on thick grass that has clumped and matted into something like an old horse-hair mattress. 'Camp away, and be happy,' the farmer told me before asking if I was going to go to the dance that night, waving a hand back down towards the head and describing how to find the community hall near the church. There'd be live music, he told me, and cocked his head and asked if I played at all myself? Or sang, even? There'd be a bar there, anyway. And the following day there'd be currach races on the other side of the head in Kilbaha. I told him I'd see how things went, and how the weather turns out.

I'd fully intended shaking out my one good shirt, pocketing a couple of harmonicas and strolling down the summer-stilled lanes to the hall. Dancing a set or two. Taking a drink. Having a chat. Flirting a bit. All in the warm fug of a late-night summer dance hall. I'd been adamant that my kayak trip around Ireland would always be as much about Ireland as kayaking, and I wouldn't become some automaton notching up sea mile after sea mile. But by the time the dance starts, my daydreams have become nightdreams and I am fast asleep, cushioned on the soft grass.

An hour or so after dawn the next morning I am back on the water. It is misplaced enthusiasm to start so early – treadmill thinking – as I am paddling against the current. I am still too inexperienced to believe that working the tides and currents is really so critical. The black cliffs slip past agonisingly slowly, so that by the time the tide has slackened and then turned in my favour, I've worn myself out for little real gain. I could have gone to the dance, frolicked till dawn, slept in till midday and covered the same distance for about the same effort and much less time and for far more pleasure.

Only in the afternoon do I finally get the benefit of the turned current as it sweeps me past Donegal Point – confusingly named, as I'm still hundreds of miles short of the real Donegal. I'm tired out and ready to camp. And after a night's sleep I'm stupid enough to get up early again the next morning and make the same mistake all over again, setting off six hours too early. Or, arguably, six hours too late. Wrong, anyway. Past Mutton Island, heading straight for Hag's Head with several hours more to go before I reach the start of the Cliffs of Moher. The shoreline parallel to my course, two or three miles away, is a dark line with the modest bulk of Slievecallan mountain inland from Spanish Point. Mid-morning I stop on the preternaturally calm waters to open a tin of tuna and a packet of oatcakes for an early lunch. The sun is hot above me, and the drifting kayak turns slowly as I eat until I find myself looking back behind me to the way I'd come. Above the land and extending for miles in every direction there is an immense black wall of thundercloud. The wind is offshore and I can hear the distant rumble of thunder being blown towards me. There are thick veils of rain, forks of lightning.

Oh, no, no, no ... this is not good, this is not good at all ... lightning ... sea ... small boat ... not good. And so I should ... ... uh, I don't know ... throw everything metal overboard? I chuck the tuna can into the water. *Not be damp?* I wipe my hands dry on my neckerchief. *Paddle like hell for shore?* That is about three miles away and will take close on an hour.

Perhaps I should get out of the kayak and hang off it, actually in the water, low down. That seems a bit extreme. Possibly wrong, too. And certainly a high-risk strategy. Especially given that I've little idea what the chance of being hit by lightning is. I am certainly the highest, and the only non-liquid, thing in many square miles. But does that make a difference? I haven't the foggiest what the effect of electricity hitting salt water will be. Not for the first time in my life I wonder if I hadn't left school a term or so too early.

So what I do is I pick up my paddles and strike out for Hag's Head, still a couple of hours paddling distant, but both away from the thunderstorm and in the direction I want to go in. The head marks the southernmost part of the Cliffs of Moher. At just under 200 metres, the cliffs are not the highest in Ireland, indeed are not even a third of the height of the cliffs on Achill Island or at Slieve League, but they are the most famous. A long black rampart marching in an almost flat plane of rock along the Atlantic coast with only a few small ripples and folds in the sheer face of rock, like a tight-drawn curtain of rock against the Atlantic chill.

Just before Hag's Head is a pock-marking of stark, white houses built on the skyline. Every time I see new-build houses and a cliff I imagine the Irish economy running off its edge like a cartoon rabbit, its legs still windmilling and pedalling as it moves out into thin air, just moments before the long drop. And that's more or less how it's turning out. Through that summer, before the crash, very few pundits were questioning the sustainability of an economy based on the financing and borrowing needed to build and buy a seemingly endless number of new houses. Foreign workers were still flooding into Ireland to work for high wages on developments across cities, on the outskirts of towns and next to small villages. Only the most cynical wondered if there weren't many more houses in Ireland than there were households to occupy them. Some developers and even government ministers were suggesting that the market for the houses being built would be filled by the 'new Irish' who'd moved into Ireland to build them, and then the next lot of emigrants would come in to build the houses needed for more incoming workers, and so on ad infinitum.

Along the tops of the cliffs themselves I see groups of walkers who have suddenly noticed me far below bouncing along in the chop. Some stop. I can see the pointy, elbows-out silhouette of someone raising binoculars to their eyes. Those who keep striding I can use as pacemakers. Now, in the late afternoon, with the current in my favour, I'm travelling considerably faster than a walking person, really flying along. Or so it seems, for it's hard to judge if that person on the cliff top whom I'm leaving behind is striding along like a Masai warrior, or shuffling at the pace of a distracted window-shopper.

There is a lower, but still airy, buttress of rock that a group have scrambled down to so they can swing hand lines out over an overhang to fish for pollock. I can see that there are two women amongst them, one hauling in a line as I pass, and the other sitting on a rug with a picnic bag next to her. The men are in T-shirts and jeans, but both women are wearing mini-skirts and crop tops; I would swear that the one on the rock edge swinging the line of hooks out is balanced on high heels. Almost certainly East Europeans who, touchingly, still dress up to the nines for any activity that isn't actually the grind of everyday work.

A little further and I am alongside tour boats, surging through the waves to bring sightseers out to the cliffs. Up above me I know is the new interpretive centre, and a car park, safety barriers, signs, footpaths and the Atlantic Edge Exhibition. Pay your entry fee and the cliffs are yours in a carefully organised and non-perilous way. Paddling below, I'm oddly disappointed in my cliffs experience.

I remember a night a decade and more ago when I'd been at the Lisdoonvarna Matchmaking Festival. Held every year at the end of September – 'after the harvest, when you have the time and the money for courting' – the get-together is several weeks of dances, introductions, drinking, flirting and loneliness either cured or heightened. I'd been doing a magazine story on Ireland's last matchmakers, Willie Daly and his daughter Maire, and for several days I'd followed them around the bars of Lisdoonvarna as they made notes in a big brown-bound ledger, huddled with men and women of all ages and backgrounds to get their details, and then made the introductions.

Through Willie I'd met Ann-Marie, a visiting Samoan-Irish girl come to town with friends looking for *craic*. We ran into each other over and over, late at night in bars, or at the morning dances. I began seeking her out, charmed and amused by her hilarious accounts of being 'matched' with hurlers and farmers and city boys, all of whom would take her for a 'test drive' round the dance floor whilst hollering bits of chat-up in her ear. We fell into an easy friendship and more, so that one night we decided to get away from the all the frenzied 'matching'. Packing some wine and a rug, we drove out to the Cliffs of Moher, where, with the car radio tuned to a local country music station, we waltzed in the moonlight on the very edge of Europe. It was our own Atlantic Edge Experience, listening to the sea far below, thrilled by the knowledge that just a few three-time steps away was a drop into darkness.

CHAPTER 9

O'Connor's Bar

AT DOOLIN I CATCH UP with Sam, who is installed in a neat, crowded campsite next to the small harbour. As I set up my own camp I notice how very green and manicured the grass is between the tents and lines of campervans and caravans. This is the opposite of wild camping: neat, organised, suburban. I revel in hot showers, a kitchen block with a roof, washing machines and driers.

Sam has met up with a pair of kayaking friends – Jukka from Finland and Nancy from the States. The three have expedition-paddled together in the past and are off out to the Aran islands while Jukka's wife and children drive around the west of Ireland. They have their charts out on the grass and are listing stores and equipment and marking up routes, very much the expedition team. The serious Finn questions me briefly and leaves me feeling the amateur muddling through on luck and a bit of local knowledge. I, in turn, bridle at his making a quasi-military campaign out of what is going to be no more than a few days' coastal paddling whilst his family drive along the shore with a car full of dry clothes. Or perhaps I feel guilty about his rumbling my poor preparation, which consists of putting up my tent and heading into town for a drink. I think we both sense that he would be a far better candidate for the thousand-miles-round-Ireland adventure – whilst I would surely be better off doing a few days of well-planned coast-hopping.

In Ireland there is always a bar to take your mind off such things, and up in O'Connor's the music is starting up. I prop myself against a pillar and listen. Perhaps there'll be some morale-raising ballads about a canny lad heading to sea and confounding everyone with his triumphing in the face of all disasters. Though a quick mental shuffle through the sea songs I know – 'Lord Franklin', 'The Greenland Whale Fishery', 'I Wish I Was Back in Liverpool' – only comes up with storms and seasickness, loss, drownings and disaster.

A trio of fiddle, flute and accordion finger out jigs and reels like touch-typists taking dictation from invisible voices. They are locals. The fiddle player has a 'farmers tan', browned gauntlets that end in white on his arms where he's pushed his sleeves higher up than he had in the fields. They are good musicians, adroitly keeping the tempos changing to discourage eager tourists from clapping along. Someone starts every now and again, but even the keenest is thrown off at the first sharp corner as the music veers into a new pace, leaving the last person's clap hanging in the air like a joke fallen flat.

The music's twists and turns don't deter a Darby O'Gill character in a tweed cap and patchwork waistcoat, though. At regular intervals he fishes a bodhran out from under the table and bangs and thuds away at it with a denturey grin. Then he gets up and hoofs away, whipping up explosive cracks and slaps from his boot soles and the concrete floor. As watchers lift their mobile phones to record him gurning and jigging, he gives a big grin and a window-cleaning whirling arm of a wave at each pointed lens.

In Dingle, in an act that mixed bravado and fear in equal measure, I'd bought a set of driver's 'L' plates, red on white squares, and stuck them on the kayak fore and aft. As I carry the kayak down the steep, weed-iced slip, a serious German on the quayside looks me and my craft over carefully. He asks if I'm just learning to paddle and if it's compulsory in Irish waters to flag my ignorance with plates. He does some kayaking himself, he tells me, and thinks it might be unwise for me to go out on my own, if I don't know what I'm doing, in this wind. 'I think you're wrong, but I totally agree with you,' I tell him, and paddle off.

Before tourist money, government grants and odd, modern streams of prosperity, the Galway Aran Islands (to differentiate them from Donegal's single Aran Island and from the Scottish Isle of Arran) were small, stark self-contained worlds. Increasing in size from east to west, the barren rockery of Inisheer, Inishmaan and Inishmore take the full brunt of the Atlantic weather, their soil so poor that agriculture was always at back-breaking subsistence level. Stones were cleared from each piece of land by hand, and then piled up as walls and windbreaks to enclose pocket-handkerchief fields. The very soil itself was created from sand, stone dust and seaweed. There were few natural resources except boulders, salt water and wind.

A way of life that had changed little over five hundred years overlapped in the twentieth century with the exigencies of modern film-making. Robert Flaherty's docudrama *Man of Aran*, shot in 1934 on the islands, famously sought to show to the modern world the unchanging lifestyle of the islanders. But in doing so, Flaherty had to sidestep the inconvenient truth that the islanders' lives had already begun to change – and quite significantly. Locals were asked to act a part, recreating events and tasks that had been fading away on the islands over the previous decades, whether harpooning basking sharks for their livers to light the winter lamps, or bringing up baskets of kelp from the shore to make 'soil' in the fields, or launching their currachs out into storms. 'Families' were featured whose members weren't actually related but had been grouped together because they seemed more photogenic, and all were dressed in 'costumes' recreated from folk-memory – raw-hide slippers and woven woollen belts for the men and long flannel skirts, petticoats and hooded cloaks for the women. The sets were real enough: the everyday fields and whitewashed stone cottages of the islanders with their reed thatched roofs tied down against the savage winds. However, it was a time when light was all important to film, so the scenes were necessarily shot in good weather, with the beaches appearing as dazzling strips of white.

This is not the Inishmore I am looking at now. Boats and ferries track in from all directions to a busy harbour, their heavy throbbing engines audible before they come out of the drizzle hiding the mainland. And with its higgle-piggle of primary-colour buildings Inishmore looks like a Monopoly board after a long and high-stakes game with every bit of real estate housed and hotelled in squares of splashy bright colours. There are sizeable buildings around the port and cars fill the roads.

Although tired, I lack the will to stop, finding myself drawn further and further along the coastline. But there is either no obvious place to land, or no flat hidden place to put up my tent. As I paddle along the shoreline, I mull over the madness and error of demanding that places such as the Aran Islands stand still in time so that those few of us with austere tastes can appreciate the experience. And I know this applies to much of my trip – my exploration of Ireland from the outside – a yearning for something already gone. It probably applies to much of my travelling life, now I come to think of it.

Through upbringing I am able to ride horses, wield hand-tools, make things out of rope and branches, sleep comfortably on the ground, match drink with drink, and speak a phrasebook's worth of foreign languages. So around the world I have mixed easily enough with cowboys, tribes people, pilgrims, subsistence farmers, fishermen, sailors, gypsies, adventurers, ramblers, gauchos and jobbing musicians. And I have the knack, if I go far enough into those wild places, of being slightly better at doing things than people's low expectations allow an outsider. But back at home I am far worse at modern, everyday things, and I feel something of a stranger here, paddling around an Ireland that has changed at its own hyper-accelerated pace.

I eventually land on a shore of tide-dried rocks covered in seaweed. It is a hundred yards and more to the shore and I am watched by a sardonic seal as I slide and trip back and forth with all the gear and then with the kayak. Above the tideline there is a maze of small fields, most with tumbled down walls. In them the machain grass has grown up and over in layers, tangling itself into a fat mattress, filling the spaces between the walls like quilted squares. Trying to put the tent pegs in is like driving nails into a pile of feather pillows. I tie the guy ropes to rocks and tufts of grass, though still the skin sags. Anything I drop – a spoon, my torch – disappears as if into a weedy pool of water.

Sleep comes deep on the layers of of grass, and I wake with sun playing across the folds of tent skin and a sharp knocking sound cracking the air. *TCHOCK ! KTOCH! KLACK! KLOCHT!* Several fields away a farmer is opening and closing the gate, *Man of Aran*-style, to put a couple of cattle into one of the bedroom-sized fields. He tumbles a gap in the rock wall, 'Ho!-Ho!'s the cattle through, and then piles the boulders up again to fill the gap behind them.

Lying on the grass, I listen to the meadow pipits rising and singing and falling, and the lazy buzz of flies and a distant horse's snort, and feel a small spider run across my stomach. I wonder how many past islanders have felt and heard and seen exactly what I am experiencing now. The warmth of the sun, the birdsong, the blue of the sky and the knock of stone on stone. The farmers before these generations, and before them the mysterious peoples who'd built the forts and the beehive huts. And how many more in the future would lie here and feel the surreal floating sensation of lying on the trampoline of grass, and hear the birdsong unchanged?

My bad moods and misanthropy come, it seems, from the weather, and have changed with the sun, which has lit the sea to the colour of an LA swimming pool. I drift away from Inishmore and set a north-western course towards the archipelago of low-lying islands that scatter the southern coast of Connemara, some barely broken free from the mainland and others still joined to it by an umbilical cord of sand and scrub. *Connemara* translates as 'close to the sea', and these scraps of land can't get much closer to the marine without actually being submerged.

In these shallow waters are a *Swallows and Amazons* scattering of names: Fools Shoal. The Big Breaker. Inner Passage. Duck Island. Doonguddle. And inland from here, in Camus Bay, comes one of Ireland's longest place names: Muckanaghederdauhaulia. I savour the word as I paddle – MUCK-ANAGH-ED-ER-DAU-HAULI-A – 'marsh of the pig between two salt seas'.

Further out at sea than I'd expected, I come to a small group of rocky islands, the Namackan Rocks. In this calm at low water, they are a proper expanse of land with lagoons and channels. But in any wind or swell they would have been nothing but tiny studs of rock washed over by the seas. I'm forgetting the bad weather. Under the azure sky in this golden calm, I imagine myself on a miniature Hy-Brazil, the mythical island said to lie south-west of Galway Bay which is shrouded in mist except for one day each seven years. Some legends say that the island, even if seen, can never be reached, though people through the centuries claim to have landed. It features on ancient maps in a confusing number of shapes, sizes and locations, allowing crypto-geographers to suggest the island as America, the Canaries – and even a rock roughly where I am now. Perhaps I've slipped through some portal to a parallel world of myth. The glorious clarity of the weather, the sparkling sunshine and the total calm suggests as much. As does the friendliness of the seals that pop up beside the kayak and look me in the face with their brown, cow-sized, myopic eyes, their stiff white whiskers twitching like antennae.

Sudden splashes and ripples mark startled pollock, which crash-dive down from basking in the warm surface waters. Paddling into a central 'pool' amongst the ring of rocks, I come upon a clinker-built boat drifting in the sun. A man has propped a rod over the side and two children are jiggling hand lines down into the depths.

The man is surprised to see me: 'God! You gave me a start. You're a long way out in your canoe.'

'Ah sure, you too, in your little boat. What a great day, though, is'nit! Don't we deserve all this now after the past weeks? Did you catch anything!?' I find myself slipping into an Irish accent a couple of notches stronger than my own, as if I don't want a dissonant voice in this lovely place.

He receives it at face value. 'Divil a one. There's no mackerel this year, at all. I don't know what's happened to them. Last year I'd be pulling up a full feathers of them, five and six at a time ... and this summer I only ever got one at a time so far, and they're small, like sprats really.'

That's all I'm hearing, along this coast, and when I've thrown a line I've not caught a thing, either. There's something up with the mackerel this year. But the sun's out, the sky enamel blue, the sea a-sparkle, and that's enough to shake off troubled thoughts.

Part Two

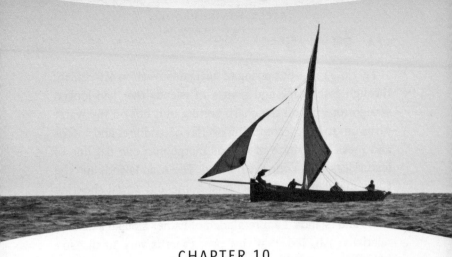

CHAPTER 10

A Quarter Down

CROSSING FROM THE ARAN ISLANDS I find I've made a significant advance. My all-Ireland small-scale road map is printed half and half on two sides of a single sheet, with the bottom of the country on one side and the top on the other. I'd started halfway along the bottom of the southern half of the map, and now need to turn the map over to see my landing on Mweenish Island. This means that I've made it a quarter of the way around Ireland. But with six weeks gone, my original maths now seems like so much hubris. At one point, early in the trip, at my most confident, I'd genuinely thought that I might be finished by this day, in late July. Still, I tell myself, there's only three-quarters of the island left to go.

I get the maps out trying to navigate myself to Mweenish, through a seascape and scatter of islands that had looked straightforward on the chart, setting out, but on the water turns out to have a confusing overlay of landlines and shores and rocks. The maze of islands merge into one flat line of featureless land along the horizon. The Aran Islands and the Clare mainland are the fictional home and actual shooting location for television's *Father Ted* and, looking at the distant rocks and islands, I am reminded of Father Dougal's take on relativity: 'Ah, Ted, that cow over there is very small, isn't it?' 'No, Dougal, it's not, it's just a long way away.' I feel that a similar misconception might sum up my trip.

My friend Tash had called before I'd left Aran to ask where I was heading. She was on her way to the Galway Arts Festival but offered to drive out and meet me with a picnic. We'd settled on Mweenish Island as a rendezvous because of its bridge to the mainland. Now, though, we are both lost. We text back and forth trying to synchronise our coordinates.

There's a causeway on the map: Have you come across it?

No, still on mainland. Where go when on island?

Take road to left, then second track to left – first beach you get to

Ah, the benefits of modern communications in arranging a shore party. I text again.

If passing shop can you get a bottle of wine? And Irish Times

When I land, the sun is pouring down and honeying the white sands and spotlighting two Mediterranean-looking trees on a spur of rock. Tash's Postman Pat red van is squeezed between two walls at the end of a boreen.

I can see Tash standing by the van. I'm looking forward to talking with her rather than to myself, anticipating doing the crossword together, brewing up some tea. This contact with someone I know well normalises the trip, neutralises the loneliness, the occasional feelings of madness. It's a summer's day, and I'm on a beach with a friend. All's perfect. Then suddenly the massive dark cloud that covers the half of the sky behind me releases a grape-shot volley of raindrops that flatten the waves and drive little craters into the sand. Tash sprints for the shelter of her van while I stand knee-deep in the sea, like a disconsolate heron, as the sky's waters flood over me.

Later the rain gives way to a strange half-light as I pitch the tent under the curious gaze of a trio of cows hanging their heads over the stone wall. Tash has already got the kettle going to make tea and we sit on the tailgate of the van doing the crossword and looking out between the doors that frame a view of the grassy lane. The view feels stagey and unreal, like some light opera lit by coloured spots, and, as if on cue, from stage left, a small blonde girl dressed in pink trousers and top, her face serious, walks into view. Followed by an identical small girl also in pink. And then another. And finally a fourth. They walk in single file up the lane and disappear over the brow of the hill.

As if the four small girls have then morphed into one, a figure then comes back over the hill a few minutes later; an elderly woman holding a pink bathing costume. 'It's lovely here, isn't it?' she calls as she passes, then stops to add, 'But it's terrible in the winter … the wrecks and the drownings this island has seen.' She gestures out to Duck Island on the horizon. 'A trawler went up on there in a gale ... all drowned ... you can see the wreckage there still ... the bodies, young men were crewing, came up on the beaches here.'

Later, with glasses of wine in our hands, we walk the sands below the camp. There is a child's wellington boot on the grey sands. In Scotland a single left boot is a bad omen, whilst finding a lone right boot is lucky and they are often nailed to a ship's mast as a talisman. I try to remember other seafaring taboos I've read about. According to region, pigs, priests, umbrellas, bananas, women and playing cards are all unlucky and kept off boats. Imagining the unluckiest boat afloat, filled with a cargo of just those things, brings to mind a surreal nursery rhyme. The owl and the pussycat, perhaps, with the runcible spoon, guitar and five-pound note, but weirder.

I've been collecting items for the totem line on the front of the kayak. There's the yellow plastic duck and a fulmar's feather plucked from the sea just after I'd seen it flutter down from the skies. Also a dolphin's vertebra, and an eroded fish-shaped piece of wood, both of which I trusted might work sympathetic magic on the seas. Then a small pumice with a hole through it, so light and floaty that I felt it might work in the manner of oppositional magic, confounding the gods that might sink me. I add two swirl-coloured beads, from Tash, to avert the evil eye, but leave the boot – which is a left one – on the sand.

A little further on, we meet the woman with the swimming costume, back from her afternoon's swimming. She has another macabre story, of a woman who came to stay here each year with her husband, then disappeared. The husband said she'd left early, and that was the last that was seen of either of them.

Walking through a small high-walled field by the two Mediterranean trees, botanising with book in hand, recognising marsh orchids, and worts and devil's bits, scabrous and other delicate confettis of yellow and red and mauve, I find the signs of a neglected smallholding, and pushing briars and grasses aside with a stick I'm startled to find a woman's face staring up at me. She has been carved subtly into a boulder set into the ground, the grass grown over her like a cascade of tousled hair.

On the rocks I strip off and swim out into the clear waters, but even while I float I find myself tense. The talk of drownings and the missing woman has turned everything into an omen. I have a sense of dread at the back of my mind, and wonder if it has been there all voyage, a part of my whole relationship with the sea. To try and clear my mind I dive down to touch the seabed, feel my chest tighten as the cold water presses in on me. A few metres down I'm amongst trance-dancing seaweeds in purples and greens and all shades of brown. The natural world, its immediacy and its simplicity, are an antidote to my sense of disquiet. I feel the weather and the waves and swell and the basking sharks and rain and everything that's happening around me as neutral. *I'll just keep moving*, I tell myself.

The next day is the regatta at Roundstone, a few miles up the coast, and the morning shipping forecast promises force six or stronger 'soon' – which means anything up to twelve hours. I launch in the morning with the kind of trepidation one feels in the calm before the storm. Because, cliché though it is, the sea is unusually still, with bathtub scale ripples along the rocks. As I paddle on from Mweenish, I notice two sailing boats – traditional Galway hookers – barely moving in the light breeze. Long bowsprits carry russet foresails out from their bows at an acute angle, whilst the mainsails billow to the side. They drift along, with their blunt black-tarred hulls driving through the waters like wedges.

Mweenish was once famed for building hookers, though no one knows exactly when or how the boats first evolved. It is hard to envisage a jump from the skin and light-ribbed frame of the currach to a fully planked boat, and some believe the clinker-built ships of the Vikings may have been their ancestor. The Irish for boat – *bád* – comes from the Norse, as do many other words specific to sailing and the sea, including *ancaire* – anchor; *stiúir* – rudder, *dorgha* – fishing line, and *trosc* – cod. But it's more likely that the hookers developed from fishing boats sailed from England and Scotland, then copied by Irish shipwrights who'd worked abroad. If so, their origins are still Viking – but by a more roundabout route.

Whichever, the hooker became a discreet, indigenous style of boat with a flattened bottom for navigating shallow coastlines, a broad beam for carrying everything from tonnes of peat, rocks or limestone, to cows to fishing gear to passengers. The *bád mór*, the 'big boat', was up to forty-five feet long; the *leath bád*, or 'half boat', somewhat shorter. A simplified sail pattern allowed the maximum amount of canvas to be put up with the minimum of gear.

Coming into Roundstone Bay, even the light sea breeze has dropped. It is the windiest summer on record but the hookers lined up to race are becalmed. The big-bellied, barrely boats wallow gently in the wavelets, their tan and cream sails hanging slack as damp sheets on clothes lines. They have open braziers fired with chunks of peat to boil up kettles to 'wet the tay' with, and in the calm the smoke hangs in the air. As I paddle through the fleet I feel like a ghostly presence in the midst of an old sea battle played out silently and in slow motion. The ships' hulls nudge up against each other, the forest of spars soaring into the blue skies, there's a smell of tar and hemp and salt, and the smoke drifts through the calm air like cannon fumes.

A tannoy from the shore is trying to impose order on the canvas-skinned racing currachs lined up off the pier head ready to start the first of the afternoon's rowing races, but the drifting tangle of hookers fills the bay. A flotilla of crash boats buzzes out from the harbour and starts pulling them out of the way. The sound of a shotgun from the land gives a soundtrack to the naval warfare ambience. Two currachs shoot forward, four rowers in each, arching over the long, square-shafted oars with the narrow blades. Bending, straightening, bending, straightening. The stroke oarsman in each boat flicks his head round to find a way through the assault course of heavy black hulls, smaller boats, and buoys. The winners are not the swiftest rowers, but the most agile. One boat gets hopelessly out of stroke as it tries to steer between two closing hookers, and ends up going round in circles like an injured black water beetle. The other currach has taken an easier route and, already round the marker, is heading back to victory.

I slip in behind the winning currach and land on a shelf of rock below the seaward bulk of the pier, where I haul *An Fulmaire* clear of the dropping tide and tether her to a rusty ring. Above me a dangle of legs hangs over the pier edge, whilst on a balcony over the water there is the sound of clinking glasses and talk. This handsome pier that I am landing on is one of the forty or so around the coast of Ireland that bear the name of the Scottish engineer Alexander Nimmo, who surveyed some two-thirds of the Irish coastline in the 1820s and then set about designing and constructing the piers and quays that would make the exposed natural harbours of the coastal villages safe berths.

I stop to listen to a hawk-nosed man in a tea-cosy hat hunched over a cherry-red accordion. A sheet of thick plywood had been lain on the ground and a plump, jolly woman is noisily hopping and skipping on it. And then the skies open and the crowds rush for shelter, squeezing into the pubs up and down the street. I make my way back to the kayak, as happy to paddle on in the rain as wait it out.

Even my detailed sea chart founders in the complexity of shoals, rocks and mini-islands along this stretch of Connemara coastline. There are long stretches of sand and dunes inland, and at sea a maze of channels between rocks and reefs. But the rain stops, and as I land and make camp I'm rewarded with a perfect sunset that intensifies from a rose tint in the west till it becomes a sheet of deep red and the waters ferment into Homer's wine-dark seas.

By the following midday, however, the wind is a relentless blow that turns the sea leaden and whips up big waves that curl and break along their ridges. I set out only because the numerous islands and low-lying shoreline inland seem to promise some chance of shelter and many escape landings. Here it is definitely waves I'm amongst and not swell – petulant local waters.

There's a sudden crackle of sound on my VHF radio, set to channel 16, the distress frequency. The coastguards are relaying that there's a missing swimmer reported somewhere off Dolan Point, ten or so kilometres behind me. I switch over to the working channel, where boats in the area are being asked to head to the point to help in the search. The lifeboat in Clifden is already out on another rescue, so there is a back and forth of messages as various yachts and boats in the area radio in and the closest of them turn towards Dolan Point.

I switch back to channel 16 and keep paddling. I'm in between Illounurra Island and the mainland, protected from the main swell and the wind, but there are white breakers on the rocks. I hear an engine long before I see the bright-orange RIB (rigid inflatable boat) coming up behind me. It's bouncing along, hitting off the wave tops and making a regular banging sound. Getting closer I see it veering off its course towards me and accelerating. I can see detail as it gets closer. The helmsman is a portly, middle-aged man, wearing some kind of fake captain's hat. The boat is brand new, with a huge outboard on the back – a 'SSIA-craft'. Five years previously the Irish government had instigated SSIAs, or 'special savings incentive accounts', adding twenty percent to any sum invested. The economic thinking behind the scheme was unclear, but it was seen as 'free money' by the Irish and, on the dot of five years, when they matured, everyone began cashing them in for new cars, patio decking, conservatories and round-the-world holidays. Not to mention irritating jet-skis and RIBs.

'Are you in trouble?' RIB Man has throttled back the engine from chainsaw-through-tin to a burbling chunter, and the boat is rolling almost on top of the kayak.

'Uh, hello, no.'

'You shouldn't be out here in these conditions; there are people in trouble already ... c'mon, take this rope and I'll take you into the shore.'

'I don't know that's necessary, y'know. I'm fine.' The RIB is rising up on the swell and threatening to pound down on top of me. I begin paddling away.

'C'mon now, these are bad conditions. I'll take you in.' The voice is drifting away behind me, the words shredded by flailing blades of wind. I purposefully set off across a low reef of rocks and then round a small headland. I can hear the yammering of the engine rising behind me. And then a few minutes later a throttling back again. My radio, on the foredeck, breaks into sound. My would-be rescuer is calling up the coastguard.

'Hello, I'm out past Dolan Point in a RIB and I've just been talking to a kayaker who's out in the bad conditions.'

Coastguard to RIB: 'What are you saying? Is that a kayaker in trouble? It's not the swimmer, no?'

'No, it's a kayaker and he says he's alright. But the conditions are very bad out here ... He's paddled away now.'

Coastguard to RIB: 'So, you're calling us to say there isn't a problem?' The radio on the deck goes silent – a long heavy pause. Then: 'So would you clear channel 16, then?'

●—●

I make my escape along the shore of Ballinleama Bay. The wind has got stronger, but it is blowing evenly now rather than gusting as I edge along towards Slyne Head, another of Ireland's 'corners', where the seas twist and turn and tangle as they hit land. Along the Cork and Kerry coasts hard edges of rock form walls of cliffs that drop straight into deep waters, but I've now crossed a line to Ireland's other geological format. Here the waters barely cover the run-off of rock from the land, and shallows extend far out to sea, making reefs and islands where harder strati of rock have withstood the waves and the wind.

Slyne Head is actually an island, some four kilometres offshore, at the end of a long headland of white beaches and low rocks and a mazey archipelago. I've insinuated my way through a narrow channel, sucked and pushed by the speeding currents as the ebbing tide rushes out. I pull out on dazzling white sand and find shelter behind a rock. Out of the wind it is warm, especially in my black rubber wetsuit, and I fall asleep in the sun. This is some kind of bliss. There are no houses here, no fences, and only a few brown and white cows wandering along the beaches. It's a timeless place, discounting the bright-coloured plastics amongst the beach waste. I imagine myself a monochrome daub, a figure to give scale to the 'distant purple hills' school of early twentieth-century Irish painting, where blocks of landscape colours are almost abstract, and the man-made details are little more than simple white cottages, rounded haystacks or wandering dirt tracks.

I awake from a doze and sit up abruptly. There is a strident twittering and the black and white flutters of two startled oystercatchers taking to the air. I imagine that my inert, black neoprene bulk laid out on the sand must have looked familiarly like a seal to them, making my sudden waving of lanky arms and legs an outrage. Later, as I paddle through the narrow gorges between rocks, I surprise them again. They fly off, bills scissoring open and shut like crimson chopsticks, shrieking their displeasure.

But which is it, 'bill' or 'beak'? Which birds have which, I puzzle to myself as I paddle slowly along the shore. An oystercatcher's bill? Oystercatcher's beak? Ducks have beaks? Except it's a duck-billed platypus ... eagle, then, definitely a beak ... linnet, a bill, or not ... a robin's beak, surely? A blackbird's bill ... dove, a bill ... parrot, a beak. I'm trying to come up with some grammatical or ornithological or even logical rule for dividing birds into the 'beaked' and the 'billed'. There doesn't seem to be one. One gets pecked by a beak, in a hurt-and-drawn-blood kind of way; being pecked by a bird with a bill would be a joke, right? So beaks are potentially painful and bills are for small little birds ... *A wonderful bird is the pelican, his beak* ... no, his bill? ... *can hold more than his belly can, he can hold in his beak* ... BEAK, that's it ... *enough food for a week, and I'm damned if I know how the hell he can.* So it's beak for big birds, then, and bills for ... let's get technical and exact ... all passerines, say ...

You really do get to thinking like this if you paddle.

●——●

Coming out of the channel I feel how strong the wind is, and beyond is an exposed length of coast with sloppy waves breaking off the surface of a big swell. Where they hit the land, they explode in huge bursts of spray and blocks of green water. But most worrying on this shore are the 'boomers'. Incoming swells are hitting undersea reefs and rocks that almost touch the surface, and exploding upwards, in angry bursts of spray and water. I'm both intrigued and concerned. If one were to rise up under me, I'd find myself thrown up into the air as if a depth charge had gone off under the kayak.

At the point where I have to leave the shelter of the small islands, I hesitate. I can already feel the sea tossing the kayak around, and the sight of the boomers is unsettling. The paradox in this paddling lark is that to stay upright one has to be relaxed and follow the flow. Dance with the water, if you will, as if steering an agile partner across a rough ballroom floor after a cocktail too many. Tighten up, as is reasonable when you're unable to read the sea, and instead of flowing with the waters you end up stiff and reactive, and too slow to match the fluidity of the waters. In other words, capsized.

I'm doing something that's stupid in kayaking – making a dash for it. The length of exposed coastline is probably only about a mile in length, and then I can duck in behind several miles of islands that will act as a sheltering reef, creating lagoons and channels and pools. But that mile of paddling does not look fun.

In the event it takes twenty minutes or so. The waves toss me around a bit. But I've got my confidence back by convincing myself that if anything goes wrong, in the worst case, with this onshore wind I'll be able to land on the rocks, if not in the kayak, then by swimming. It's a cathartic moment, battling the feeling of dread. And it's exhilarating, too, toiling past the big seas smashing against the shoreline.

Once inside the 'reef', there is a different set of problems. Studying the chart, I'm not convinced there is a permanent route through the labyrinth of islands and channels here – just a chance that at high tide some of the fault lines in the rocks make narrow streams that join up. But the tide is dropping and I push my way into dead ends and pools that shrink visibly around me. The surface of these waters is matted with a brown sea grass that makes each stroke like trying to fork a decent portion of tagliatelle out of a pan.

At one point I land the kayak on a reef of weed-covered rocks and climb up to look ahead. There's a possible network of cuts that, like the best of mazes, turn back on themselves and zigzag back and forth. But the water is going down too fast and soon I find myself looking between two pillars of dried rock facing each other like Tangiers and Gibraltar. Beyond is a mini-beach of sand and then some more rock like a miniature pass through a chain of mountains, and beyond that an expanding Sahara of rippled sand that drops back down into the sea far beyond. I feel as if I've entered a Lilliputian world, in a kayak the size of a supertanker. I could unload here and carry everything through the pass and across the sands, and then reload and paddle onwards for another hour or so till dark, but the logic of laziness suggests that if I'm going to unpack everything I might as well set up camp on one of the shag-grassed heights above my miniature seascape.

I'm relaxed now, lulled by a good day behind me, and by having found calm. So I sit in the kayak letting peace drift over me. Even within ten or fifteen minutes the waters drop by a foot or so, and looking back I see that I'm now floating in a pool, and not an inlet. In the cockpit of the kayak sealed in by the spray-deck and in my cagoule and hat I'm warm and feel as if I'm in a gently rocking cradle. My pool is now only slightly bigger than the kayak. This is a moment of perfect stillness, just before 'duskus' as locals have the time of falling darkness.

The night wind coming in off the sea is brisk and cold as I set up the tent and light the stove. I can see the tide below my patch of grass coming in again slowly across the sands and realise that to launch the kayak, with the minimum of carrying, will mean starting at about three in the morning. I wonder idly if the waters will fully join up across the 'pass' or whether I've compromised my circumnavigation by going across what is de facto land.

The tide is far out again when I wake. I've overslept and, having broken camp, must carry everything across the sands, back and forth on four trips, laden like a Sherpa. The day is breezy still, but the sun is out and the waters are shimmering. Like the weather my mood has changed. The waves don't seem as big today but that might only be because I'm rested and heading towards Clifden, only a few hours' paddling along the coast.

As I come out into Mannin Bay the chart marks *Testy Breakers and Knock Breakers* further out to sea. I'm beginning to understand the boomer phenomenon now, not as random eruptions but rather with a rough tempo in specific places above rocks and reefs. There's an almost predictable exploding boomer above Doolick Rock. Curious, I steer my course close to its position. Though I don't know exactly when the boomer will burst upwards, I do know where it is, and this is enough to embolden me and draw me in close. I wait for the waters to up-rush, a little fearful that I've miscalculated and am about to be thrown up like a ping-pong ball on a jet of water.

I'm seaward of the rock as a big swell passes under the kayak and I sink down into its trough. Then, as the seas twist and swirl onto Doolick, they suddenly lift straight up into the air with a huge, breathy whoosh. Spray is caught on the wind, as the heavy bulk of water crashes back into the sea. I'm fascinated as if by the northern lights, a volcano or a big wind whipping through trees; the power of natural forces. It's hydraulic fireworks.

I paddle in a long course round to the landward side of the rocks and wait for another boomer. Now I'm downwind and downcurrent of the exploding water. I see the next boomer as a glassy green wall of water that rises so high into the air that even a hundred foot away it seems to tower above me. Almost immediately the wind slices off its crest and a shower of spume and drizzle blows over the kayak. An onward pulse of torn-up waters drives on from the rocks and throws the kayak around.

I feel a dangerous fascination pulling me closer; fear has gone now and I'm hypnotised by the boomers, wondering what it would feel like to actually have one go up right under the kayak. This is a dumb thought. I can feel myself lured by a sort of hydro-vertigo. With the sea and the wind calm compared to yesterday, the boomers have taken on an almost playful aspect, and paddling on toward Clifden I find myself drifting closer to them as if on safari, watching something big and unpredictable but currently quiet, like a gently grazing rhino.

CHAPTER 11

Thinking about Thinking

AFTER ALL MY PRACTICE in Dingle, I was beginning to get paddling and towns right. At Clifden, I left the kayak and most of its contents at the sailing club. An hour after that I was showered and changed. The good feeling was to not feel like a paddler. To not stink of sweat and salt and seaweed. Not feel damp. Not feel the pressure of the weather and the tides and the wind dictating action and inaction. It was good to sleep in a bed and feel like a tourist. My pleasure in the late afternoon was to walk around the town, shopping. I had been losing hats at a steady rate – first a floppy stetson with long chin-strings, then, somewhere around Doolin, a peaked cap with a Foreign Legionnaire's neck flap. So I spent an enjoyable hour looking through all of Clifden's many hat possibilities – tweed berets, trilbies, baseball caps that feature wings and beer-can-holders – and in the end opt for a locally made Hatman brown peaked cap. I note with pleasure how many things I am buying on the trip are Irish. Especially now that I've switched from wine to Jameson's and Murphy's.

I catch up on the news, too. Which means the weather. It has been bad throughout Ireland – allegedly it has rained every day for the past six weeks – but it has been even worse in England. Gloucestershire, Worcestershire, Oxfordshire and Berkshire have had biblical rain, flooding rivers and turning some towns into actual islands, and a rescue operation described as the biggest in peacetime Britain is underway. I wonder if I shouldn't postpone my do-any-time tour of Ireland for a once-in-a-lifetime chance to kayak through the Cotswolds.

Given the state of the flooded towns and my relative comfort, it seems unfair that I am the one picking up food parcels. But back in Dingle I'd had an email from my friend Melanie in London: *What do you want? Mackerel lures? Or a jolly good Dundee Cake filled with booze. I could cut it up and send slices to poste restante addresses. Other people I know have taken my cakes up Everest, round bottom of S America in canoe and Richard Branson took one up in his balloon. Let me know.*

A whole cake has been waiting in the post office in Clifden for more than a week, and as I come into the office I pick up a rich spicy odour. Handing the heavy package over, the postmistress asks what's inside. When I tell her it's cake, she licks her lips. 'It's been getting stronger every day,' she tells me, 'we're going to miss the smell.' Out in the square I can't help opening the package and penknifing off a thin slice. The cake is pure fuel. I pack it carefully back in its jacket of foil, disciplining myself for ounce-by-ounce rewards over the challenges to come.

I sit in the square warming in the rare sun. Having been at sea and camping out amongst birds and dolphins for the past weeks, I now have a sense of people as wildlife. What catches my eye here, as with birds, are exotics, the migrants. East European workers, in particular, the men sporting razor-sharp haircuts and D&G tight T-shirts to show off their muscles and flaunt the money they've spent on themselves, the girls tanned and coiffed like Russian gangster molls. They bring a hedonistic glamour to the streets for as long as the sun is out.

There are British families, too, with more drab plumage – Boden cords and country pastel jumpers and Barbours and Hunters, and large estate cars that have brought them in from rented houses, and friends' farms, and shooting lodges and fishing cottages. The French show their holiday savvy and chic credentials by dressing in elegant winter country clothing. The dollar-hobbled Americans, devalued against Eurotourism, are a more fleeting presence in dowdy leisurewear; at the approach of rain they pull on the cheap plastic anoraks sold in local shops. And huddled around the metal obelisk at the centre of the square, with rucksacks acting as couches, there are New Age travellers, alternative and neo-hippies, in a mix of decommissioned military surplus and ethnic tat and home-cobbled leather.

At various stages of my life I could have fitted in with many of these subspecies, but now, in warm checked shirt and polished leather shoes, dry-bag bulging with notebooks,

I don't feel I quite belong. But I feel like company and at my hotel happily discover an Italian and a French woman in a similar frame of mind. I overhear them discussing where to go that evening in their lingua franca of Spanish and, as I speak Spanish, too, suggest we join forces and go to the King's pub to hear a local band. The guitarist, Mick, is one of the Clifden lifeboat men; I'd met him and another RNLI volunteer, Taff, at the sailing club when I'd landed the kayak there.

The band is called Glór, and with guitar, accordion, banjo and vocals are roaring through 'Star of the County Down' as we squeeze into the bar. Once again the vintners are profiting from the poor weather and everyone's need to find shelter. It is too loud to talk, and too rude to shout unless at the bar staff to order drinks, so the three of us listen to the music and tap our feet to a mix of traditional tunes and Americana songs and an accordion-driven fandango.

Afterwards we head back the hotel, where a French cajun band are playing. Badly. They want to play concert music and are upset at an audience that wants just to drink and dance. The band keep the dance floor empty. I nod up another stout. Later, going up the few steps and into the small dark corridor that leads to the toilets, a man reels out of the Ladies, followed by screams of laughter. 'My gawd,' he gasps in a drink-slurred American accent, 'I sure got that wrong ... I don't know, man, it's just that I thought it read *Laddies* ... you know, like, er ... *Lads*.'

In Ireland, toilet nomenclature can be a challenge. It's normal to label the loos, in Irish, as *Mna* for 'women' and *Fir* for 'men', and as a foreigner you don't have to be more than mildly dyslexic or middling drunk to assume a typo. Or to assume that the Irish are themselves chronically dyslexic and also don't understand the difference between singular and plural, nor, indeed, gender.

The next morning I leave Clifden. It's Sunday and I find the earliest open cafe for breakfast, which is blasting heavy metal for the early-shift staff to wake themselves up. Outside streets are being cordoned off for a vintage car rally. The front page news on one of the Irish tabloids screams 'Great White Sharks Off Irish Coast'. Turns out a 'shark' had been seen off a Cornish beach – so, arguably, 'off' the Irish coast – and there are pictures and various eyewitness accounts of a possible shark attacking a possible dolphin.

My taxi, when it came, had to join the lines of veteran and vintage cars processing up to Market Square. Red-faced stewards are instigating a marque hierarchy. Smart Jaguars, and Bentleys, and the very oldest and most venerable of ancient motoring history, are ushered to park in poll place, whilst Cortinas and Volkswagens and other less ancient 'family' cars are directed up along the street. An amiable voice burbles like a well-tuned engine over the PA: *A very nice silver Mer-say-dees now, a coo-pay, a beautiful car indeed, and that's followed by an Ameri-can car, a Mus-tang ... and just behind that is a lov-erly Roh-ver.* The Rover is the exact same model that my grandfather had. I remember going for 'drives' in it as a small boy, around Sussex or just the few hundred yards down to the shingle beach and the sea. I suppose the grey and jangling pebble beach at Worthing was my first experience of the sea when only a few years old.

Grandpa Winn always put on driving gloves for his feats of pilotage. Here in the warm sun and in my memory I smell the overheated oil, the painted metal and the plasticised leather of old cars. There are Escorts and Triumphs and Morris Minors and Anglias – the economy cars of 1970s Ireland and my teenage years, now become collectables, to be polished and paraded. Many of the cars on display have a toy model of themselves glued to the dashboard. One car has shuddered and ground to a halt in the street, the bonnet is up and two men are bent over it with spanners and screwdrivers and rags coaxing it back to life. A car breaking down and being fixed again by its driver is something you only see nowadays in Africa or Asia. You don't see many picnic hampers or car coats or driving gloves, either.

The commentary continues: *An M a-G is next up the street, these were indeed a great car, and that is a Jag-a-wuar, a 1962 Jag-a-wuar, coming along next and, now, bringing up the rear we have a Scania Statoil delivery lorry, driven by the great Malachy. Malachy, how's it going?*

Good-naturedly given the hold-up in his rounds, the Great Malachy raises his hand regally as he steers his tanker up through the crowds. My taxi, a modern something or other, pulls up beside me in the middle of the street. I throw my bags into the boot and supply my own commentary in my head: *And the Toyota people carrier coming past us now is carrying some deluded eejit who only thinks he's a fecking Eskimo paddling his can-ooo around Ireland ...*

I have a sense of elation heading out of the narrow bay away from Clifden. I think it's because, for once on this trip, I am not worrying about something that might happen, or is actually happening. Not today. The sun is shining and it's warm, and I have a sense of familiarity about what I'm doing. Heading off round the coast in a kayak has finally become normal and I've latched on to a feeling of simplicity in having all I need to shelter, to eat, to survive, packed into the kayak. Perhaps it's knowing I've got Melanie's cake.

Before, when I've done long trips, it's almost always been with horses. I've been reflecting on the similarities of saddle and paddle, and as I go with the tide straight across the wavelets there's a sharp, regular up-and-downing like the 2/4 time of trot. Then, after I cross the shallow waters between Turbot Island and the mainland, I come out at an angle to the bigger swell and into quartering waves from the open sea. Now *An Fulmaire* has a lilting rocking and sideways dip at the bow as she first rises at an angle up each wave and then tilts and slides down the other side, giving a waltz time, a cantering, if you will.

On these even waters, at cantering pace, I fall into reveries about words and horses and boats – of the first peoples on these islands and the origins of the sleek, plastic boat carrying me across the sea – and conjure up a mythology that connects all three. I am imagining a time back before history when the horse tribes spread in all directions from the Asian steppes, and westwards into Europe, mobile, fast, courageous and ruthless, until their meeting with the sea that mirrored the vastness of the grasslands of their atavistic memory and folklore. I am dreaming up the logic in the creation of sea-horses in the form of skin boats.

Sullivan O'Bere, the Irish Chieftain, had done exactly that. Routed by the English after the Battle of Kinsale in 1601, he led a thousand followers two hundred miles north to Leitrim and, arriving at the Shannon in midwinter flood, they killed their remaining horses and then used the hides as boat-skins. The two groups of men – Beara and Connaught soldiers – made the boats according to their own local designs. The long thin 'Beara' currach worked well, but the rounded northern style, perhaps an oversized form of the ancient coracles used on the more placid River Boyne till modern times, sank on its first crossing.

I'd read in books on traditional boats and noted from museums and hanging around harbours that the words for skin or small boats are often remarkably similar. Or, with allowances made only for pronunciation, exactly the same. Now the words tumble into my mind. So, there's the Irish *curach*, which sounds like kayak, and the Welsh *coracle* on the west coast of Europe, and the *kajjikk* in Malta and the *caique* in Turkey, no hang on in Greece, because in Turkish it's *kayik* ... and Turkish is the root language of much of the steppes and so it's probably there that the word and maybe the concept of small ribbed, skinned boats originates.

I know this is simply a linguistic flight of fancy, but I'm hooked. I think of those old photographs of travellers I've seen. Is it Gertrude Bell – one of those big hats and no-nonsense-skirts women, anyway – crossing the Tigris or Euphrates on rafts of inflated skins? And there's something similar I've seen from Pakistan called *zak*, so half of a *kay-zak*? So, if both the idea of the skin boat and the name for it spread from Central Asia and finally to the Pacific coasts, then maybe the word went across the Bering Straits and in North America became attached to the Eskimo kayak. Which means – OH YES! HOME RUN! – with the Inuit word in Greenland for a skin boat being *qajaq*, that if Saint Brendan going west in his skin *curach* reached Greenland, which he almost certainly did, then the skin boat and the one single word for the skin boat had circled the whole world centuries, maybe millennia, before anyone knew that the world *was* circular.

Long hours – I've been at sea now for three hours – of rhythmic paddle strokes are a luxury. Like long walks, providing pause for peripatetic pondering. Erika had asked me what I thought about as I paddle, and now as I think about thinking I am surprised how little I consciously do think at sea. Before setting off, I'd fondly imagined I'd have the time and inclination to remember past events as a sort of in-flight movie, or would be able to develop interesting trains of thought. But my linguistic kayak rambling is a rare snatch of almost-joined-up thinking.

For the act of kayaking, I realise, is far more complex and less repetitious than I'd expected; most of my time on the water requires the same body–mind coordination as juggling; the ability to concentrate without too much thought. Indeed, actual thought about the mechanics of kayaking is to be avoided. Paddle in, shift weight as kayak tips on wave, lift paddle, lean into dip, other blade in, pull lightly as waters drop down blade and reduce resistance, compensate for gust of wind, shift arse before it goes numb, push rudder pedal over a bit, lift paddle, move from hips as kayak rolls. You have to do all that in automatic.

Is this what becoming skilful at something means? As when after hundreds of hours I could finally sew a line of stitches through leather without having to plan and place each awl hole. Or after thousands of hours of fumbling practice, at last, complex chords – E-flat augmented fifths, F-sharp suspended ninths, diminisheds, minors – fell under my hands when I picked up a guitar. But I'm flattering myself. That's not the ease I have in a kayak. Not yet. Only sometimes does the movement of sea and craft and my body seem totally balanced. I'm still caught by surprise. Though less and less.

Still, when the conditions are as good as now, I have the luxury of being able to think. And given that chance I'm thinking like a madman, with theories and notions and ideas and crazed words pouring out with my paddle strokes. So next off, tumbling through my mind, come those horse tribes of Asia – Scythians, Huns, Magyars and perhaps, too, proto-Celts, moving inexorably westwards across Europe, crossing mountains, subjugating or destroying more peaceful tillers of the earth. They leave few traces of the stone, pottery and worked metal that archaeologists like. Rather the horse tribes, and the skin-boat people, lay down the strati of language, myth, music and belief that has lasted far longer. Ideas and knowledge. How to make skin boats, or handle horses: language and stories and song verses passed from lip to lip.

The day passes easily, and in the dropping sun – it must already be seven o'clock or more – I stop to loiter. Free for once from lashing rain, I try out the trick of local fishermen who estimate the time towards the end of the day by holding up their hand at arm's length. The width of the full four fingers fills the distance between the horizon and the dropping sun when there is an hour left to sunset. Two hand-widths, one on top of the other, is two hours. So it is roughly a finger to each remaining quarter of an hour before dusk. But those would be broad, heavy fingers of a tough rope-hauling fisherman's hands, whilst I've got the digits of a guitar-chording typist, so I try to make some adjustment.

It's more than three of my hand-widths between sun and the earth's rim. So I've at least two hours.

I'm rocking on the sea a mile or so from Inishbofin Island and several miles off the mainland. Using fishing as the time-honoured excuse to do little, I reach behind me to take the hand line and feathered hooks out from under the elastics, and pay out the orange twine as the half-pound lead plumb pulls the hooks down out of sight. With fifty or sixty feet out, I jig the line between thumb and forefinger for a while. There's a sudden faint thrumming in the line. I hand over hand the line in, loops and coils floating off on the other side of the kayak. Then a quick pull and a sudden snatch and the feeling of more weight, and the tightened line turns a tight circle.

Pulling up more line, I can see flashes of colour and silver darting below, and then two mackerel: the small one that I first hooked and a larger one. I pull in the first, bigger, fish and loop the line in a hitch round the spray-deck handle to tether the other fish in the water. I grasp the mackerel firmly in one hand, feeling its cool, pulsing shape. The hook twists easily out of its mouth, and one-handed I open the knife attached to my float and cut forwards from behind each pectoral fin through to the back of the mackerel's head, severing it. Another cut back to the vent and a hooked finger run along the cut, and I've shucked the intestines, the swim bladder and the heart into the water, where they sink slowly in a swirling mist of diluted blood. I tuck what is now a neat fillet of fish into a bag, and do the same to the other one. That's my supper sorted. I recoil the line and pick up the paddle again.

CHAPTER 12

Freeriding

I AM ON THE WATER EARLY on Reeks Sunday – the last
Sunday in July. Over on the mainland, almost within
sight, is Croagh Patrick, the mountain where Saint
Patrick is said to have fasted for forty days before
banishing all the snakes from Ireland. On the radio early
that morning the weather forecast exhorts walkers – thousands of people climb the seven hundred or so metres to
the summit on this day – to wear warm clothing and suit-
able footwear. Many of the pilgrims, even so, will still walk
barefoot as penitents.

The radio news has more about the great white shark,
too. It has been seen off a beach on the Cornish coast,
which newspapers are calling the Irish Sea, to add more of

a frisson. It is a silly-season story with fins that looks set to swim and swim. Some marine biologists are suggesting that the whole coast has been swarming with great white sharks for years. One expert claims that global warming is drawing sharks into our waters. Others scoff at this, pointing out that *Carcharodon carcharias* actually prefers cooler waters. Spoilsports (and I fall into their camp) suggest that the average person can't tell a great white from a basking shark. Or, indeed, a dolphin.

I am more drawn into another news item. Kevin Murphy, an endurance swimmer who's ploughed his way across the English Channel some thirty-two times, almost with the regularity of a Dover–Calais ferry, and has swum from Scotland to Ireland in 11 hours and 20 minutes, has been frustrated by the weather from his attempt to swim the fourteen miles across Dingle Bay. I relive my long hours of paddling across the bay, trying to think what it might be like out there without even the benefit of a kayak.

By mid-morning the sun has risen up into heavy grey clouds, and the wind freshened. I am cutting across the mouth of Clew Bay. At the head of the bay are tens, hundreds even, of diminutive islands, like a scatter of jigsaw pieces waiting to be assembled into a simpler picture of sea on one side and land on the other.

In 1967, one of these uninhabited outcrops, Dorinish, had been bought by John Lennon. He had a brightly painted caravan shipped from London to the island – probably the first appearance of psychedelia in the west of Ireland. Paddy Quinn, a boat-builder from nearby Inishcuttle Island who was charged with rafting the caravan out to Dorinish, seemed to think so. 'Beatlemania and the Swinging Sixties have not reached the west of Ireland,' he told reporters, admitting that he couldn't quite put a face to his customer. Lennon visited the island just once, by helicopter with Yoko, before giving custodianship of 'Beatle Island' to a group called The Diggers to set up a commune. Accommodation was in tents, and travel on and off the island was by hitching lifts with passing fishing boats. Letters arrived addressed to 'Hippie Island, Ireland'. The experiment in near-self-sufficiency lasted two years.

This sets me to thinking about my parents' own decision to move to West Cork in the 1960s. I know some of the reasons: Irish roots, and Irish friends, cheap property and more freedom and opportunity than was offered by the 'rat race' in England. For my mother there was the appeal of keeping horses and dogs. And, for my father, living in Ireland allowed him to set up a factory to create remote control vehicles and under-sea machines, as well as having the pleasure of a ruined tenth-century castle and yards of buildings to restore, and then fill with vintage cars and his 'museum of technology'. There was a coastline to sail steam boats on, and a runway to fly his aged planes out of, to get to somewhere else as often as possible.

I suspect that neither of my parents gave much thought to Irishness. And neither did I as a boy, although I was aware of standing out amongst the native Irish like a goat in a flock of sheep. I loved Irish music and culture, but I was aware of being unschooled in its ways – and clanless. Three decades on, things are entirely different. In the mad, late-booming economy, East Europeans, Spanish and French arrived in Ireland to earn wages, as did Nigerians, Thais, Filipinos, Pakistanis and Chinese, and I find myself counted, most often, among the sheep. Paradoxically, too, I feel all the more Irish for having been abroad so much.

After several hours of paddling across the lumpy sea I arrive under the dark cliffs of Clare Island. Above me is the 1500-feet height of Knockmore Mountain. This is a common tautology in Ireland's geography, *cnoc* being the Irish for a mountain, making Clare's highest point 'Big Mountain Mountain', just as *inis* meaning 'island' makes for a redundancy in all the Inis- and Ininish- and Inish-whatever islands marked on maps.

Apart from Melanie's fruitcake and two tins of fish and some rice and couple of bruised onions, I am pretty much out of food. I'm short on water, too. And I feel that time is running out as well. Progress is slow, and in finding a rhythm that carries me over the sharply serrated wave tops I can see and feel that these seas have become bigger, rougher and more unpredictable than any I've chosen to go out in so far, with the wind blowing a four and gusting to five. I look to the birds for some clues. There are gannets sweeping low down to the waves and a fulmar soars past, circling me once, looking at me eye-to-eye. They don't seem unduly bothered or purposefully seeking shelter.

The birds prove right in their insouciance. In the hour and a half it takes to cover the five miles to the mainland, the wind blows itself out and the sea begins to subsidise. I now have a decision to make, and again I leave it to instinct. Ahead is Achill Island, largest of the Irish islands, barely cut off from the mainland by a muddy and tidal sound that is little more than a river for some of its length. The sound offers me a short-cut through to the north-west coast of Mayo, saving several days of big-sea paddling, but does this mean I'd be selling myself short? It doesn't feel quite right, but then nor does the sea forecast for the coming days: more high winds, more swell, more big seas. Going outside Achill Island means long lengths of exposed coast, under Ireland's highest sea-cliffs. I can see myself getting marooned in remote bays for days, whilst waiting for weather good enough to get round outside Achill. To hell with purity. I'll settle for get-round-Ireland-however.

Achillbeg, the island at the entrance to the sound, contains another of those seemingly dyslexic and contrary Irish words, like *mna* for 'women'. *Beg* might sound like 'big' but means the opposite. In behind Little Achill, what wind is still blowing is blocked by the land to the north, whilst in the sound the waters have calmed to a flat, barely rippling sheet like crumpled paper carefully flattened out again. The sky too clears, and setting up camp I light a small fire of driftwood and cook up what I call a 'Jameson's stew', made by pouring a tin cup of whiskey to sip until the water boils, and it's time to add rice, tinned tuna, chopped onion, tomato paste and dried herbs. Then another tot of whiskey whilst stirring the simmering ingredients into a mush. The result, a nourishing stew, with a whiskey tang. There ought to be blob of peanut butter, too, but ship's supplies are exhausted. It's all I can do to leave enough water for coffee in the morning, which I'll need to drink early. To catch the tide, I'll have to be afloat before five.

Contemplating sleep, I watch a returning fishing boat plough across the wide expanse of golden waters beyond the sands, leaving a furrowed wake behind it. Then there is a sudden explosion, and another and another, as if the sea is being strafed from below by torpedoes. It is a school of dolphins, leaping out of the water in line, behind the boat, and then turning back on themselves in tight circles. I try to count them. Eight? Twelve? Twenty? It is like keeping track of a handful of steel ball bearings rolling around a silver tray. But then the dolphins start a game so child-simple that even I can understand its dynamics. One at a time they burst straight out from under the sea, shooting as high into the air as possible, flipping and wriggling like kids on a trampoline, almost flying before crashing back into the water in great splashing belly flops.

Watching and listening to the dolphins playing first elates and then saddens me, as I think of Fungi – that stranded intermediary between my world and that of the wild dolphins. I wonder about the dolphins' experience of the sea as they surf across and arrow through and under the waves, their movement so different from my slow, slogging paddle over the water's skin. Watching this tribe of wild dolphins I now feel closer to the cranky Cetacean of Dingle. Like Fungi I am well fed, fit and comfortable but alone. When I'd spent days rain-locked in my tent I'd been oddly happy to spend hours watching the activities of oyster-catchers probing the shoreline, the glide, dive and flutter of gannets, the step and skip of grey wagtails engaged in a courtly minuet on a puddle's edge. My brain was willing to be engaged by the antics of another, any other, species. If a couple of mullet had come along and offered to pull me in my kayak around the bay for twenty minutes, I'd have been off like a shot. So I could hardly blame Fungi for riding along on the bow waves of the boats come out to see him.

Under the bright full moon there seems to have hardly been a night separating the day's end from the dawning of the next morning. I wake in grey mist and silence at four. No breakfast. A four-knot favourable current is too good to lose. The water is totally stilled, yet even as I push off from the sand, my feet numbed with cold from wading calf-deep to board, the current begins to pull me rapidly along the shoreline. The weather forecast the night before had promised rain and high winds but the sky is clear and cloudless. Not even a cat's paw pattering on the water's surface. The landlubbery smell of new-mown hay, cow shit, meadow flowers and drying peat rises from the banks on either side of me. In the waters under me I can make out pewter-coloured darts of mullet, and a grey seal freeriding with me on the tide. We surge past a heron standing in the salty shallows, darting forward to chopstick up small fry with its long sharp beak-bill.

At the Michael Davitt swing bridge, connecting Achill to the mainland, I come to a halt. The seawaters rushing in from both ends of the sound meet here in a swirling force between the piers. By waiting for the tide to turn, I can get another free ride to complete the remaining half of the distance as the waters empty out again to the north. I ground the kayak on a slipway and look towards a picnic breakfast of muesli, milk powder and instant coffee when I notice the hotel across the far side of the road. With two hours to wait till the tide turns, I pull out my cleanest trousers, and slightly cleaner shirt, and my leather shoes, plaster scummy seawater through my hair with a comb, and minutes later I am sitting in a bay window, drinking proper coffee, reading the day's *Irish Times* and contemplating a battery of hotplates, tureens and toasters.

Waitresses, when not pouring me more coffee, are laying tables and folding napkins. They seem happy to have a non-resident kayaker making camp on the best table in the house, and seemingly capable of working his way through all the buffet breakfast on his own. It was worth the €8.50 just for the pleasures of polished silver cutlery, matching plates and ironed linen. And yet, perhaps it was a mistake. For hotels are about company and nights before, whilst this breakfast is a solitary occasion that leaves an ache of loneliness.

But there is no time to indulge in such feelings just now. I have to be back in my wetsuit before the tide turns.

Launching into the ebb that is pulling me further around Ireland, with very little effort on my behalf, after a perfect breakfast I ought to be a little more happy. But loneliness is a tough companion to ditch and I'm beginning to feel overly sentimental, not helped by the totem line on my kayak, whose new treasures include a tiny wooden Sami-carved ptarmigan and a bouquet of small feathers that Erika sent in her poste restante letter to Clifden.

And maybe there is something lonely about Achill. It's a place I've been intrigued by, as the one time home of German novelist Heinrich Böll, who wrote of his bitter-sweet years on the island in his *Irish Journal*, and of Graham Greene, who came here in the 1960s, both to write and in pursuit of his mistress Catherine Walston, who rented a cottage at Dooagh. Greene, it seemed, was happy on the island: 'I long for somewhere like Achill or Capri where there are no telephones,' he wrote while working on *The Heart of the Matter* and *The Fallen Idol*. He later recalled the time in a poem: 'A mattress was spread on a cottage floor/And a door closed on a world/but another door opened ...'

Paddling north, rocking in small wavelets under hot sun, I turn on the radio to hear the lunchtime shipping forecast and catch chat-show talk about the great white sharks 'in Irish waters'. The worst summer weather in living memory may yet be enlivened by a bit of *Jaws* drama. The vague, if not dubious, sightings off the coast of Cornwall, have now seemingly become fact to be commented on by sport fishermen who really did see great whites circling around them in 1999. And that same year, the radio asserts, there were reliable shark sightings in Scotland, including one that followed a group of sea-kayakers in the Hebrides. But Cornwall seems to be the epicentre of great white sightings, as it is for big cats, UFOs and fairies.

Nic Slocum, whom I know from his whale-watching trips run out of Castlehaven, is a lone sceptic. The Irish waters are a little warm for them, he tells the radio presenter, and the sightings are likely young basking shark or big dolphins or wave-shadows in the sunlight. Any concerns I have about big predatory sharks stalking me fade away. If I really wanted to find a great white shark in Irish waters – where they almost certainly don't exist – what would the chance be of paddling around in a bright-yellow kayak for a few days amidst an infinity of sea and actually coming across one? Very close to zero. I think I can safely take sharks off the list of things to worry about.

Unlike the weather, which remains a very real concern.

●━━━●

It might be sunny and still-aired now, but the shipping forecast foretells a deep depression coming in from the Atlantic. It seems that yet another period of low pressure is sweeping, bringing rain and – again – high winds. Once more I'm in a quandary. Coming out of Achill Sound I'd been planning to go out to sea again, follow the seaward side of the Mullet Peninsula beside the Inishkea islands, before reaching the oceanic expanse of Donegal Bay.

The Inishkea – some of the remotest and least visited islands off the Irish coast – have caught my fancy. Though abandoned today, they once held a thriving population given to piracy and distilling *poitín*, Ireland's generic moonshine, while a small islet called Rusheen was an outpost of the Norwegian whaling fleet into the twentieth century. But it's the events that led to their abandonment that gives me pause. In October 1927, the islands were battered by an autumn gale that kept the fishing currachs ashore for too long. A lull in the storm, the calm eye at its centre, lured young men out to fish, not just from the Inishkeas but from numerous ports and islands along the Mayo coast. The second blast of the storm came so suddenly that few made it back to shore. On the Inishkeas, five currachs, each crewed by two brothers, were lost.

It wasn't just the deaths of the young men that was tragic but also the loss of the man strength needed to tip the balance in the islanders' annual struggle to survive. Losing so many men in one day was the catalyst for many communities electing to 'come ashore' over the following years, abandoning satellite settlements that had been in a stilled orbit around Ireland's coastline since before the first Irish saints and their monasteries.

By going outside the peninsula I might get wind-bound for days on end, or lose a week. I was low on food. I'd supplemented my rations with bread rolls and butter pats filched from my breakfast table, and had half of Melanie's plutonium-heavy cake in the hold, but not enough to be happily cast away on an uninhabited island. By going up the inside of the peninsula to the town of Belmullet I was relying on a rumour I'd heard about a short-cut through to Mayo's north coast: a narrow channel, a few hundred metres long, that ran right through the middle of the town, deep enough to bring a small boat through.

I decide there's not much choice about it, and paddle up the bay in a heat haze that conceals land only a few miles away. It feels like the calm before a storm, and makes me uneasy. Belmullet, at the head of the bay, is built on an isthmus of land so narrow that the peninsula looks on the map like a ripe fruit barely held by a brittle stalk. If a channel through to Broad Haven still exists, I tell myself, then the Mullet is actually snapped off and I am still going 'around' Ireland. Below the town children are running along the muddy sands. There isn't a wetsuit amongst them. A gang of boys are building some kind of raft out of flotsam at one end of the beach as I paddle along the shoreline looking for an entrance to the channel. They gather in a tight, sullen-looking group to watch me. One of them ducks down to pick up a stone, uncoiling quickly to send it thrumming through the air in my direction. My plan to leave the kayak and find a shop seems unwise. And I'm still unsure about the rumoured channel.

Then I notice some heavy nineteenth-century stonework, like the outflow of a particularly well-wrought storm drain, and a ruler-straight line of water leading below high walls. It's the cut. I paddle under a tantalising ribbon of town roofs, garage awnings, house tops and shop signs and debouch into a muddy and stinking estuary, snaking away from decrepit quays. A desire to just keep paddling drives me on, catching the tide as it begins falling and pulls me in a wide arc past fields and salt-grass mud-islands and abandoned boat hulls till I can see the lighthouse beyond Knocknalina, where the coast opens out into the wide expanse of Broad Haven.

It's nearly dark and the wind has crept up notch by notch so that, as I come round the point under the lighthouse, there is a big swell and choppy waves. After a day spent twisting between fields on estuaries, and crossing calm bays and in the urban channel of Belmullet, it's a shock to be back in the raw, powerful sea. Where there had been forty shades of green, now it's an infinite number of greys. And where I smelt flowers and grass and earth, my nose is filled again with salt, and decayed fish and iodine.

It is a slippery and tiring climb to pull everything from the water and carry it to a field where in the coarse grass on a tiny area of flat I make camp, and supper, using up the few paltry supplies I have left. It rains and batters all night, and by early the next morning it is blowing a force six. The sea below me has set into big swells with foam blowing off their tops. The distant cliffs of Benwee Head are a black line. I've pretty much run out of food and hunger's going to push me on. Not just hunger for food but a hunger to keep going. Yesterday's mileage – nearly fifty kilometres – was so good that I feel confident now, even facing the churning waters, even knowing that I'm heading into the remotest and harshest stretch of coastline on the whole trip, where massive cliffs face the Atlantic.

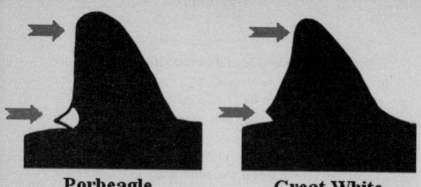

Porbeagle   **Great White**

CHAPTER 13

Seeing Sharks

THE RAIN IS SLUICING down persistently and the wind is howling, but I decide to launch and see how things feel on the water. Launching means half-jumping, half-wriggling into the cockpit as it bucks and twists in the swell and shears up and down the rocks. Actually paddling out into the waves seems easier. They're big – fridge-freezer height – but in regularly spaced blocks coming straight on the bow, so the kayak feels stable under me. I've got my hood cinched around my face and am getting the rain full on the nose. My bearing is towards Kid Island, a huge block of rock marking the southernmost edge of Donegal Bay. East from there, past two more stark, lofty, rocky islands, the Stags of Broad Haven bay, the cliffs march along the coast of Mayo into Sligo.

Far out into Broad Haven I decide to go on. It's hard to know if this is a logical decision or a gut feeling or the start of a mistake. The wind is far stronger than any I've ever chosen to go out in. Great rushing gusts. Force five rising to a six and even stronger for minutes at a time. The sea is grey and surfing, the distant cliffs black and forbidding. The rain is so cold and stinging, it makes me narrow my eyes. And the coast line from here has only two possible landing places in the next twelve miles. The wind has increased but it's actually flattening the sea and it's in my face which is good; slow going but stable. With the wind noise and the waves sloshing over me it feels brutal, but all my time on the water has changed me. I feel I can handle this.

I'm under the cliffs. Great Gothic cathedral walls with flying buttresses of rock, and towers and caves like huge doors into darkness. There are winds punching down over the cliff edge – katabatic, they're called – which are like an avalanche of pressed, roiling heavy air; an unexpected gust can push on the paddle blades and twist my body almost round on itself. To avoid the worst of them, I move in closer to the rocks but now I pick up a second evil – clapotis – as the swell deflects off the dark rock walls and back into the waves. There is nowhere to bring the kayak in. But my eyes run along the cliff face at sea level, spotting a ledge here, a knob of rock there; I'm just noting handholds, escape routes, the slivers of salvation if things go wrong and I come out of the kayak.

There is a touch of Zen about paddling at the very edge of one's ability. Like any other edge one's stumbling along, it concentrates the mind wonderfully. The sense of loneliness

I'd paddled with all the previous day has been quite literally blown from me, and instead I'm allowing myself to travel rather like a fulmar, riding the thermals and responding moment by moment to the elements.

If I'd been thinking objectively at this point I would have been numbed by the most frightening aspect of sea-kayaking: the total commitment required. This is like practising a martial art ... all the training, the endless repetition, or in my case the several hundred miles I've already paddled, provide an instinctive repertoire of moves. I've just got to keep loose, enjoy being tossed around by the wind and waves and the feeling of being on the edge, and if I can do that without a break in my concentration, but also without losing an easy sense of relaxation, and for several more hours, beyond this long line of cliffs, it will have been another successful returning from the sea.

It occurs to me that the whole meaning of this circum-navigation is about proving I can commit to something; and that, knowing myself, I've picked a challenge that is both simple – go round Ireland in a kayak – and finite, so that however long it takes it still won't go on for ever. Almost any other endurance activity allows one to give up, or at least surrender to passivity when things get really bad. Set off to run across hills and if you 'bonk', then you can just stop – lie down, even – and catch your breath. Cycling's the same; you can put your feet on the ground and get off any time it gets too much. But not sea-kayaking. It doesn't matter how bad things get; you have to keep paddling to stay upright, until you hit land. Or you'll just turn over, come out of the kayak and, very probably, drown.

I've been paddling now for two hours. I'm stunned by the beauty of where I am. Amongst the flurries of rain and the spray, I can see the Stags as great towering chunks of rock. One island is pierced right through by a huge tunnel. I'm following a line inshore using the tide and the more sheltered waters behind stacks and turns in the cliff to find the easiest path. This coastal world has slowly become my environment and I've learnt to read it like a book – albeit a LARGE PRINT simplified vocabulary book. Over the past weeks, things I would never have noticed before catch my attention. My eyesight and hearing and sense of smell are tuned. A peregrine falcon slipping down a cliff face to disappear round a headland. The flicker of fin from a sunbathing pollock even as it dives. The faintest change in the patterning of clouds showing a change in the weather. The smell of new-cut silage coming off land in a fog, when I can't even see the land. The sound from the blowhole of a dolphin.

I've come in behind a fold in the cliffs and the wind has been shuttered down. I'm in a relative calm, and I ease up on paddling for a quick glance at the chart in its waterproof see-through cover. In less than a mile I'll reach Pig Island. I can see its bulk ahead, almost joined to the land, and just beyond there is a possible landing place. I have the feeling of being watched; a sense I've come to acknowledge as the paddling days have run by. Usually I find I can scan the cliffs and spot a tiny figure – a fox, a gannet, a raven – almost hidden on a cliff face looking down on the yellow dot that is me and *An Fulmaire*. I scan the cliffs here. They're rain-soused slabs of sheer black rock. Not a sheep nor a person in sight. Out at sea there is not even a gull in this wind. Then I twist round to look behind me and my heart leaps. Just at the back of the kayak, fin out of the water, is a large dolphin, Fungi-sized, swimming only two or three metres back from the rudder, following in my exact path. I feel a sense of companionship; I'm being not so much watched as accompanied.

Stories of dolphins rescuing people, or guiding lost ships into port, are as old as the Greek myth where the poet Arion throws himself off a pirate boat rather than remain captive and is carried to land by a dolphin. Dolphins are mammals. They're nearly 'us'.

I turn forward again; I can't afford to remain unbalanced in these waters. And then a freezing, spine-tingling jolt hits me. Dolphins and whales have horizontal tail flukes. Fish tails are vertical. The 'dolphin' behind me, I realise, had a tail fin sticking up. This changes everything, and considerably for the worse. I am being followed by a shark. Only a few feet behind me, and almost the length of the kayak. And sharks and mankind don't have nearly so cuddly a shared history as dolphins and us. Especially given the news stories of the past week.

I've already used up all my adrenalin and fear kayaking through these waters, being thrown around by seas that could roll me in a second's inattention, and the shark is an element I find myself considering with a surprising calm. I twist around again. Maybe it is a young basking shark. It is still there, closer now, and I can clearly see its head, not with the pointed Pinnocchio nose of a basker but ending in the rounded nose of a shark kind of shark. I note how little effort it needs to keep up with my wind assisted five knots or so. How long has it been behind me, before I noticed?

I take another look round and that rounded nose is now only a metre from the stern of the kayak. Five or six feet back there's a thick dark dorsal fin and further back still – another seven feet? – the tip of the tail, moving lazily, powerfully from side to side. I face forward again. I can hear the roar of surf against the wall of cliff, and behind me the wind whistling around the buttress of rock. I can smell my own damp skin. I can feel the waves roiling under the kayak. I know one thing. I must not capsize.

Keeping careful balance, I slow the kayak to a wallowing halt and use the paddles for support strokes. Looking around for a fourth time I see the shark drive down out of sight to one side of me. A few seconds later its fin surfaces tens of metres away. The speed, added to that blunt nose, rules out a basking shark.

I am now in a smallish area of sea with a large shark that has been quite obviously following me and is now no longer in sight. I begin paddling onwards, keeping close to the cliff side and scan the waters around me. I am still being challenged by the waves and the wind, and my senses are relaxed. By the time I pass Pig Island I have seen many places I could have made a forced exit but I realise that, bizarrely, the shark hasn't scared me. I've felt the sense of privileged excitement that comes from seeing something big and dangerous – a lion, perhaps – in its natural habitat and realising that its danger is not directed at you. Or not on this day. I have kept paddling.

The first port and shelter is Belderg, where I make my way behind the breakwater and into a stark little concrete harbour. It is a harsh-looking place. Mayo folk like to flag up the toughness of their county by saying, 'Mayo', and then adding as a reflex, 'God help us.' Belderg's shoreline is all rocks and stones and drops, with no obvious level to pitch the tent on except for a small flat, rough platform next to a derelict boat house. It is still raining as I put up the tent using stones as weight-pegs and a car draws up. The woman driver points out a cottage across the beach: the owners of the patch of land I was camping on. The Caulfields, who open the door to me, seem only slightly put out by my fait accompli and offer to drive me to the local shop, six miles away. In the close, warm confines of their car my damp clothes steam the atmosphere, as if the Caulfields are transporting a pressure cooker of simmering cabbage.

The shop itself is like a return to the wooden-shelved, needle-to-an-anchor village shops of my rural Cork childhood. Processed cheese, sliced white bread, a meagre assortment of root vegetables and an array of tinned foods: Fray Bentos pies in flat tins, peas, rice pudding, sardines. Basic foods designed to be left in cupboards, or carried in sacks or in boat holds or on picnics or to last for long weeks on a shop's shelves when there is no one around to buy them. Heavy on carbohydrates and cheap proteins. Nothing fancy. A perfect assortment of groceries for a kayaker. Victualled for a few more days, I cast a longing eye at the adjoining pub – not quite a shop-pub of the Dingle kind, but able to fulfil the same function.

At the tent I cook up a familiar menu with the added luxury of rice pudding, watched by the curious, lozenge-pupilled eyes of a brace of sheep. A watery sun sinks back along the cliffs and the sea is calming. Cars drive down to the harbour, and people get out and stand chatting and looking at the sea. I amble down, too, and get talking to a man who fishes out of the bay and is down checking his boat, which has reared up on its mooring.

Sharks, he mulls; well, there would have been basking sharks one time, but they were never common on this coast. He hadn't seen one for years and years. Other sharks? Well, there were blue sharks, of course, little fellas you'd see up on the surface some time, or catch in the nets the odd occasion. Big sharks? How big now? Bigger than a blue shark? Ah, sure there were stories all right ... there's always someone has seen something odd. But sure, a decent-sized mackerel was a hard enough thing to find nowadays.

Back at the tent I note down exactly what I had seen. The rounded nose, the dorsal and tail fin, the dark colour and the length of maybe ten or twelve feet, the speed when it dived from behind the kayak and reappeared in the waves. I still have no idea what it was. A not-so-great white? A monster blue shark? Or, most likely, a porbeagle, the commonest big shark native to these waters. A record specimen caught off the Scottish coast in 1993 weighed 507 pounds. If a porbeagle it was, I'd been in little danger, even if I had capsized; there have only been four confirmed attacks by a porbeagle on humans, and none fatal. That compares to white sharks, which have been responsible for 430 attacks and 63 fatalities.

I sleep badly. In the few hours of darkness, sheep press between my tent and the shed wall for shelter, knocking the guy lines. The wind flaps the loose tent fabric. My mind plays over and over the day before. Not just the shark but the five hours of paddling amongst big rocks, big cliffs, in big winds and rains. In the half-light of dawn, I again wonder if I am really up to the task I've set myself.

In the event, my launch is postponed. Dr Caulfield strolls over to invite me for breakfast and, perhaps inspired by my car ride with them, a shower. As Ann cooks up a proper fry,

Seamus and I talk about the landscape outside his window. His father, a local schoolteacher, had noted remains of field systems under the bog. The full import of the Céide Fields, as they became known, was only realised when Seamus became an archaeologist and began probing and excavating the blanket bog that had covered this corner of Ireland and given it the bleak aspect we looked out on now. Under the compressed moss and vegetation, as if under an ice cap, was a preserved five-thousand-year-old set of fields, villages, houses and tombs. They were amongst the oldest known field systems in the world and told of a Neolithic culture of early cattle herders and agriculturalists, with complex beliefs in an afterlife and mythic resonances with cultures across Europe. But these doughty farmers, having cleared trees to make their fields and grazing lands, had set up the very conditions to create the blanket bog that had submerged their works under moss and plants and water, rather as I'd noticed the walls and stones on Inishmore sinking into the thick mattress of grass. In his poem, 'Beldberg', Seamus Heaney writes of 'landscape fossilized' and a culture that has migrated away.

Having seen the coast cliffs and rough seas and paucity of safe landing places to the west, it seemed unlikely that these early Irish had much to do with boats. Or perhaps they did and were just better and braver seamen than me, because on a jutting promontory there were buildings that might well have been fish-spotting stations. This lofty headland, Seamus explained, had finally been cut off by the sea a century ago and turned into a towering stack. In the 1980s, he organised a team to be helicoptered out there to camp the night and survey the remains. His then eighty-year-old father had insisted on coming along, as well as the elderly woman who owned the land. He described a motley bunch preparing to spend the night on a patch of grass the size of a football pitch with sheer drops to the sea on all sides. It was, I supposed, like spending a night on top of some plinth or column. The helicopter's down draught as it left had blown various crucial surveying maps and items over the edge, leaving the team peering helplessly over the drop to where they floated, inaccessible, far, far below.

The Caulfields also tell me that they had watched one of the greats of endurance-kayaking land on their beach. Peter Bray had first set off on a millennial trip, in 2000, to paddle solo across the Atlantic, west to east, against the currents. His boat foundered and he was lucky to be picked up from the sea after a day and half in icy waters. But the next year he set off again from St Johns in Newfoundland, and seventy-six days later he'd come ashore just below the Caulfields' cottage. I try and extrapolate from my own experience of being hours out in big seas what it might be like to spend days and nights, whole weeks, in a kayak. But it's past imagining – what it might be like not getting back to shore as dark comes in and instead snatching a few hours of sleep with the waves slapping against the hull of the kayak; not being able to stretch your legs on each landfall, and walk around, run even, to warm up; and having noone to talk to once out of radio contact. My attempt to circle Ireland seems almost attractive by comparison, with all its shore leave and pubs.

CHAPTER 14

Reading Melville

WHEN I RELAUNCH IN the light afternoon sunshine the cliffs have lost their forbidding aspect and appear like the spines of shelved books, regular and multicoloured. I pass the stack that Seamus and his team had camped on – and where, he said, legend has it that Saint Patrick, representing a new Christianity, cast out the old pagan deity in the figure of Crom Dubh, the 'bent dark one'. Legend tells of their fight as a Tolkienesque duel of fire bolts and transformations until finally the saint drove his adversary onto the headland and collapsed the landbridge – to create the very stack I was looking up at. Imprisoned as if on a pillar, like a stylite, the old god was tortured to death by midges.

The midges were certainly no figment. They had clouded around me the previous night as I'd camped out, rising out of the grass and stones to settle on every inch of my skin, crawling up under sleeves and trouser cuffs, and into my ears. In Ireland, people tend to call midges 'midgets', which gives a proper sense of them as tiny but substantial foes.

Ahead, past Downpatrick Head, in the sparkling wavelets, there's an odd shape flopping up and down. Getting closer, I see, just under the surface of the water, a huge round disc with a loose triangle attached. When I glide in on a collision course the blob comes into focus as a sunfish, laid out on its side in these almost-semitropical waters. It levers itself upright with a triangle of dorsal fin before sinking out of sight. It's a fish that could have been designed by a six-year-old – a construct of crudely drawn circles and exuberantly elongated triangles – and is another giant of the seas, a flabby and unthreatening grotesque.

The water is so clear I see as if through a prism into the depths, and so spot an odd blob coming up from several feet away. At first I think it some kind of jellyfish, and it's only when it drifts right under the kayak that I see it's a white bra, swelling and pulsing in the current. I imagine whole shoals of lingerie migrating under me. Slips and cami-knickers and stockings, like turbot, squid and eels. This is the way my mind has come to work, paddling out at sea, especially when the tempo of the waves is light and my strokes a physical and hypnotic mantra that frees the mind to wander.

That night I spend in Rathlackan harbour, arriving as a swimming class of children are braving the chill of the first of August. Some are already on the jetty, blue-lipped with cold, swaddled in bath towels or leaping into cars. The harbour very soon empties around me.

I talk with a couple of fishermen, or, as they tell me, ex-fishermen. One of them was a salmon netter but gave up when the government began buying up licences in an attempt to increase the numbers of fish reaching Irish rivers to spawn. He was going to stop anyway, he says, seeing as how there was little enough money and few enough fish. But he tells me that some of the luckier salmon netters had got as much as a hundred thousand euros in compensation. Most people moved onto crabs, he says – which are big business, with some boats out round the clock tending lines of hundreds of pots. But there's a worry now that crabs, like local lobster, which are too scarce to pot, will get fished out. And what will there be after that? 'Pollock,' one of the men suggests. 'There are fancy restaurants putting it on the menu now, though it tastes like shite whatever price you put on it.'

Licence lotteries aside, making a living from the sea has always been a tough life, and a reliable path to death, too, if you spend enough time on it. My new friend gestures towards a life-sized bronze statue of a diver, fins in hand, mask off and looking towards the horizon. Ah, a terrible sad story, the once-salmon-netter tells me; a group took a currach deep back into a cave near here, a German man and a local family, a man, a woman and their child, and then the currach got flipped over and they were all thrown up on a wee beach at the back of the cave with the tide on the rise. And it was two local divers – that's Michael Heffernan there, the statue – that went into the cave in a mighty swell, and one diver was washed out again barely alive. And then, when the *gardai* divers arrived, brought here by helicopter, in they went and they found the German and Heffernan drowned, up on the beach next to the family – who were still alive, and they'd taken the clothes off the dead man to stay warm and built a wall of stones against the waters, and God knows it was hard getting them out in a little boat pulled on a rope. The whole thing was dreadful. It won't be forgotten around here.

It was a coastline of drownings. A plaque near the harbour gave memory to nine men drowned in the same October storm in 1927 that had decimated the Inishkea islands. Of the nine men, four came from one family, the Goldricks, and three from another, the Kearneys.

Like every landing I'd made on the Mayo coast, there was almost no level ground at Rathlackan big enough to take even my small tent's floor space. Finally I pitched it on the beaten and flattened earth of the cliff path above the harbour on the edge of a twenty-foot drop to the sea below, tying off the guy lines to tufts of bracken and heather dangling over space. It was the night of Lúnasa, the Celtic festival of harvest and fertility, and machinery whirred and clanked late into the night as farmers cut and tedded and baled hay in the fields inland, taking advantage of one of the few dry days in the summer. Traditionally Lúnasa is celebrated with feasting, bonfires and orgies, but there didn't seem a whole lot of anything going on. I open an extra tin of tuna to go in my rice slop, just as my tetchy petrol stove flares up into a hissing sputtering fireball that threatens to immolate the tent, the kayak and me. And then I sleep, a stretched sheet of nylon away from the cliff drop, haunted by drowning dreams, waking up gasping for breath.

●━━━━●

The wind increases through the morning, pushing up big waves. Out in open water, crossing the mouth of Killala Bay the occasional faceful of spray is merely refreshing, but as

I close on the coast again and round Lenadoon Point I can see breaking waves all along the coast ahead of me, and far out to sea, and hear the rush of surf coming from behind as waves run me down in a flurry of bubbles. Every few minutes a combination of big wave and swell and undersea profile combine to make a monster wave that lifts the kayak's stern so high so that the whole craft tips onto its pointy bow and careers down the wave.

On the shore I can see that the waves make an unbroken watery cliff of breaking surf. I am fenced out at sea. Inland I spot a church spire and a thick, green cloud of trees at Easkey and a square tower that marks the breakwater and harbour. I can also see lines of camper vans, awnings and cars dwarfed by roofracks piled high with surfboards. What is good for surfers is almost by definition bad for kayakers.

But the waves breaking on the reef are so big that most surfers have left their boards on their cars. Only a very few are paddling out into the break. I pass a couple of them. We have different agendas; whilst they wait for the big waves, I time my inward rush for gaps between. Every breaking wave submerges the hull altogether and some come up as far as my shoulders. A reef throws up massive breakers off the head and I gamble on the water's energy and power having been absorbed enough by the rocks to surf in on a trough, paddling hard to keep ahead of the waves chasing me down from behind. I am very nearly too slow. As I drive the kayak ashore and jump out, a four- or five-foot-high wave breaks over the kayak, filling the cockpit with water and then begins pulling the dead-weight of boat out and down into deep water. I have to fling myself into the waves to grab the ropes at the bow and haul it in. With the next incoming wave I get the kayak a bit further up the shingle, my bare feet battered by the churning stones. These include spheres of black and white rock, shot through with the cores of fossilised plants and sea creatures, whilst whole slabs of stone hold the full imprints of fronds, stalks and leaves. It is a primeval beach. With primeval weather.

I get the tent up just as the rain begins. Great sluicing curtains of water are drawn across the sea and land by the wind. Cooking is impossible, and I root in bags for the last of my foods as the rain batters the cracking nylon above my head. I mix porridge oats, a tin of sardines in tomato sauce and a finely chopped raw onion together in a bowl and spoon it down. Though my sense of hearing, smell and vision have all become sharpened by my survivalist existence on this trip, my sense of taste – thank Christ – has become dulled, making for a survival strategy in itself. I feel that I could probably eat boiled kelp, carrion seal meat or even pollock happily enough if I needed the calories. I lie down to wait out the wind and rain and rummage through the ship's library for *Moby Dick*.

Call me Ishmael. Some years ago – never mind how long precisely – having little or no money in my purse, and nothing particular to interest me on shore, I thought I would sail about a little and see the watery part of the world ... Whenever I find myself growing grim about the mouth; whenever it is a damp, drizzly November in my soul ... then, I account it high time to get to sea as soon as I can.

The opening lines should have given me pleasure; I was doing just what Melville was suggesting as a cure for melancholy. But if the cure when tired of life is going to sea, what is the reverse when tired of sea? Going to sea more? Or is it time to walk away with solid ground beneath my feet? Perhaps I am just sad and depressed because in this Irish summer I am paddling through a damp, drizzly November climate. Then leafing through the book I find the name Anna-Mei – a girlfriend of many years before – inscribed on the flysheet and my melancholy is complete.

⚫————⚫

Next morning the big surf is still beating on the shore, trapping me on land, and I walk the few miles to Easkey. The kayak, the tent and most of my kit, I leave on the headland. A masochist with no morals and a desire to kayak around Ireland could have packed everything up and headed off and would surely have wished them well.

But maybe it is all about breakfast. At Easkey, a cafe produces a fine fry-up and a pile of newspapers. Looking out on the world and far beyond at the sea from behind glass, as my clothes dry on me, and with the clatter of the kitchen and the sound of holiday families around me, I wondered if my despondency at the thwarted trip is less about the weather and more about being alone. But the previous day's *Irish Times* puts the weather in pole position. 'Washout Summer Beats Winter With 49 Days' Rain In A Row,' laments the front-page headline. And that is just the rain. Twenty-one of the twenty-six previous days have been subject to 'small craft warnings', when winds were predicted to hit force six or considerably more. There have been six gale warnings in the same period. The weather in June and July has been the worst since the Irish Met service started keeping records, and two days into August it doesn't look as if it is going to get much better.

The rain sluices through Easkey all day, as I circle between cafe, shops and bars. But in the evening there is only a light drizzle, lit by a watery sun, as I trudge back to my camp. I pass lines of surfers parked along the shoreline looking out to sea, a few of the most skilled or foolhardy bobbing around out in the waves, looking like seals.

I wake to the sound of the tent flapping damply around me, the wind strengthening again. I feel like a jail-bird going through the dull ritual of imprisonment as I seal up my tent, put on damp clothes and return through the rain to the cafe, for an even longer breakfast. In the shop I buy basics: tomato ketchup, a pack of rice cakes, chocolate biscuits, a tin of corned beef, a bottle of Italian wine. Then I add a packet of smoked salmon and a bottle of Jameson's.

Passing McGowan's I can't resist a first drink of the day. A mix of local and surfers' pub, it is decorated with kitsch model boats and galleons, a framed proclamation of Ireland's Independence, a window made out of a wagon wheel and photographs of mad nights in the bar. Now, though there are only a few fishermen drinking quietly in a corner, and three bored teenagers playing pool. Christy Moore's *Prosperous* plays from the speakers behind the bar, and CDs by Andy Irvine, Planxty, Stockton's Wing and other Irish bands are piled amongst the boxes of Tayto crisps. Everything reminds me of the small-town bars I hung out in through my teenage years, and then played music in when I'd rambled further afield into the west of Ireland. More lonesome memories.

When I get back to my camp, I am soaking wet and chilled. One hand's fingers are numb from the drag of the thin handles of the plastic bag carried for two miles. I strip off and towel down before diving into the tent. It is too wet – again – to fire up the stove and cook, so I experiment with a supper of tomato sauce squeezed over rice cakes, and find I like them. I switch the radio to country music and drink the bottle of wine. The tent, with its yellow inner and green outer skin, feels like a generous body-bag.

I try a bit more of *Moby Dick*, opening the book at random: *Like one who after a night of drunken revelry hies to his bed, still reeling, but with conscience yet pricking him,* I read, aloud, *Jonah's prodigy of ponderous misery drags him drowning down to sleep.* Except I can't sleep. The wind outside is coming and going in great buffeting blasts. Long calms and then a sudden bang against the tent that cants it far over to one side as if I'm being run over by a steamroller made of feather cushions.

I unscrew the whiskey bottle and pour a long slug into my tin cup, and at last move into dreams in which, constricted by the tube of my sleeping bag, I struggle to escape the great maw of a basking shark or some more shadowy sea monster that is swallowing me down.

CHAPTER 15

And Now Crusoe

I WAKE IN THE MORNING clear-headed, knowing that I have to leave. The struggle to get out beyond the breakers is a reversal of my surf landing, though this time I can see the waters that, ahead, are trying to ambush me. I have to paddle strongly to keep the kayak straight and to punch through the top ridge of water. At one point breakers submerge me, sweeping cameras, and map case, and compass, off the front deck in a tangle of restraining lines. Gushes of cold water pour down my neck. But a quarter of a mile out, the waves subside into a regular rolling swell and I have broken free of the heavy gravity holding me ashore.

As if on cue, the sky clears and, though the seas remain big, the wind has abated to a sharp breeze. Far ahead I can see Inishmurray island, about three hours' distant, and turn away from the land across the quartering sea towards its dark shape. I experience a vague disquiet. The island is too far away. The surging and gurgling of the water along the hull is making me uneasy. There is too much pressure. Ah, that's it: I really need a piss. I could turn back for the mainland shore, losing both time and distance, or – no, absolutely not – pee into my wetsuit in the time-honoured way of surfers and divers. There is another way, I decide, reaching for the razor-sharp rescue knife attached to my buoyancy aid. In a big swell like this the operation is going to be tricky, and not without risk, but I put down the paddles and with the precision of a heart surgeon cut along the crotch seams of my long-johns to make a Y-front opening. If all this goes wrong, I realise I'm going to be found hanging upside down in a kayak, arms bound to my waist by the spray-deck, having apparently chosen to self-mutilate myself with a clasp-knife. But it works and, having retailored my wetsuit, I hack a plastic water bottle into a bedpan and I'm away again.

●———●

Inishmurray lies some four miles off the coast of Sligo. The small population came ashore in the late 1940s. It had always been a hard island to live on, with no natural landing place – only crevices in the rocks that would just take a currach or small boat on a calm day. The stone and concrete pier jutting out of the landward side of the island seems a good place to head for, but it offers little protection in the surging waters. Rows of shags stand along the top of the jetty, high above me, in their formal black plumage and with craning necks looking down like the front row of a balcony audience in an opera house. With the swell surging up and down across the rocky shore five and six feet at a time, there seems little chance of making a safe landing and I sit offshore studying the shoreline.

Then I spot a bulwark of reef and beyond it a flattish sheet of rock that the waters surge onto and then drain off, leaving it no more than a few inches deep between waves. Waiting for a lull between swells, I drive the kayak ashore on an incoming wave, shoot across the slab and scrabble for purchase to stop myself being pulled back out again. I spring out of the cockpit, bare feet scraping and bruising on limpets and skidding on the gel-sludge of seaweed. The next wave catches the kayak and whirls it round, driving it full into my shins. I hold on and pull it up the rocks. The next wave barely reaches the kayak, and I manage to drag it aground on a shore of boulders.

It occurs to me, rather too late, that I've stranded myself on a deserted island in the face of oncoming bad weather. Like in climbing, where it's often only too easy to scramble up a rockface that then proves impossible to climb back down, landing a kayak can be easier than relaunching again. But at least I have land under me, even if I've swapped *Moby Dick* for *Robinson Crusoe*.

With the tent set up on a meadow of thick meadow grass, and a tripod of paddles holding my wet clothing up to dry in the gusting breeze, I set off to explore my new domain. On higher ground, there is an old schoolhouse, recently reroofed, with benches outside, a burnt patch in the grass from a driftwood fire and a water butt of green slimy rainwater. The building is locked. Beyond it are the remains of the village – a row of neatly built single-storey houses ending in a row of bigger, barn-like buildings and beyond them a small church. All are roofless, doorless and with only holes for windows. In one house I find a message written in red paint: LEFT 1948 PARENTS MIKE AND EILEEN. Down the pillar of a porch are daubed the names of BOYS: five sons and three nephews – MICHAEL, MIKE AND MICHAEL. On the other side are eight GIRLS, NIECES and a G.CHILD. A date at the end – 6.8.84 – presumably marks a family reunion on the island. Around the church are the older, more permanent graffiti of gravestones. Rabbits scuttle across the felted grass between the walls.

I set off to walk to the other end of the island, half a mile away. From the highest shore I can look down on the sea below and watch as huge waves course in from the expanse of Donegal Bay, rearing up like sheets of glass before exploding in shards against the cliff face. On the ocean side is a high-water line of mangled forty-five-gallon barrels, great splintered wooden beams and drifts of plastic bottles. In a rare cove of sheltered water, a female eider duck paddles in tight circles in pursuit of its small fluffy chick.

In the sixth century, Saint Molaise established a monastery here on the island, and its simple but awesome bulk of stones remains atop a rise above the village. I circle the high defensive wall of stones, wide enough on top for several people to walk abreast, until I find the tight entrance gateway, almost a tunnel, burrowing through the ramparts. Within is a jumble of chapels, altars, crosses, graves, and an oval-domed oratory whose central chamber is reached through twisting stone corridors. A perfect beehive of stone, it is as magical and impressive as a Mayan temple, and equally old. Inside one of the chapels is a line of rounded 'cursing' stones, some of them carved with ornate crosses and patterns, all the size of bowling balls. Turn the stones and incant the right words, it is said, and one can direct pain and death on the deserving. A century ago, the islanders used them on a gang of excise men who were making it hard to distil Inishmurray's famed *poitín*, then watched their boat overturn and the men drown. A few decades later a woman came over from the mainland to curse Hitler and took credit for the outcome of the Second World War. Before that, penitents had carried the stones around the island's sacred spots, sins given an actual weight of punishment.

In the dull evening light I make my way back into the stone oratory and sit on a small stone bench in the stilled air. There is the slight murmur of silence like putting one's ear to a shell. I wonder how life must have been in these monasteries of Ireland's Golden Age, flourishing at a time when the Romans had left Britain to the Norse. The picture I have is something like a hippie commune with good food, daft clothing, a bit of singing, half-skilled crafts and a good bit of art. The numerous references to the daughters and sons of bishops, priests and nuns in early Irish literature suggests that the idea of celibacy came late to the western shores of Christianity. Life in early Irish monasteries was in all probability far more comfortable than for the average farmer or tribal follower of the same period, and quite a bit more fun. But the Golden Age was over by the late 800s, as even in this remote monastery a Norse raiding party arrived and slaughtered the last abbot and his monks.

Back at my camp it is almost dark as I light the stove, cook up another combination of unlikely ingredients, and listen to the seabirds flying overhead, their lives ordered by the tides rather than by light and darkness. As, indeed, for the moment, is my own.

The next morning, the wind is warm but blustery and there are still big seas. I accept the fact of being marooned for another day and set off around my island in the sun. First I check the rain tank under the schoolhouse roof; I am low on water but not so desperate that the green liquid sluiced with gull shit from the roof looks tempting. Then I pick up a tennis-ball-sized round stone with the idea of bowling a rabbit for the pot. I assume the rabbits had been imported as an easily captured food source. Inishmurray is one of the first islands of any size where I've not found sheep grazing.

Botanising as I ramble, the island produces ragwort, burdock and thistles – far too many for my bare feet – and in every sheltered spot there's a combination of dock, scarlet pimpernel, thrift, self-heal, nettles and other wild plants. There's not a garden plant to be seen, oddly enough, though the birds fossicking among the weeds are those of a suburban backyard – blackbirds, starlings and wrens.

Feeling peaceful and warm, I lie for hours looking at the mainland and the looming bulk of Benbulben, a five-hundred-metre-high shoulder of rock scoured during the last ice age from the surrounding Sligo landscape by glaciers. It stands out like an Irish Ayers Rock. Formations like Benbulben are called *nunataks* – islands of exposed rock once surrounded by ice, as they still are in Greenland. Like kayak, *nunatak* is another word of Inuit origin.

At dawn next day the wind is gusting strongly again. My stay on the island is becoming slightly alarming. I ration out my remaining water for drinking, and filter a few litres from the water butt through a handkerchief to use for cooking and to boil up for coffee. My petrol is running out as well, though there is ample driftwood here to make fires.

Before the trip started, and even in the first days, I'd imagined myself foraging and fishing and hunting, living off the land as much as out of shops. I'd planned to unsheath old skills and hook out edible crabs from rockpools and net shrimps, pick samphire off the mud flats, boil up mussels, and at night whilst camped out I'd set snares for the rabbits which seemed to infest every island around the coast. But the reality was that I didn't have the energy. I'd rather eat something dull and easy out of a tin cooked to mush with rice, or even go hungry, than stir myself to find or chase down wild foods. A handful of early blackberries had been my bounty from nature so far, and a couple of undersized mackerel. All my focus was brought to bear on just paddling on.

In the past five days I've made only one forward move and I work out that, on a pro-rata basis, to complete the circumnavigation I'll have to keep paddling until February. I pace my island again. Taking a book, I find a hollow out of the wind, and in the sun strip down to sunbathe. Later in the afternoon I see a dark cloud gathering over the mainland, and then unfurling itself across the sea and over the island. I feel the first heavy drops of rain as I run back to camp; I'd taken advantage of the breeze and sun that morning to put everything – sleeping bag, bag-liner, clothes – out onto lines or weighted down with stones to dry and air. In the torrential rain, everything, including the clothes I am wearing, is soaked. At the camp I bundle it all into the tent, stripping off my clothes to throw in afterwards, and then howl outrage and obscenities at the storm. It drains me of anger, as does the sight of a perfect rainbow looping over the raked sides of Benbulben, and the sun shining out from under the clouds and lighting up the seas.

The pounding rain has also calmed the waters a bit, I think. So I suddenly feel the need and chance to leave the island. I pack quickly, pull on the wet wetsuit, which warms quickly against my body, and set the loaded kayak on the flat sheet of rock where I'd landed, sitting in it as the final surges of big waves lap up to its hull. The kayak slews and bounces off stones and skids in the whirling foam, but I paddle and pole and push to reach the regular waters beyond the shore.

This is probably a stupid move. It is late afternoon, going into evening, the weather is poor and due to get worse, and I am setting off on an eighteen-mile open-water paddle across the longest sweep of the biggest bay in Ireland. All I know about the coast I am heading towards is that it has some of the highest sea cliffs in Europe – 600 metres in places – and so offers little chance of an emergency exit, should I need one.

CHAPTER 16

Donegal Bay

S TRIKING OUT ACROSS DONEGAL BAY, I feel a peculiar exhilaration about the whole commitment that's demanded of this journey – the longest stretch of open sea I'll be cutting across. The going is relentlessly hard, with a steep roller coaster of swell that a few miles off Inishmurray rolls into great explosions of surf on the rocks at Shaddan. But after an hour or two of paddling, time loses meaning and soon I'm into a zone of pretty much pure concentration. I spot the occasional bird, flying down the corridors of shelter between the big swells, but the wind and the waves are churning each other up and it's not fishing weather for gannets or auks. They're all determinedly travelling. And so am I.

After what I'm guessing might be three hours, the swell has got bigger and the waves, too, but this mostly makes it easier to kayak; higher peaks, yes, but coming less often, so my arms are pacing me across the water. Every now and again a big swell coincides with a big wave and I'm left scrambling with the paddles, first one side and then the other, to keep my balance.

I do have one concern. I left the island late in the day and now, well into evening, I'm far out to sea, maybe seven miles from shore, and the light is going to start going in another hour or so. The coast is a dark shadow on the horizon and Malin Beg, where I'm aiming for, is a tiny harbour in an inhospitable coast. On a grizzly, grey day like this it would be difficult enough to pinpoint in the daylight, but in darkness it may be impossible. I study the chart whilst there is still light. The long stretch of coastline before Malin Beg is marked with cliffs and uncharted rocks.

I'll get some idea of direction from the Rathlin O'Birne Island lighthouse; if I see it flashing white, then I'm well offshore, which means safe, but maybe too far off to be able to find the harbour. If I see it as red I'll be in amongst, or even on, the rocks.

For four hours now, my actions have been automatic and mechanical, the slow swing of my shoulders and push and pull of my arms very much like a simple two-stroke engine. I find myself reflecting that in sea-paddling there's really nothing between the extremes of drowning and a safe trip. Unlike climbing, say, or riding horses, or indeed nearly every other adventure activity, there's little chance of ending up in a wheelchair or on crutches. Water can be chilly and fast-moving but it's essentially soft. One doesn't have crashes or falls at sea. And to avoid drowning one only has to keep upright and paddling. It's like being a clowning acrobat pedalling a bicycle back and forth on a tightrope high up in the big top. No more than gentle exercise, really, slightly comic, except there is no stopping until the end of the line; no putting one's feet down mid-trip and getting off.

Bit by bit on this trip I've been nullifying one fear after another. Not fit enough? Well, it seems I am. Sharks? Seen 'em, and been stalked by one. Big seas? Washed over me, and I floated on. Rising winds? Every day. Miles of coast-line with no landing? Well, that's the whole west coast. Marooned on offshore islands? Loved it. But I've circled round the one genuine, practical horror – drowning. And as other worries get crossed off the list, it's increasingly preying upon my mind.

In fact, now that I've acknowledged it, memories are flooding into my mind. I've come close to drowning how often? Well, there was a time on the Danube when the wide stretch I'd been swimming across abruptly turned narrow and deep as it squeezed into a gorge, and strong currents pulled me down under the surface over and over, making each struggle to the surface ever harder. Then I had managed to grasp a bush that grew from the sheer rockface and keep hold on it till a boat pulled me to safety. Another time, in Corfu, I was pulled by a rip-tide from the mouth of a bay around a headland in cold November waters, muscles stiffening and head sinking lower in the bustling waters as I headed out to sea. And once, stupidly fully dressed, weighted down, plunging to the muddy bottom of a lake in the Norfolk Broads, standing upright, looking up at my boat's hull a few yards above me in the evening gloom.

The thought of Kevin Murphy on his swim across Dingle Bay horrifies me. And then my mind spins off into thoughts of the myths of the underworld below. The realms of mermaids, *selkies, rusalka, krakena* or the *aughisky* – an Irish water-horse spirit that carries the incautious down into the depths to be ripped apart and eaten.

Sitting on a beach once in Morocco, I'd seen a body wash gently out from the waves and onto the sand, as if still alive, crawling a few feet forward with each incoming swell. There were Moroccan families picnicking on the beach, and most of the men, all of the children and none of the women ran to gather around the corpse. The dead man was still wrapped in the more resistant of his clothes, his trousers a lace-work of holes and tatters, with only the double- and treble-thickness seams and the fly and pockets wholly intact. Boots or shoes gone. A heavy, yellow oilskin jacket, ripped open and held by a single button. A teenager pushed at one wrinkled foot with the toe of his blue plastic sandal and the whole leg shifted heavily. Then after a while nearly everyone returned to their picnic blankets, the families closest to the corpse moving a little further away. Someone trudged up through the sand to a distant cafe to call the *gendarmes*. When they came – a Laurel and Hardy duo in heavy grey uniforms, sweating as they strutted across the sands – they turned the body over, rifled its pockets and found a *carte d'identité*. 'Pêcheur!' announced one. Reading out the dead man's occupation from the card constituted detective work of a kind and he looked pleased with himself. They left to call an ambulance and the body was left facing the blue infinity of sky, eyes sunken under closed eyelids, hair still crisply curled.

There's a popular idea that drowning isn't the worst way to die. Not messy. Not so very painful. Not too brutish and nasty. A bit like going for a dip and then falling into sleep –

a very long sleep – whilst bobbing around in and then under the water. Drowning is different from other deaths. Even the word is strangely specific. Die by any other means – old age, overdose, Ebola disease, loose gravel under the wheels of a too-fast car taking a bend, cancer – and you've just 'died'. Even the word 'killed' adds little to a general idea of death except the suggestion of violence and perhaps some idea of surprise and tragedy. You can be killed by things as varied as a falling brick, pneumonia, friendly fire, a knifing, a maverick doctor or an irate stingray. But if you drown, then that's what *you* have done.

Maybe it's because the medical process of drowning allows for spectacular Lazarine returnings from the dead. Blacked-out inert bodies can be pulled from the waters, especially if it's been cold water, and revived hours after 'dying'. It's a maxim in water rescue situations that life hasn't been lost until a body is both warm and dead.

Perhaps drowning is different, because the seas and rivers and lakes are themselves a dark mystery, subverting the norms of the land, forming a mirror-image world. The drama of drowning takes place out of sight, in a too-swift reversal of evolution, from land-based mammal back to sea creature, from human to amphibian, from air-breather to – briefly – water-inhaler. And there is another level, which seems almost natural. Our bodies are skin-bags of liquid, holding minerals and salts and trillions of tiny lifeforms in suspension, very like a miniature sea in itself. So this returning of our waters to a wider more universal water makes more sense than going 'dust to dust'.

And, while my mind is on these things, I recall something else – a particular and personal flaw. I have negative buoyancy, caused by heavy bones and not much fat. This means that I can't do the 'drown-proof' method of floating, when you bob around in the water in a relaxed foetal position, raising your head every fifteen seconds or so to take a breath. If I 'bob', I start sinking. Either I'm actively swimming or I'm drowning.

Out here at sea in fading light, with the wind howling and the waves peaking and crashing and surging around me, I sense, with a shock of recognition, yet another danger. I am unafraid. Paddling to stay upright and winch my way across the miles to harbour is so dynamic that all these thoughts are abstractions, like a radio playing in the background. Either I'm kayaking at the very peak of my skills and am right to be unafraid or I'm sadly deluded and in fact only one sneaky wave from losing the plot and tumbling over. The danger of overconfidence, however, is that you feel you could go on for ever.

I reflect on my reading about sea-kayaking. How long-distance paddlers who have set off on trans-ocean kayak voyages have nearly all been successful on their first epic adventure. And how most of them have gone to make another trip, usually more ambitious, and if they survived it, then another trip after that, until one by one they made one landing too few and dropped from the roster.

Perhaps the most famous of these kayaking greats was Franz Romer, who successfully kayaked across the Atlantic from Portugal to Puerto Rico in 1928, covering nearly four thousand miles over two months at sea. From Puerto Rico he set off again to paddle on to mainland America, then disappeared in a hurricane. But only a few months before I'd set off on my journey, adventurer Andrew McAuley went missing almost within sight of land after crossing the 1200 miles from Tasmania to New Zealand. In previous years he'd kayaked across Bass Strait between Australia and Tasmania, and across Australia's huge Gulf of Carpentaria, and on an expedition taking him on an 500-mile journey inside the Antarctic Circle. His empty kayak was found, but not his body.

With darkness falling I'd like to be able to identify the particular piece of dark horizon that holds the break in the cliffs that is Malin Beg harbour. But if I don't find it ... then what? Do I keep paddling for ever? I've got my 'Y-front' long-john wetsuit, and under the net in front of me are the odd bits of remaining food – carrots, an easy-open tin of kippers, a few oat biscuits. There's a bottle of water behind the seat, and the mix of hats and gloves and sweat shirts and cagoules needed to keep me warm. My world has shrunk to this little cockpit of yellow – and at the same time it has grown to include all the world's waters.

Then I spot the harbour – an opening of grey and silvery waters cut back into black cliffs. The haven turns out to be almost vertical, its slipway a steep slide of concrete with steps and levels hewed into the rock. In the surge of water up and down the concrete slope, landing and getting the bags out is difficult. At one point a big swell throws the kayak up and in against my shin bones with an agonising crack. I've begun swearing, quite loudly and blasphemously. A release after the tensions of six hours of paddling in big seas, and a very direct response to the bags sliding back down past me and into the sea. Finally I drag the kayak up to the first level of jetty, some twenty feet above the water. There a woman and a small boy are fooling around with a fishing rod. I realise that the acoustics means she will have spent the last quarter of an hour trying to shield her six-year-old from my foul oaths – the majority having to do with procreative acts, some involving the kayak and Jesus and the Mother of God, tricky to explain out of context. It's forgiving of her to respond to my embarrassed 'Ah! Eve'ning' with a cordial-sounding greeting. Perhaps, though, she takes a bit too much relish in pointing out there isn't a shop within miles, nor a pub, either.

I leave the kayak on a slab of concrete next to coils of rope, piles of lobster pots and a fleet of landed boats painted in sky blue and bright white. The local fishermen lower and raise their craft in and out of the water with various engined winches and steel cables from the top of the slip. It's a long haul up steps and slopes to the clifftop. I've carried only what I need for the night, leaving the rest of the kit in the kayak. I've very little food left, so that's a saving on the portage. And all I really need is my sleeping bag and tent, thrown on a patch of grass on the cliff edge. Weariness and relief will send me to sleep.

CHAPTER 17

Earthly Delights

MALIN BEG WAKES to a blue sky, a stiff breeze and a sea that has quietened down considerably. Lowering the packed kayak down into the water with gravity on my side takes minutes, and with no swearing I'm heading for Árainn Mhór, the second largest island off the Irish coastline.

It's more than twenty miles away, but I'm sun-warmed, hungry and ready to paddle. I've learnt to measure out the hours of paddling in small, discreet rewards, spaced as far apart as possible. An hour's paddle and then a biscuit. Another hour and a gulp of water. Maybe two hours more and I stop and wiggle around in the cockpit pulling at the spray-deck and wetsuit to take a piss, concern that the act might capsize me not helping. I'm careful not to allow my worries about navigation to prompt too-frequent stops to look at the charts. Paddling is like working on an assembly line, but being paid on piece work and not by the hour. There's no reward in idling.

A pomarine skua skeets over the waves. Three yachts pass much further out to sea. Now that I've hit on a relatively easy day – open sea, lightish wind, a soft swell, sunny – I can afford to daydream again and my thoughts drift towards the things that I'm going to do when I get to the island. The list starts off modestly enough. Buying some food, for a start. And sinking a pint or two in a bar. And picking up a letter from poste restante. But then, as the hours pass, I begin adding to the list of pleasures. I've done so well I deserve a restaurant meal; I go through a virtual menu and choose steak and a salad, though I can't decide on a starter, and think I'll wait until I'm actually sitting at the table to make that decision. But I'll definitely have a bottle of wine. I'll check my email whilst I'm ashore, too. And to hell with camping: I'll have a night in a hostel and get a shower and dry all my kit. Maybe I'll take the next day off altogether and explore the island, lounge around on a beach in the sun, go to a few sessions in the evening. I deserve a massage, too, and by having made so much distance in these two days I've effectively saved – so, really *made* – money. Which means I can get a haircut, as well. And there'll be music.

In my mind I've recreated Árainn Mhór as a mix of Dingle, Dublin and my own idea of the garden of earthly delights. The anticipation is enough to keep me good-tempered, even when, confused by the haze and the long distances, I mis-navigate myself into the maze of islands that lie inland from

Árainn Mhór and so add quite a few miles to my route. In recompense I mentally upgrade myself to a better bottle of wine amidst the coming pleasures.

Approaching the island at its south-east corner I'm heading for the small village of Ballintra and I scan the higgledy-piggledly scatter of houses and buildings above the harbour for an off-licence, restaurants, shops, a hostel, the striped pole announcing a barber. It doesn't look hopeful. Indeed, as far as I can see, there is nothing but houses in the village. I keep circling the island anticlockwise, heading round Cloghcor Point and into the South Sound. A bright-orange speed-ferry shoots past me northwards and into the harbour at Leabgarrow. This looks a lot more promising. There's a bigger ferry disgorging cars. Boats and even full-sized trawlers up on blocks ready to be worked on. And, painted on the seaward side of a rambling building just above the beach, a shaky, but large-printed single word: 'BAR'.

The evening is turning drizzly and a cold breeze is adding wind chill to what has been a warm day. After nine hours at sea, I'm physically tired and very hungry; I haven't had a satisfying meal in three days, not since Easkey. It's an effort to pull out on the slip. There are tight groups of children and teenagers, coalesced into age groups, hanging out on the quay, or sheltering from the wind behind derelict buildings, some smoking cigarettes in the cupped-hand way of old lags and furtive schoolkids. It's like the patches of waste ground colonised by bored gangs in an inner-city estate. But here the background isn't high-rises and factories but the green and russet slopes of the island's hills.

I walk past the restaurant I've already spotted from the water. It's firmly closed, with a sign saying it will reopen in two days' time. There's a funeral on the island. The packs of children roaming around are the pupils sent from Irish cities to learn Irish in the *gaeltacht* summer schools, Árainn Mhór being a noted heartland of the language. Maybe that explains the graffiti on walls, the drifts of chocolate wrappers and soft-drinks cans in the ditches and the glass kicked out of the phone box. The hostel is wreathed in acrid smoke clouding out from the back yard as a family set fire to sausages and chicken legs on a barbecue. Young boys are running in and out of the hostel screaming, and there is the crash of breaking glass and swearing as someone lurches into a table and bottles of beer crash to the ground.

Item by item I'm crossing pleasures of my list. I'm down to needing just the basics now. Food. And drink. And a place to camp. Walking up the street I see a bunch of yachties, arms filled with boxes of food and drink, heading back to the harbour. Ah bad luck, they tell me in English accents. I've just missed the shop. It was closing as they were leaving.

I walk on to the bar. I'm still in my wetsuit and cagoule. There are smokers trying to evade the wind at the door. The floor inside is raw concrete, and it's a big spacious room. Groups of drinkers sit glumly around tables on benches. There's no food. And probably not, tonight, anywhere this side of the island, the barman tells me. There's three flavours of crisps, though, he adds helpfully, as he pours a pint. I'm going to be having stout for supper, it seems.

I walk back through the drizzle to the harbour, where a chip van has driven in. My island of pleasures is reduced to a paper wadded with chips and a chunk of battered fish, eaten sitting on damp concrete next to a metal barrel overflowing with rubbish. I've already had a bit of jeering from one bunch of early teens: 'Hey miss-ta, wha's tha y'wear'n ... it looks like a fookin' rubber johnny.' 'Is tha' y boat, th' can-oo ting you came in on?' These aren't rural accents, nor rural manners, and they unsettle me. Looking at the chart I note Calf Island only a little offshore. Its moated position seems like a reassuring camp spot. Wearily I climb into the kayak again. The rain has stopped and it's a still evening as I paddle towards the rock and grass.

Passing a yacht at anchor on the way, I'm hailed from the cockpit by one of the box-carrying sailors. 'We saw you yesterday,' he explains, 'out in Donegal Bay ... when it was nearly dark. You made it okay, obviously?' I paddle up to the stern and a row of faces look down on me. 'Actually, we were pretty worried about you ... big seas, and we'd get a glimpse of you and then you'd disappear ... We nearly turned around and came back to see if you were okay, but you looked happy enough, or afloat, at least ... Why don't you come up and have a drink? Beer? Glass of wine? Tie your kayak off the stern ... you bloody deserve a drink ... how many miles is that you've done today?'

I haul myself up the stern ladder and lounge against the taff-rail at the back, aware of smelling of damp neoprene, while my new friends – crewing the yacht back to Scotland – bring up bottles and glasses. There is easy talk about the sea, the weather, and at some point it is assumed, or perhaps it is just my assumption, that I am staying to eat. A heaped plate of pasta is passed up to me, along with yet another glass of wine. And, with spirits renewed, I find myself extolling the pleasures and pains of kayaking, even in this miserable summer; indeed that I can't think of a better way to see the coast ... And then, with a shot of Jaegermeister in hand, it occurs to me that I *can* – and this is it. Yachting. I feel like Mr Toad, sitting in comfort, poop-pooping at this new way of life.

Seemingly I've found my wish list for Árainn Mhór aboard this yacht, the *Kaparda*, and as another shot of *digestif* drowns some small part of my brain, I wonder about asking if anyone is drunk enough to cut my hair, or give me a massage. Instead, in the dark, on a chorus of good fellowship, I lower myself into the kayak and staggle – half-paddle, half-stagger – over the few hundred metres of water to Calf Island. The tide has dropped in the hours that I've spent on the yacht and the water's edge is separated from dry land by a long expanse of seaweed-draped rocks and deep pools of water. I have to negotiate this booby-trapped landscape six times in the dark, carrying all my gear. The sextet aboard the yacht must be hearing a comic soundtrack of splashes and crashes as things drop onto the shingle amid curses and loud yelps of pain.

The next morning I wake late, with the tent in festoons of slack skin between the poles, a dump of bags around me, and my wetsuit thrown on the grass. It's grey and cold and a strong wind is blowing. The *Kaparda* has already drawn anchor and sailed. I pack and kayak back to the slip.

The same group of kids is hanging out on the quay and a grumpy leisure sailor is poking around with an oar in the shallows. 'Some little feckers threw all the cushions and mats in off my boat.' He gestures up to a small fibreglass cruiser propped up in the shadow of a grounded trawler.

Leaving my kayak on the quay seems foolish. But I want breakfast, and expect mail at the post office, and need stores and petrol, too, for my stove. These simple needs tax the island to and beyond its limits. 'No petrol around here,'

I am told in the post office as the clerk confirms that none of my letters have arrived. He wants a forwarding address, so I struggle to work out a location, based on when the letters might arrive here, how quickly they would be sent onwards and how far I might have travelled in that time. It is all beyond me, and finally I plump for a friend's address in Dublin, good for days, weeks or months.

'Breakfast, is it?' I'm not yet within Northern Ireland's political borders, but there's been a sea change in accent since crossing Donegal Bay. In the tones of the north, positives sound melodic and possible, but negatives – petrol, my mail and, now, possibly, breakfast – are couched in harsh and obdurate words. Raised in the south, in the Republic, much of my experience of the North has been years of the 'Troubles' on the news, and the endless, bleak, intransigent litany of 'NO! NO! NO!' between one side and the other. Grating Northern politicians have mouthed and spat negatives at each other decade after decade.

Enquiring about petrol, the blunt 'nos' and 'you can't get that here' emerge as if in response to indecent proposals. But the chance of breakfast has become more promising. 'You'll have to go round to the hotel at Ballintra, but it's only a wee walk ... and there'll be plenty of people going to the funeral ...' – an automatic signing off the cross – 'so you might even get a spin off someone, in all likelihood.'

An elderly farmer in a ramshackle Volvo stops beside me in the middle of the road. His is a gentle voice, slow paced as if to talk cows into letting down their milk. We drive through a landscape of old houses twinned by newly built bungalows – Árainn Mhór has the Irish building craze, albeit on a personal, haphazard scale, many of the back-garden building sites just walls and eaves and rafters, waiting for roofs. 'Of course,' said my driver, 'some will never get finished. Islands have good times and hard, and we have all the new ferries and grants and tourists, and times have been good enough to us, thank God, but I wonder can it last?' I judge his age to be around eighty; old enough, anyway, to have seen many things fail to last. His was a benign detachment. 'Ah, yes, the childre' can be a bit rough, rowdy b'times ... They come out here for the Irish schools and they run a bit wild, but on an island they can't do much mischief, and God knows they keep the place alive.'

In the hotel dining room I sit by a window overlooking the waters I'd paddled across the day before. From my airy height I can see the twisted back-and-forthing I'd made through the islands, and the direct route I'd missed – now looking as obvious as a glittering trunk road.

Back on the quay, I duck into the small blockhouse shop. Wooden shelves hold sweets, convenience foods and souvenirs. A dreamy girl with long hair and a Pre-Raphaelite Celtic face is lost in a book. Looking up at me she asks 'Is that your boat, the yellow canoe on the slip? I saw you coming in yesterday.' She's animated now, looking out of the window and across the scattering of islands. 'Can you go anywhere in it? Far out to sea, and to deserted islands?' The magic-carpet aspect of the kayak was opening up its possibilities to her as it had to me. 'What do you see out there?'

I run through the highlights of paddling around the coast, like some huckster selling real estate. The birds, the basking sharks, the immensity of the cliffs, making camp on islands, the changeability (if not the bleakness) of the weather, the dolphins. 'Dolphins? Would they jump up from the water? Oh! My! God! That must be lovely.'

On the quay a gang of children seems to be dismantling a dried-out trawler with their bare hands. Equipment tough enough to withstand winter storms and fishermen is being kicked and beaten and pried apart. They stop their work to watch me as I pack the kayak, climb into the cockpit and begin pushing myself off. 'Hey, Mistah! You, Mistah! Will that ting fall over?' I ignore the conversational gambit. Another voice comes in. 'If it goes over, can you swim? Will yah drown, will yah?' My grim silence seems to frustrate my questioners and I leave to a chorus of catcalls, fading away behind me into the squabbling jabber of seabirds.

CHAPTER 18

Companions

OUT ON THE WATER the weather jukebox is still set on random play. There's a thick mist rolling in as I nudge the kayak into the oily swell and line up compass and chart to calibrate my optimum course north towards Bloody Foreland, and then readjust it by a generous amount so that, however wrong I might get the tides and currents, I'll still end up hitting land somewhere rather than sailing past the top right corner of Ireland and out to sea.

After an hour the mist begins to dissolve, like a second dawn, revealing the islands of Owey and Cruit, either side of me. I'm glad that I'd already worked out that was where they should have been, with the island of Gola straight ahead. And I'm making good time, pulled northwards by the ebbing tide. One of the reasons that I'd wasted so much time faffing around onshore looking for breakfast, doing the crossword, chatting, was because the tide doesn't turn till mid-afternoon. Finally I've learnt to prioritise the elements of seafaring in their correct order of importance. Weather, always weather, first. Sea conditions next, and their interface with the land. Then tide. The triumvirate. But overawed by the weather and the seas, I'd often overlooked the importance of the tides in the equation. I'd missed favourable tides, or impatiently headed out into contrary waters without realising the difference that the push or the pull of the currents might make to six or seven hours' of paddling. I had been locked into the landlubbers' solar clock, getting up in the morning and going out to spend the day paddling as I might have gone out to shovel earth out of a ditch. But I'd at last got wise to the effects – positive and negative – of the tidal flow and the ever-changing coastal currents it set up. Instead of following the sun, I'd gone lunar.

Each tidal cycle is out of kilter with the sun but goes in and out in time with the moon, and full moons, when our twin is closer to us, exert even more pull, making for fuller, stronger spring tides. The currents flowing around Ireland change direction and even speed in time with the tides, spinning through 360 degrees of direction in every tidal cycle. So, in each twelve hours, for about six hours the current will either be with me or not actively against me, whilst for the following six hours the moving waters will not – to put it lightly – be that helpful. Electing to go against the current is like choosing to join a traffic jam of contraflow cars on a busy bank holiday. Getting it right can give an extra mile, or even two, for every hour paddled.

When I'd started paddling I'd vaguely known all of this, but on my limited kayak expeditions the pulsings and turnings of the currents had been masked by the more dramatic stops and starts of foul weather, big seas and my own incompetence. Now, as I've got fitter and more confident, and as the windows of paddle-good weather widen, so the currents and tides assume prime importance.

I paddle at roughly three knots – a bit more than three miles an hour – a comfortable strolling pace. On average the current might be half or even a full knot either with or against me. But along parts of the coast, when the waters are accelerated by being forced through straits or around headlands, the waters might be travelling at six knots or even faster. Be on these waters at the right time and you get a free roller-coaster ride. Even just sitting on a favourable tidal stream, eating biscuits and watching the seagulls and dozing for a quarter of a day, I'll be carried along like a suitcase on a luggage carousel.

Towards dusk, with the sky both clearing and darkening, I'm rushing along. I can see deep 'V' ripples around the buoys above lobster pots, showing the speed and direction of the current. Far inland I see, for the first time, the surprising outline of Mount Errigal – a 2500-foot-high mountain of pure conical perfection that looks like Fujiyama, white-topped from quartz instead of snow, colouring rose now in the sunset. I know it well from doing childhood wet-weather jigsaws.

I can picture the exact puzzle, shaped, cleverly, to my boy mind, like Ireland itself and with images of Irishness – the Cliffs of Moher, Benbulben, the round tower at Glendalough, the Lakes of Killarney, the Giant's Causeway, Errigal – printed roughly in their correct place on the silhouette. Along with the geographical landmarks there were women shrouded in all-enveloping Kinsale cloaks, donkeys with creels of turf, a fellow fly fishing on the Mayo lakes, stout lads leaping up in the air hurling and a view of Dublin's O'Connell Street. I recall the unflagging joy of fitting its several hundred pieces together, seeing the coastline grow under my fingers, and wonder if there isn't something of the same pleasure in this journey, fitting together tides, cliffs, landings and weathers as I move slowly around Ireland's rim, putting off filling in the more complicated and puzzling centre of the island until later.

It is on the very edge of blue-black dusk over the mainland when I land on the mud and shingle exposed by the fallen tide on Inishsirrer Island.

I hump my gear across a landscape of rubble – perfectly rounded stones from billiard ball to spacehopper, all covered by thick matted grass. Grass knots around my ankles as I erect the tent over an expanse of thatched rocks and beachcomb by torchlight for firewood to cook with. Finally I relax in the flicker of the flames from my small rock hearth and stare up into the stars. It's the first clear night for weeks, and I circle my gaze around them, ticking off familiar constellations. The Great and the Little Bear, and the Pole Star northwards over Bloody Foreland – the next headland – then Taurus and, within it, my favourite celestial companion, the star cluster of the Pleiades. Lying on my back I see the flashing navigation lights of planes rushing westwards to America. Then a sudden light moving from horizon to horizon. It takes just a few minutes, and if

I hadn't made a note in my journal after reading a newspaper article I would have thought it a sluggish shooting star, but it's not, it's the International Space Station. Strange to look up and know that there are people, more people than on this island, above me in this expensive tin-can – at $100 billion, the most costly 'thing' ever made by humans – orbiting through space.

On the island I can see an abandoned *clachan* of houses as faint rhomboids, triangles and squares on the horizon against the last fading of the western light. I imagine them abandoned the usual five or so decades before, the population already decimated by half a century of drownings and winter deaths from illness and accidents too far from the medical help on the mainland, followed by the pull of economic emigration, and finally the inevitable reality that it was cheaper, and easier, to bring the islanders ashore to the newly electrified Ireland of welfare state and schooling than to take the modern world out to the islands. And once a critical mass of islanders were gone, then all had to follow. For places like this were nothing if not communities; there was little scope for solitary hermits and misanthropic stay-behinds in traditional Irish coastal life. The harsh climate necessitated that people should work together, share the tasks of fishing, building or harvesting, as well as evening get-togethers when warmth, words and common experience were gathered into one room around one fire, with songs and a drop or two of *poitín* or porter.

The abandoned island had a sadness to it. But I feel, too, a joy on taking possession of a solitary home. Perhaps in this I'm not typically Irish – in my contentment and even need to be alone for long periods. Or perhaps it's just a question of privilege, not having to rely directly on others for my survival, being able to indulge my hermit-lite adventures and intersperse them in my own time with carnival, sing-ongs and intrigue.

But I'm glad that I'm alone here, and that I'm making this trip alone. And for the first time I don't feel I need to rationalise this in any way or alleviate it by playfully talking out loud, in other voices. Tonight I'm silent, and happy with it.

●━━●

To catch the tide I'm up just after dawn. Groggy from sleep, watching the approaching clear-skied sunrise, it's too time-consuming to light a fire, so I mix up oatmeal and milk powder and water, and stir in a generous spoon of instant coffee powder. Possibly an efficiency too far. But I slurp it down anyway. The water is bubbling lightly round the rocks and the kayak ripples forward with each paddle stroke. Errigal is a dark truncated triangle against the eastern light. Bloody Foreland comes up fast. It's a landmark, where I turn east across Ireland, setting off on the third and shortest side of this island's unbalanced rhomboid shape.

Out to sea is Tory Island, another community I'm going to scutter past in my growing obsession with completing this circumnavigation. Today things seem to be on my side. Not only is the current flowing eastwards at a knot or so, but a westerly wind, the first in days, and the only time it's been helpful so far, is at my back, pushing me along like the big hand a father puts behind a toddler on a tricycle to keep them moving. I straight-line through the channels between Inishbofin and Inishdooey islands towards the cliffs at Horn Head, some five miles of open sea away.

On this trip I've noticed how my distance from land is marked off in contour lines of bird species. Inshore under cliffs I see peregrines Stuka-ing rock doves, and ravens and hoody crows, rarely more than a glide away from solid land. The black-backed gulls and kittiwakes, too, seemingly keep an eye on shore, as do the shags and cormorants, standing on rocks, wings spread. If I get really close up I can see the cormorants' subtle sequinning of bronzed feather tips, and the dried-out shags' flicked-forward, cow-lick quiffs.

Several hundreds of yards offshore, I'm paddling through rafts of razorbills and guillemots. The smell of raw fish drifts from them with a whiff like opening a can of tuna. As I pass them, the closest birds to the kayak begin to vibrate, the frantic effort of their legs thrashing away under them as they pull out of my way. Closer still and they duck forward and dive, changing direction as soon as they're submerged. Sometimes this brings them back under the kayak and I see them flying through the water, their stubby wings half extended and moving in short staccato beats that pulse them forward, squeezing out a silver contrail of tiny air bubbles from their plumage.

Further out still and I spot solitary puffins. In summer their beaks are like an outsized clown's nose, snapped on moments before ducking out into the ring, and almost obscuring their sad eyes emphasised by the sweep of eye-liner. Watching the puffins fly is heart-stopping, their wings buzzing yet barely creating lift enough to pull them clear of the water and, like me, liable to be capsized back into the water by a bigger than expected wave passing below them. They don't so much land on land, but tumble into it in a succession of pratfalls and mournful-faced crashes. But, like the best of clowns, artfully concealed by the slapstick is a real talent, a mix of juggling and acrobatics. Once under the water the puffin's whirring wings, now in their hydronautical element, shoot them in somersaults, arcs, dives and rolls in pursuit of sprats and sand eels. As it labours back onto the surface and into the air to carry food back to its burrow and waiting infants, one sees not a single sprat but rows of fish neatly hanging in rows either side of its beak as neatly packed as tinned sardines. Somehow whilst performing barrel-rolls and dashes, the puffin keeps those fish he's already caught neatly clamped in his beak, whilst still being able to snap up another and another and another.

A mile and more out to sea you are left with just the cruciforms of gannets against the sky and Manx shear-waters, and stormy petrels. The petrels are tiny, dark, fluttering bat-birds. Seemingly too frail for the sea, like drab moths caught in a strong wind and blown offshore, it seems unlikely that they can survive out here or even stay aloft for long. Their habit of pattering their feet over the wave tops as they fly makes them look inept, as if they're merely trying out flight to see if, with just a bit more prac-tice, it might work. And yet, apart from this brief period of summer nesting and the need for land to cradle their eggs and chicks, the petrels will spend the rest of the year and all the winter storms far out at sea.

Fluttering, I note as I dip and splash my paddles, is an efficient way of staying aloft, and looking inept is not actual proof of inability when it comes to survival at sea, though perhaps genuine ineptness is still a very real handicap. The bigger shearwaters, though, look like they can really fly, stiletto wings flicked out and held taut as they skim the jostling waves and rotate on their own axis so that first one wing tip runs along the surface and then the other, like knife points cutting the water's skin so one expects the greenish, watery tops of the waves to fall apart like swiftly sliced slivers of cucumber.

Off Horn Head the seas are piling up and falling over each other in great tumbling blocks. There are races and eddies; lovely for the birds who dip and wheel into the upwellings of waters, and morsels, from deep down, but a rough ride for me until I slide out into smooth water beyond the head and into the wide bay of Sheep Haven. Tying off my paddle I sit back to rest and eat a biscuit and a carrot for lunch. While I eat, for the first time on the voyage a passing fulmar lands on the water beside me, settling easily and companionably onto the surface.

This afternoon even the wind has died. There is hot sun and regular swell and, when the tide and the current turn and flow against me, it isn't strong enough to slow me much. For the first time on the trip I have the conditions I'd hoped for – and how different it seems. Here I am, winching my way across the north of Ireland, paddle stroke by paddle stroke, one after another until by early evening I've covered some forty miles, and am within sight of Malin Head, Ireland's most northerly point and my halfway mark. If this is to be the new paddling reality, then I'll round the head the next day and scoot down the far side of Ireland in a few weeks. I land feeling tired but jubilant on a steep-shelving shingle beach. Malin Head is lit in the last of the sunlight.

The beach is backed by piles of flotsam, jetsam and driftwood, and rough grass with cattle grazing the shoreline. Beyond them is a fence recycled out of car parts, bedsteads and baulks of sea timber. Keen to stretch my cramped legs I climb the chained and padlocked gate and stroll up a lane. In a yard a man is working under the cab of a lorry. 'I've just landed on the strand below,' I hail him. 'Would it be okay to camp there just for the night?'

'Below on the strand, is it? I couldn't say.'

'Do you know the owner? He wouldn't mind me camping there, would he?' I persist. Without another word he turns back to the surgery on his truck, dismissing me.

Further inland is a cluster of houses and a small, white-washed pub. Inside the lounge two smartly dressed middle-aged couples are talking quietly. Aware of my wetsuit and matted hair, I get to the bones of my self-introduction quickly, and ask about camping on the beach. There is a silence. The owner might be the man at the small farm up the road, offers one woman cautiously. I walk up to the house and bang on the door. A ferrety, cringing collie tied on a rope squirms and whines and snarls at me from the yard. There is no answer.

As I walk back downhill, one of the couples has come out from the pub and they call me across the road. The farmer is away on his honeymoon, they tell me. The best thing would be if I carry my kayak up the hill to their garden to camp. Too heavy, I explain. The woman takes a deep breath. 'Oh, well, you know ... if it's the man I'm thinking of, he might be a bit, um, funny about his land.'

There it is, as close as you get to a warning in a small community: the chained gate, the lorry surgeon's reticence, the awkwardness in the pub. Of course, I don't know exactly what 'funny' might mean, but I assume that being found camped on his land means that appeals to reason, legalese about foreshore rights and the niceties of trespass law or claims of ignorance won't cut the mustard. 'Funny' might mean shouting or even fists, or a waving shotgun. Or it might not. It seems somewhat unlikely that a man on his honeymoon will arrive back late at night and walk his boundaries ... and if he does, surely his recent conjugal pleasures might make him lightly amused by my presence rather than seriously 'funny'.

It is too late to move on. But the spectre of the land-owner crouches over my evening. I don't return to the pub. Nor light a fire to cook. I sleep uneasily, waking at first light to find a thick fog and chill air. The shipping forecast predicting imminent strong winds is at variance with what I can see from my tent. And it is at odds, too, with the coastal report from the coastguard station and weather observatory on Malin Head, just across the bay. They are obviously looking at the same weather as me and confirm no wind and no visibility.

I launch into the fog, dependent on chart and compass to get me the next twelve miles. Crossing the wide mouth of Lough Swilly I find my hearing sharpens as I pick up the slosh of the swell against Dunaft Head long before I see the blackness of the rockface. From this landmark I set a new course, one of a series of straight lines plotted around the inside of the wide curve of the headland, so that every half an hour or so I touch land and know that I am still on course, and that there is shelter if the forecast winds suddenly blow up. But the periods away from land are strange and disorientating. The thick grey fog cocoons and muffles, and the paddling is as monotonous as a gym rowing machine, seemingly going nowhere.

Inside the fog, my shrink-wrapped world seems weirdly noisy. The small splash of each stroke sounds like a bucket being emptied down a drain; the water pushed apart by the bow like the hissing roar of a pub's urinal. Even my breath, or the rub of cagoule sleeve against spray-deck, rasps in my ears. Sounds from beyond are, by contrast, muffled and fuzzy. The sound of waters swilling over rocks is like faint white noise and difficult to pinpoint. I'm wary that my cautious navigation has been subverted by currents or tide and I have already missed the head and the next stop will be South Uist. Or the polar icecap.

Then I note a darkening in the fog ahead and to one side, giving direction to the splashing. And then both sound and vision come into focus together – the splashing matched by a tumble of rocks and small cliffs. As I nose forward, my field of focus presents a perfect Tang painting – a brushstroke to show a rock, a shrub, a frond and all the rest hinted at in washes and voids. I half expect to see a jolly Taoist monk sitting on a ledge to give it all scale.

CHAPTER 19

Malin Head (without a donkey)

MALIN, LIKE THE MIZEN, is a psychological and physical challenge. Its currents are infamous, especially when against the wind, and outside of a rare combination of calm weather and benign tides the waters off the head are long miles of overfalls, standing waves and rips. Its steeply cliffed shores offer no escape. As I approach, a light breeze has been pushing its way through the fog, very gently at first, then stronger so that the mist rolls across the steepening waves like smoke. Gusts and channels of clear air open up, creating long vistas of grey sea down corridors of mist. The kayak is rolling back and forth. The gusts grow stronger, blowing hard, reducing the fog to wisps and then to clear air so that I can see to the horizon in a dull mono-chrome. A long way to my right is the dark in-curve of Malin Peninsula. The head is framed by explosions of surf. It's not passable in this weather and I turn for land and the small harbour of Port Ronan, surfing in on big rollers to land on an exposed concrete slip.

An hour later I'm installed at the Sandrock Holiday Hostel, showered, warm and, with my clothes spinning around a washing machine, I sit looking out of a wide-screen picture window and watch the sea churning and crashing on the rocks below, and the spray lifted up and driven against the glass in a scuzzy, foaming deluge. It feels as if the room is being driven through a car wash.

I made the right decision. In fact, even sitting here, I feel drained. The hostel is half full, its attraction as Ireland's 'most northerly' point is tempered by its utter remote-ness, but there's a scattering of Irish and foreign tourists, looking for romantic grandeur. Most haven't got up when I settle myself in a chair, and when they emerge blearily to make themselves breakfast they find me comfortable and content like a cat that's been out all night prowling and hunting.

'If only I'd said I was going to paddle the length of Ireland, I'd be finished now,' I lament to Margaret and Rodney, the couple who own the hostel. 'I just got a couple of words wrong.' They give me news of Sam, who had kayaked in the week before. 'He was here for a few days,' says Rodney, looking out the window, 'and it seems you might be, too, so make yourself at home. You kayakers are getting to be good for business – are there any more behind you?' He points out shelves of books, suggests a fisherman who might have lobsters to sell for supper and gives me a map of the lanes and roads around the head showing the route to the shops and pubs at Malin Pier. 'Oh, and if you play guitar or banjo, there's a few in the office ...'

Late in the afternoon I walk a couple of miles through drizzle to the village pub. I chat to the bargirl as she pulls me a pint and calls my order through to the kitchen. 'Going round the whole of Ireland in a kayak ... God, you're very brave.' That's what I want to hear. 'Aren't you frightened out there – drowning and all? Storms? Sharks?'

Ah, no, I tell her. It's all common sense: knowing when to stay out of the sea, like today, pick a bit of easy to round Malin, then it's all downhill back to Cork. At which point a wiry, handsome man with a broken nose, and a recently scarred-up cheek and a blackened eye, leans in towards us. 'Canoeing? I did canoeing in the paras. Fucking exercises, paddle out to some place, cold as be-jaysus, guns and all. Norway. I'd do that. I'd go out in that.'

He jerks his thumb out at the sea, slugging down a mouthful of drink. 'I'm breaking horses now. Mad bastard did that to me the other day.' He felt his cheek. The bargirl had gone out to the kitchen. 'Do you know how to tame a horse? Get your t'umb and finger into its nose,' he pinched his together and made a hard fist with the effort, 'then throw him to the ground and give him a kicking, get in there and punch him and give him the knee,' his body jerked and twitched, 'and that'll tame him. Do you get me? You didn't know that, did you?' He moves in closer as if measuring up my nostrils for the finger and thumb hold. The arm coming towards me drapes itself over my shoulder.

'Ah, right, man. You know what I'm talking about, you done it, you know how I love those horses.'

I am saved by a group filling the door into the bar next door, who call my new friend back in to his drink. The bar-girl when she brings out my steak is philosophical; 'He's a bit excited, isn't he ..? It's the weather, getting too much for people ... What else is there to do but stay inside the dry and have a drink and ..? Well, it's a miserable summer!'

The next morning the wind is still strong and the seas wild when I walk back to the same restaurant for a late breakfast. The cowboy-para comes out of the lounge towards the toilets, bandy-legged but upright. Either never having stopped drinking in the bar, or back there again, but still lucid. 'Hey, you man, how's it going? C'mon, c'mon and have a drink and I'll tell you about horses. Right, finish your breakfast so, but come in later.'

The *Irish Times* is gloomy about the day's weather, and the coming days too. Journalists are piling on the 'worst summer' statistics. I feel a sympathy for my bragging new friend and the countless others who've retreated into the pubs of Ireland for the summer. I've been doing the same when opportunity has allowed. A stroll through damp lanes and past the harbour brings me to Farran's, whose small, panelled rooms are already filled at noon with a mix of farmers in dark suits, local fishermen and Irish holidaymakers. Mobs of children dart in and out of the door depending on whether it is raining outside or not.

It is a friendly, sober retreat from the weather. Talk along the counter is of a man who's just arrived on Malin Head, having come all the way from the Mizen by his own muscle power. 'God, he's some fella, isn't he?' I heard. 'And the bad weather and everything; but wasn't it a great idea – do you think he had to buy any drink for himself the whole way, what with the old stuffed donkey?'

The man who'd made a journey of free drinks is Tim Goodacre, a young Australian who had set off to walk from the Mizen to Malin carrying a large soft-toy donkey and – the hook that caught everyone's admiration – stopping in every pub he passed for a drink. He'd strode into Malin some hundred and fifty pubs later and become a local celebrity. His wider fame was assured by a national radio appeal for the return of his donkey when it had been ass-napped from a bar en route. I do some pen and paper calculations next to my crossword. 'Well, if he did buy his own drinks it would have cost him about €600, allowing for the odd half pint and a few nights on the batter ... but I'd say you're right, and that he got stood a drink every time ... which makes it a great idea.'

Why didn't I think of a gimmick? My own trip doesn't strike anyone as nearly so clever, what with the weather and being out at sea. Voices rehearse the dangers of getting around Malin, and I try to tell which are those of experienced fishermen and boatmen, which those of tourists and farmers who've merely looked down on the seas from Dunaldragh Head, Ireland's northernmost point.

Malin's position as the Irish John O'Groats seemed to bring the villagers some amusement. But the conversation has served to make my trip seem simultaneously daft and stupidly uncomfortable, not to mention lacking in imagination, with no drinking plan or stuffed accessory. I decide to walk out to the point and look at the sea.

At Bamba's Crown by Dunaldragh – 'Fort of the flock of birds' – seagulls blow like confetti in the updraughts and over the Napoleonic-era watchtower. Lloyd's of London had monitored shipping passing here on the North Altantic route between America and the ports of Liverpool, Belfast and Dublin, signalling to them at first with semaphore and from the beginning of the twentieth century with Marconi's new wireless. In the kind of financial gambling and juggling not confined to our own times, Lloyd's would reduce the insurance on boats arriving safely from the Atlantic past Malin and transfer the cover to those heading out to sea. The messages passed between ships and shore often brought more sensational news than mere 'all okay' signals; the first that Europe heard of the assassination of Abe Lincoln, the Californian Gold Rush and America's entry into World War One came via Malin Head, and a description sent by radio led to the arrest of Crippen as he took ship to America.

Lloyd's and Marconi established Malin as a state-of-the-art communications hub, and so it was natural that for more than a century the Irish Coast Guard and Meteorological Service have had stations up here. Behind the village I'd seen a network of poles towering into the air and carrying grids of wires in all directions. These radio aerials were tracking Ireland's coastal traffic and incoming weather whilst allowing for out-of-the-window, eye-of-the-storm climate measurement. But all this geographical immediacy from Malin, and from Valentia, was about to come to an end. In an era of government when the mantra of decentralisation had dispersed many civil service offices from Dublin to the most unlikely hinterlands (the Irish Prison Service was moved to Longford, a peaceful, rural county which doesn't have a prison), it seemed strange that both the Valentia and Malin coastguard stations were due to be closed and moved to the east coast, whilst the Malin Met station would be automated and run from Dublin Airport. Feelings in Malin, which already felt remote and forgotten, were running high against this deletion of part of their history, employment and infrastructure.

On the cliff tops I join knots of tourists looking down from Ard na Merica, the American Field, where fires were lit to give emigrants shipping out to the States their last sight of Ireland. On the slopes below, stones were set out and painted white to spell out 'EIRE' in massive letters, informing World War Two pilots that they'd crossed into neutral territory. Over the years more stones had been collected and arranged in rockery-graffiti to spell out names and words, or reduced parts of them: 'PAT', 'MICK', 'FIICI OI F'.

As Rodney predicts, I'm in Malin for a while, the foul-weather days edging into a second week. One wet afternoon, on a whim, I call into the coastguard station, under its netting of antennae and aerials. Three of the crew – Manus Patten, Patrick Canning and Pat Lynch – are on duty, all ex-Irish Merchant Navy with their rank in stripes on the sleeves of their white shirts. They are part of a six-man team who crew the centre twenty-four hours a day, year round. There are banks of pagers, radios, computers, maps on walls, all Ireland charts and clocks. Whilst I'm there, one of the men looks up and checks the time and goes on air to read the forecast – it is strange and reassuring to put faces to the voices that have been with me for the previous month, charting my expectations around the whole west coast.

Suddenly there's a Mayday. A sailing dinghy is sinking. One of the crew has got through on his mobile phone.

The whole place swings into action: everyone bursts back in, manning phones, computers, scouring maps. 'Mayday, Mayday. Report received of a vessel sinking in Mannin Bay, Errislannan Head. Any vessel in the vicinity ...?'

It's strange to equate all this technical stuff in a warm office filled with computers and paper and phones with real wet sea and fear. The Clifden lifeboat comes on air and is briefed: 'The buoyancy tanks are gone – they're up to their oxters in water ... they've got lifejackets and nothing else ... He says they're actually in the water now ... '

The lifeboat – I think of Taff and Mick, whom I'd met all those weeks ago, and wonder if they're in the crew – has been launched and it's only a few minutes since the call. Everything is happening at speed: one officer is on maps and charts, another on radio and phone, the third on computer. 'Clifden lifeboat will be out in the search zone in fifteen minutes ... are they definitely wearing lifejackets? I've tried calling them back but there's no answer, so I suppose they're in the water ... There's an ambulance waiting on the pier if it's needed.' I visualise, too easily, what it must be like being in the water out there amongst the boomers with your boat submerged.

The lifeboat radio-phone crackles over the speaker: 'We're in the bay now and about to commence search.' The dinghy skipper's wife – Pam – phones in. The coastguard is reassuring. 'It's looking good: we have a lifeboat out there now searching, they're wearing lifejackets ... though how many of them, do you know?' Another voice: 'What's the helicopter's ETA?' 'Uh, oh, that's the lifeboat, they have a visual! Oh, that's good.' The lifeboat radio comes on: 'We've recovered two casualties ... there were only two crew. They're fine ... no need for medical attention.'

Pat phones Pam: 'Just to let you know we've recovered your husband and the other person.' The lifeboat drops off the casualties and goes back out to pick up the swamped dinghy. This is not just a nice gesture – the wreckage is a danger to shipping. Then there is the tidying up to do: sending back helicopters and alerting nearby boats going to rescue: 'Mayday relay, Mayday relay, reference small boat sinking in Mannin Bay – lifeboat has rescued them, cancel Mayday.' There is a phone call from the rescued crew. 'Ah, that's nice, You'd be surprised ... very few people get back in touch to thank us.'

Pinned down by bad weather, Malin has landlocked me, just like Dingle. I wonder about carrying the kayak and all my kit the mile or so across the head and so getting on my way again. But there's a defining aspect to Malin that can't be bypassed. I take to tuning in to the early-morning VHF coastguard weather reports, propping the radio beside a chair in the picture window, looking out to sea. The Sandrock has emptied and filled again since I've been here, most recently with a huge family group who arrived in a squadron of cars with bags of food and took over all available space in the communal kitchen-dining room. 'Ah, that's a great feed,' the patriarch sighs contentedly when their feast had been laid along the table. 'You can't have too much food ... no, you'd rather be looking *at* it than *for* it.'

A night of music at the Crossroads promises a diversion and I trek down – through the rain, as ever – with two German sisters, Franziska and Elizabeth. At the bar we find a man called Shunie playing waltzes and Tom Jones songs on a keyboard to an empty dancefloor. The men are buying drinks while the women wait, groomed and glossy, at the tables. We drink pints and talk about dancing. The sisters are keen, and Franziska tells me about her favourite, the 'disco fox', which she steps out with her fingers on the table. A drink or two later, I get to dance with them both and can't help but relish the uncomplicated holding and touch and movement. Then the sisters dance together – the disco fox – and the two blondes, long legs entwined, have every head turning.

Then I have an idea. At the hostel the night before I had been playing guitar and the sisters had sung gorgeous harmony. I go over to the keyboard player and tell him the girls are singers. He looks sceptical but uncoils a mic on a lead and the two of them launch into a heart-stopping version of the Everly Brothers' 'Dream' and then tentatively ask if we would like to hear a German folk song, 'Kein Shoener Land'. They sing this unaccompanied, while I sit back with a pint, relishing my new role as promoter. At the end of the evening, we leave the lights behind, and walk back together to the hostel looking for shooting stars above the windy autumnal lane.

The coastguard officers had given me a precise formula for getting round the head. Too precise, perhaps. I needed calm weather, they said, with what wind there was coming from the west – and then an hour after slack water I'd have a window of opportunity. Or, to put it another way, as a local boatman had: 'If you go too late after the tide has turned or too early, or if there's too much wind or any wind at all from the wrong direction, it'll be a bloody mess out there.'

And so one morning I wake to find the wind no more than a gusty breeze and hurriedly stuff my kit into bags and load them into *An Fulmaire*. A big, slopping chop slaps against the rocks and throws spray over me, suggesting that perhaps it isn't such a good day after all, but I've waited a week and this seems at last, and at least, a porthole of opportunity.

A mile up the coast, I turn across the waves and under the black cliffs of the head look up to see the Lloyds tower. Under me the waves suddenly become hard and angular, as if the water has solidified, and then shatter into a jumble of big blocks, grinding and crashing against each other. The kayak bucks and judders, racing forward one moment and stopping dead the next. The paddle is either shaken as if seized in the mouth of an enraged dog or – worse – digs into an airy waterless void, risking capsizing.

When worried on the trip, I've fallen into the habit of singing to keep my mind distracted. When truly scared I've always bawled out the same song, a traditional west of Ireland ballad called 'Seven Drunken Nights':

As I went home on Monday night as drunk as drunk could be,

I saw a horse outside the door where my old horse should be.

Well, I called me wife and I said to her: 'Will you kindly tell to me

Who owns that horse outside the door where my old horse should be?'

'Ah, you're drunk, you're drunk, you silly old fool, still you cannot see

That's a lovely sow that me mother sent to me.'

Well, it's many a day I've travelled a hundred miles or more,

But a saddle on a sow, sure I never saw before.

The following nights are filled with ever-clearer signs of cuckoldry. A pipe on a chair is passed off as a lovely tin whistle; boots beneath the bed as geranium pots. By Friday I'm singing lustily about a head on a pillow, explained away as a 'lovely boy child with his whiskers on'.

I'd first learnt the song as a boy child myself, from a Dubliners' record, and been excited by the smutty humour suggested by Ronnie Drew's gravelly tones saying, 'This is "Seven Drunken Nights" ... but we're only allowed to sing five of them'. Now for the first time on the trip I'm singing my way through the Saturday night ('Two hands on her breasts ...'). I'm very worried. The current is dead against the tide. The swell is quartering across both and the wind is far stronger than I'd thought, swirling in all directions. It's like climbing up an endless escalator, the wrong way. But then, as I launch into the obscenities of the seventh night, a jerking paddle stroke propels me into calmer, ordered water. The turmoil drops, quite suddenly, and big but unconfused waves roll an easy rhythm. I've rounded Malin.

The cliffs beyond Malin aren't the soaring dark battlements of the west coast, but they are starkly intimidating and offer no break or shelter. I've hardly paddled past the head and I'm looking around for a place to land.

I'm in luck. There's a small bay, formed where a stream has cut a channel down from the fields. A patch of rank, flotsam-matted grass extends from a beach of rotting kelp and stones, and a rusting winch, bolted to rocks, signals a tiny, overgrown track that zigzags its way upwards. It is a haven of sorts but not one that I've got to myself. I've barely got the tent up and sat down to cook when midges rise out of the grass in their thousands and colonise every inch of my exposed skin. I pull on long trousers, shirts, wrap a towel round my neck, but still they find postage-stamp-sized patches of my skin and frank them with tens of tiny itching red-dot bites.

It's a hot evening. I drip sweat into my layers of clothes as I gather firewood, get a fire going, then throw handfuls of damp grass on the coals to smoke off the midges. On the embers, I set up my Kelly Kettle, a century old design, sold by generations of a Mayo fly-fishing dynasty, and a piece of kit I've come to rely on over this journey. It's a classic design. You pour water into the outer chamber of a double-skin aluminium cone, kindle a few twigs in the fire-pan below and a roaring volcano of flame shoots up through the centre chimney hole, boiling water in minutes and providing a fire-pan for cooking. It's made the expensive petrol stove redundant and is a piece of kit I've come to think of as 'jack-proof', as seamen like to say, impervious to weeks of damp, salt water and rough handling.

On this trip I've come to appreciate the jack-proof: items so tough and simple that even the roughest of sailors can't destroy them. I've been using the same items over and over each day, and could have done the trip with pretty much the clothes I stood up in, the sleeping bag, tent, a pot, a spoon, the Kelly Kettle, my transistor radio. Everything else is stuff held on to for 'what might happen' but never has.

What is really proving jack-proof is the kayak. A sailing friend of mine once explained the graduations of ruggedness as 'yacht built,' 'trawler built' and 'dog rough.' The yachtie stuff is smart, over-priced kit from a chandlers, the fishing equipment simple, heavy gear at keen prices, and the 'dog rough' stuff the cheap or free chunky stuff cobbled together from whatever is at hand. On my trip the light stuff is failing, or like the camera and VHF radio has to be constantly fussed over and protected. But *An Fulmaire*, despite being overloaded, crashed onto rocks, dragged across shingle and banged for hour after hour over big waves, is standing up well; she is definitely trawler-built.

And myself? Despite my week ashore, washed clothes, rest and even a hair cut, I'm probably dog rough. I have aches and pains from spending hours at sea, bent into the same 'L' shape, doing thousands of stomach crunches and shoulder twists each day, but they were the kind of kinks that unknotted as I slept and left me strong the next day. My skin and hair are salt cured. I've perfected a dull but easy diet that balances input-for-output. I am probably half-way to being jack-proof.

The fears of Malin are dropping away and I'm in danger of a certain smugness. I've passed the geographical halfway mark and have conquered the big brawling seas of the west coast. Now I have the the easier eastern half to do. However, no sooner do I begin thinking like this than I am fretting again at the realities. When I'd started, I'd been unfocused in my ambition. Easily distracted. Looking for excuses for days of rest. But Malin has put another dent in the diary and I realise that August is almost gone. Real calendar-winter is approaching, adding a new urgency to the itinerary.

I know that sometime in September the equinoctial gales will start to sweep in from the Atlantic and the days will become shorter and shorter. Though the summer has been windy, autumnal even, the equinoctials could keep me pinned down for weeks on end, however much I want to keep going. The trip would continue as a stop-start affair, clawing out miles on the odd stilled day and waiting out bad weather in my tent, and then real winter would arrive behind the gales. I'm convinced right now that I really can complete the round-trip. But I need to have a single goal: get round. No slacking, use every advantage, don't get distracted.

The next morning I am on the water at optimum time to catch tide and currents across the mouth of Lough Foyle and cross into Northern Ireland.

Part Three

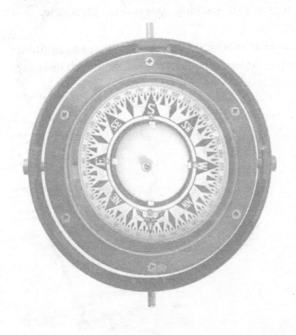

MALIN HEAD

RATHLIN ISLAND

GIANTS CAUSEWAY

MULL OF KINTYRE

FAIR HEAD

ANTRIM COAST

LOUGH FOYLE

BELFAST LOUGH

BELFAST

STRANGFORD LOUGH

MOURNE MNTS

CARLINGFORD LOUGH

ST JOHN'S LIGHTHOUSE

DUNDALK BAY

SKERRIES

LAMBAY ISLAND

DUBLIN

DALKEY ISLAND

WICKLOW MNTS

WICKLOW

WEXFORD

Silos and seals

WATERFORD

ROSSLARE HEAD

HOOK HEAD

GOLD COAST

CORK

BALLYCOTTON

KILBRITTAIN

CORK HARBOUR

HOLE-OPEN BAY

BALTIMORE

OLD HEAD OF KINSALE

GALLEY HEAD

HOWE STRAND

RABBIT ISLAND

COURTMACSHERRY BAY

FINISH REEN SPIT

CHAPTER 20

Coast Preventive

ACCORDING TO THE NAUTICAL ALMANACS, I should contact the Coast Preventive Man to announce my arrival in Northern Ireland from the Republic. But it sounds Moonfleetish, like the Excise Men, and I decide to smuggle myself along the coast. After all, it's not that I don't have things to concern myself with – notably the sweep of waters coming out of Lough Foyle. The huge expanse of the lough's waters are expelled out to sea through a narrow channel between Magilligan Point and Inishowen Head, and in a kayak these sheets of sliding sea feel like driving a car on black ice.

Evening seems to come early. Paddling throughout the afternoon, empty-minded, listening to music, I note it getting

235

chillier around four and by the time I pass Portstewart, and am off Portrush, dusk has come down. I've done one of my longest mileages and, leaving aside the Lough Foyle turbulence, the coastline I've looked in on has been low-lying and sheltered. I'm in a different place now, and Portrush, as I come in closer, looks different to me as well. More 'English', I think, even as I wonder if that's really the case or whether I'm just trying to identify a difference.

I look in from the sea at a low bulwark of rock, and then a strip of very green grass, and above that a parking lot backed by a row of four-storey houses, Edwardian, I think, or maybe later, with big, heavy-built bow windows and important-looking doors. Their colours are muted whites, creams, duck-egg blues. Oddly, the cars parked out front are like those of Ireland a decade earlier. Only the occasional new Jeep, or this year's top of the range saloon. A lone cabriolet. Every other set of wheels is a modest, often elderly, sensible car – the kind that in boomtown Ireland has been scrapped, or given to student offspring to drive, whilst everyone else, it seems, has upgraded to muscly off-roaders, sports cars or spacious executive saloons.

Beyond the town there are miles of sand beach, backed by peaked and rolling dunes. I'd got used to the almost empty beaches of Ireland, but here the sands are dotted with evening strollers, dog walkers, late-picnicking families, joggers ploughing through the dry sand.

I'd intended to camp in the dunes and land the kayak on the beach, but with the surf dumping onto it I reconsider. From out at sea, waves curling over and running onto the sand can look like no more than ripples with a bit of white tracery along their tops. But they're easily misjudged and you can find yourself, especially with a fully laden canoe, coming in fast and crash-landing your craft from five or six feet up in the air. Even quite small waves like this can twist a kayak around and roll it over and leave you crawling ashore in a scatter of possessions turned to flotsam.

I don't have a chance of landing here. Once again I'm fenced out at sea and have to keep going.

There are cliffs again and in the gloom I can't see any landing places until the Hollywood B-movie silhouette of Dunluce Castle rears up on a craggy, black headland. It feels like I've paddled into Transylvania. Above me the MacDonnell clans' towers and ramparts crown a forbidding stack of rock joined to the mainland by a narrow bridge. I land on a jumble of rocks at the castle's foot. A scattering of gulls flutter off rock ledges and fly around in dark, crepuscular bat shapes. On the shore above the broken spars, plastic debris and old barrels of the tideline, there is no flat space for the tent. I have to make do with a pitch of grass-covered boulders.

As I look up, it's clear that the cliff face and the castle itself are in the process of erosion. In the seventeenth century a large chunk of the head, supporting the kitchen wing of the castle, had collapsed into the sea, taking that night's supper and most of the kitchen staff with it. In a less dramatic way a similar fate befalls me. After landing, I drop the food bag into the water as I unpack the kayak and my fresh stores – bread, oatmeal, onion and a packet of biscuits – are soaked. Ill-fed and with a bed of rocks, sleep evades me and I am relieved to welcome the dawn and get back on the water.

❧

There's decent weather, and for the first time in weeks I have a fair bit of company out at sea. In fact, there are more recreational boats up here than I've seen since the Cork coast. Small tubs sprouting rods, yachts gusting along in the breeze, speed boats shredding the silence. I am just wondering at the lack of patrol boats in this border area when a military-sized RIB changes course and roars up to intercept me. The Coast Prevention Man?

'Have you cleared Customs? I need to see your passport and papers.'

I am being questioned and ordered about in shouty northern tones by a boxer-jawed giant in a knitted watch-cap that looks like a tea-cosy. But it's an act. The man is Robin Ruddock and his official credentials are compromised by a large inflatable yellow 'banana' towed behind his RIB, with six children astride it. He's a man I've been told to look up if I made it this far – and he has more news of Sam, who stayed a night with him the week before. 'He said you were on your way.' Robin reached out a big hand to shake mine. 'Now, is there anything you need, any help I can give?'

Robin is a sailor who knows this Irish coastline as well as anyone. He famously captained a replica currach to retrace the route of the early missionary monks from Ireland to Iona, adding to the challenge by dressing in authentic coarse woollen robes and living off eighth-century monkish fare on the voyage.

His bluff enthusiasm and good humour is a tonic in itself. 'Fantastic weather today,' he enthuses. 'You'll race along, though be sure to call into John Johnson's little museum at Dunseverick and tell him I sent you, and say hello to Jim when you're back in Cork, and who are you going to see when you're down around Dublin waters? Anyway, go on now. All the best.'

The boat revs up and with its shrieking banana load is off, leaving me to paddle towards another of those jigsaw-puzzle icons – the Giant's Causeway.

Rounding the headland I can see coachloads of tourists looking down upon the natural wonder of these hexagonal basalt columns. They run from under the cliffs out into the bay, each one at a different height, forming stepped podiums like the stage set of a musical, the tourists tottering down the heights in bright-coloured leisure clothes and rain jackets like some Busby Berkeley chorus. From the kayak I look down on hundreds more pillars disappearing under the water's surface, admire how perfect the hexagons are, each interlocking but separate from its neighbours.

These forty thousand pillars were 'discovered' when they were described in 1693 in an announcement to the Royal Society, though it's just possible that the odd local might have noticed their geometric precision before then. They were one of Ireland's first tourist sights – attracting the attention of Dr Johnson, who acidly reported that the causeway was 'worth seeing but not worth going to see'.

A century before the Royal Society's discovery, the surreal landscape had caught the eye of a fleet of Spanish galleons on the run from Sir Walter Raleigh, who apparently spent some time cannonballing one of the headlands under the misapprehension that it was Dunluce Castle. The coast's revenge was to sink one of the ships, the *Girona*, overladen with more than a thousand men, only a very few of whom survived. The MacDonnells then nipped round from the real Dunluce to bear off the ship's cannons – still seen on the ramparts – and seize treasure enough to finance increased fortifications of their castle, quite possibly including the overambitious kitchen wing.

I press on in warm sunshine towards John Johnson's museum at Dunseverick, mooring the kayak on a small pier outside the cluster of old harbour cottages. Inside, I am left alone to wander the sprawl of rooms and its eclectic collections. These are, as Robin had promised, well worth the time of day, indeed might even have impressed Dr Johnson. They remind me of the Pitt Rivers Museum in Oxford, where exhibits are displayed not according to an exact system of scientific classification but because perhaps they seemed similarly interesting.

It is the museum as curio cabinet, or art work, a poetry of things. There are lumps of coal from the *Titanic*'s bunkers, whale vertebrae, portholes and anchors, boards with examples of nautical knots, brass propeller logs, gas masks and guns. A whole cabinet is given over to First World War medical supplies; packages of drugs, bandages and syringes. There are numerous model boats, including a naïve sculpture embodying the essence of boatness with a poem printed on its sail: *The way I can do what I want because I am free*, it begins. There are inflatable fishing floats of greased canvas, a ship's brass bell and numerous bits of wood that look like wreckage washed ashore. I find myself wondering if I might sneak some of my dead weight – the gummed-up petrol stove, the unused shore-shoes, my already-read novels – ashore and into the museum to be hidden among the exhibits.

●━━━●

The English influence is apparent in one obvious way in the North, a way which feels foreign to me each time I land: there are no complications with trespass or private land.

Seemingly everywhere I pull the kayak ashore is 'owned' by the National Trust, with clear-cut, unarguable right of access, and with all the car parks, warning signs, toilet blocks, fences and lists of rules to prove it.

Around the Irish coastline I'd nearly always land on private property and then seek permission to camp for the night, or more often trespass – happily protected by the remoteness of the islands, beaches and headlands, and an unspoken tradition of grace and favour. This feels natural to me. Ireland has little public land and very few rights of way. As a boy, and even more as a teenager, I'd negotiated the complex codes and types of Irish trespass, skulking and hiding and path-finding my way across fields and through woods, assessing who didn't mind a kid in pursuit of bird sightings and who was 'funny' about their land.

The moral landscape was made all the more contoured because my own father was well known for being 'funny' about his land. Having a castle, albeit a ruined one, as a home meant a steady trickle of interested visitors wandering up to look round – and generally being dispatched with curt words. For a brief time, this took on a farcical bent, as my parents, at a low financial ebb, opened their home to the public. For two pounds a head my father would take tours of his 'museum of technology' and the upper castle rooms.

Those visitors who bored him would be galloped round in fifteen minutes flat, but those who had interesting conversation would be given a command performance, including a long tale about the castle's changing hands back and forth between the MacCarthy and de Courcy clans, once (I forget the exact details) upon the death of a white weasel, and minute explanations of each piece in the museum. There would be a rendition of 'The Dambuster's March' on the renovated theatre organ and a trot around the vintage cars, old railway carriages and bits of farm machinery, before tea laid on by my mother. It was a disastrous business venture, as my mother described it: an afternoon lost to them both, and the ticket fees swallowed up by the cost of cakes and biscuits.

Around the next headland I'm in view of the Antrim coast's top tourist attraction – even more popular than the Giant's Causeway. This is the Carrick-a-Rede Rope Bridge, a light suspension bridge dipped between a headland and a small but lofty islet. In pre-tourist days, local salmon fishermen twisted thick ropes of straw each summer to make a simple rope bridge that allowed them to wobble out to the island and fish for running salmon, camping out in one of the huts that dot the shore. Now lines of tourists sway across a bridge, which I'm fairly sure Health and Safety directives have insisted is made out of steel hawsers. Having crossed the bridge people sit dotted across the high grassy slopes of the island, whilst the sea crashes below.

I weigh up whether to risk running the gauntlet of rocks and breaking waves under the bridge, and decide against it.

Carrick-a-Rede is an odd five-star tourist attraction – a bridge to nowhere, and back. It delivers a bit of a thrill, then a spot of peace and tranquillity contemplating the return trip, and a simulacrum of authenticity following the steps of the old fishermen. Perhaps a flash of annoyance, too, at so many others who have decided to do the same thing, as well as a joy in the shared experience of sun on skin, the birds scattering overhead, the shimmer of the sea far below. If there were two bridges, I reflect, one onto and one off the island, so the tourists could make a circular trip, then they'd be doing roughly what I was doing as I circumnavigated Ireland, but with less time, energy and euros expended. Adventuring, whatever the scale, is an odd affair. Thrill and fear two sides of the same coin.

The late afternoon has turned into the stillest, hottest day of the summer and it takes self-discipline to continue past Ballintoy, a tiny village of whitewashed cottages built around a small neat harbour. In the bright sun, with the sea rippling aquamarine, it looks like a 1950s Mediterranean fishing port, and indeed has a yellow kerchief of glittering sand and a jolly-looking cafe on the harbour side. But where my imagination and hopes evoke Pernod and Brigitte Bardot, my knowledge promises milky tea and a National Trust giftshop.

I keep paddling, too, because the waters here, however calm, are being funnelled into a narrow strait. So, whether ebbing or flowing, they have to speed up to get water in and out between the landmasses of Ireland and Scotland. Even here, where I'm just on the lip of the funnel, I'm picking up a favourable current that is speeding me onwards. It gives an odd sense of sledging on a tin tray, picking up speed and bumping and crashing as the water piles along under me.

For the first time on this voyage I am kayaking due south, or, as I like to think of it, downhill.

CHAPTER 21

Charybdis

GOING ROUND FAIRHEAD, I realise that I am actually looking beyond Ireland at the Mull of Kintyre. Scotland is an easy paddle from here and for a moment I'm tempted to strike across. I don't – recalling my commitment of only a day before – but I do recall the exploits of the 'Canoe Boys', two young Scottish nationalists, Alastair Dunnett and Seumas Adam, who in the summer of 1934 set off up the west coast of Scotland. Their craft were two open-cockpit kayaks, heavy plywood prototypes designed to break down into three pieces for transport. They had inflated motorbike inner tubes as buoyancy aids and paddled into autumnal weather in singlets and shorts, pulling on simple cagoules for really foul days. In

Dunnett's book, *Quest By Canoe*, he extolled the pleasures of wild camping and the joy of being fed in return for helping with farm tasks; otherwise, their diet was the staple *drammach*, oats in cold water. The book had inspired me with its gungho good humour, courage and simplicity. Compared to them I am hideously over-equipped, but seeing Mull, I find myself taking pride in the similarities – the harsh weather overcome, a growing sense of seamanship, the kindness of people I was meeting. I'm grateful, though, for modern kayak technology. Their canoes were far less seaworthy, the tensioning wire that held the three parts together a constant worry, threatening to part in rough seas.

I try to focus on the Canoe Boys as I paddle beyond sight of Mull, to distract myself from playing in my head the McCartneys' shortbread'n'kilts paean. It's not an easy song to displace, once the idea takes root. I even try singing the slightly lesser evil of Rod Stewart's 'Sailing', but 'Mull of Kintyre' keeps edging its way back. The Canoe Boys were relative latecomers to the Scottish paddle scene. Almost a lifetime before them, a tough bird called John MacGregor had launched the recreational kayak touring craze with his self-designed canoe, 'Rob Roy'. In the 1860s, he'd paddled many of the rivers of England, and then the Danube, Rhine and Seine, before putting a fair number of Swiss and Italian lakes under his keel. *A Thousand Miles in the Rob Roy Canoe* was a bestseller in his day, and inspired Robert Louis Stevenson to paddle around Belgium and northern France.

In *An Inland Voyage*, his account of this journey, Stevenson writes of the abject tedium of paddling for hours bringing on the 'apotheosis of stupidity [as] the great wheels of intelligence turned idly in my head, like fly-wheels, grinding no grist'. A couple of years later he had ditched the canoe in favour of a donkey, trotting around the Cevennes. I do wonder, however, if he'd have felt differently about paddling if he'd ventured out a while into open sea.

It's time to camp. So tuned have I become to the sea beneath me that I feel the full gallop of current slow to a canter and then to a trot. Now the waters are moving restlessly on the spot under me, and are about to turn and bolt back the way I've come. I paddle ashore in the dusk, to an Arcadian landscape that looks like it could hold deer, or even unicorns, as easily as cattle. A wall of steep hills, thick dark woods and swards of green turf extends from the tiny shingle beach, behind a reef of jagged rocks. I've just started staking out my tent when I hear the familiar dull pounding thud and whining of an approaching RIB. This one is an RNLI inshore rescue boat with a lifeboat crew in full immersion gear and helmets. They spot me and turn to hover just off the rocks, backing and forth on the engine to hold their position. I scramble as far out towards them as possible. The wind snatches and rips at my voice and at that of the hollering guy in the bows of the RIB.

'Hell–looh!'

'Are you th– noo– trub–?'

'Wha?'

'Are yoooo th– noo– trub–?'

I'd have thought it fairly obvious that I wasn't in trouble, but happily ashore and setting up camp, at least until I had to struggle to the edge of the rocks and get soaked by the waves. But they bring the RIB in closer, an act of non-rescue that is putting us all in some danger. They've had a report of a kayak in trouble, it seems. I suppose somebody up on the clifftops – I'd seen little stick figures looking down – has seen me bobbing and swirling along in the big waves far below and assumed that I was ... what ... being swept away? 'I'm fine,' I holler; 'just camping for the night here, and then going on tomorrow.'

The crew seem disappointed. Having been called out and having found a kayaker, they seem keen to add an actual rescue to their tally board. 'C'mon, we'll take you down the coast, where it's safer.' The waves are rising higher and I'm getting doused by spray. I'm also keen to get back to my supper. This is getting silly. *I'm paddling around Ireland*, I shout back. They're virtually pleading with me now. They'll bring me back to the same spot tomorrow so I can continue but won't I get picked up? *No, I won't*, and finally they spin the boat round and roar off down the coast.

I've hardly scrambled back across the rocks and got the stove lit when I hear the RIB returning. Wearily, I make my way to the end of the rocks again. They want my name, for their records. Mine isn't the easiest name to understand shouted into a gusting wind. I suspect that the records at Red Bay Inshore Lifeboat Station will show a call out to a James Quinn, a kayaker who flat refused to be rescued.

In the morning I fine-tune my new improved Beaufort Scale. In the early nineteenth century the eponymous Sir Francis Beaufort, an Irish-born admiral in the British navy, suggested a system for measuring wind speed and its effects, and others since have added on signs denoting each force on land and at sea. So we have a force one – a 'light air' at around two knots that barely ripples the sea. A force five, on the other hand, pushes up crested wavelets, whilst a six produces white horses and makes it hard to use an umbrella. A gale force makes it difficult to walk, and streaks the ocean with foam. Force ten is a storm, capable of uprooting trees and producing heavy shockwaves.

I've come up with a more personal wind scale based on my own experiences:

0   Calm. Midges unimpeded.

1   Light air. A mythical balminess found only in Irish mythology, and abroad.

2   Light breeze. Blows smoke in your face on whichever side of the fire you sit.

3   Gentle breeze. Too chill for only a shirt, but a jumper is too warm.

4   Moderate breeze. Tent skin flaps irritatingly, but not enough force to clear drizzle.

5   Fresh breeze. At sea, blows spray in face; on land, blows dry clothing into sea.

6   Strong breeze. Blows rain sideways, and coffee mug over. At sea, blows you somewhere you really don't want to be.

7   Near gale. If on water, sense of doom. If ashore, no paddling today. Nor tomorrow. Nor anytime soon.

8   Gale. Wetsuit blows away, along with rocks it's tied to. In pub, so probably won't notice.

9   Severe gale. Tent and all kit blown away. Still in pub, so as above.

10 Storm. Part of pub roof blows off. Kayak tied to tree; both disappeared.

Waking this morning, I reckon it's a force five. The tent skin is banging and my shorts have blown from the guy lines into a stagnant pool of water. A sudden gust – force six – knocks my undrunk coffee over. The falling rain is being pushed along at an angle of forty-five degrees.

I pack and launch, all the same. The benefit of having made it round the corner to the sheltered side of Ireland is almost no swell, and this more benign, domesticated shore offers opportunities for emergency landings at regular intervals. Unlike on the Atlantic coast, I don't have to commit to three- and four-hour paddles to get past lengths of cliffs and there aren't the clashing swells and waves that throw up freak seas. Oh, and I really am – if only from sheer hours of on-the-job training – a fitter, better kayaker. Cocky, in short.

The current is just starting to run in my favour as I launch, and it builds in speed as I shadow the coastline towards Torr Head. A line of white across the sea's surface ahead is mystifying at first. Off to my right I can see the lump of the headland, a few figures standing on its gentle curves to cast lines far out into the ... ah ... right ... into a big broil of surf running straight out from the head. And I am heading that way, too – faster than I've travelled the whole way here. It's a peculiar sensation in a nominally 3mph kayak – like strolling down a railway carriage and seeing the landscape outside ripping past at train speed – and it is suddenly alarming. The current is being slung off the headland and accelerated before hitting an up-welling of water from a shallow reef. I'm in a rip-tide, hurtling towards a point where the speeding waters crash into each other.

Back-paddling doesn't slow me down much but allows a few minutes to consider the situation. The bubbling line of snowy wavelets seems from my water-level vantage point neither very wide nor so very big. There is a wall of stand-ing waves along the edge but no more than three or four feet high. But even as I drive the nose of *An Fulmaire* into them, I know I've underestimated what I am getting into. The waters burst up from under me, stopping the kayak dead as the sea explodes and pops all around me like a salvo of depth-charges. It is only a few canoe lengths to get through to calm waters but I am being whirled around and rolled wildly from side to side. Without a massive paddle attack to drive me on, the waves might hold me here for hours or carry me far out to sea.

I have what seems a lucky break, bursting through onto a sheet of calm water, but realise that I've been fooled again. The surface is indeed flat, unnaturally so, but it isn't still. The waters are welling up from below in great blocks that turn into oily snaking currents, flexing across the surface before spiralling tighter and faster to vortex back down into the depths through tight black-centred whirlpools. These look too small to suck down more than a paper boat, but I can feel the kayak juddering and whipping and snapping, and a disconcerting thrumming through the bottom of the boat as if some huge force is vibrating under me. And then total silence. The fresh wind must be travelling at about the same speed as the kayak, leaving me inside a balloon of still air. I see, too, how the rip current has carried me out and away and past the head-land. Frighteningly fast.

The squirming, sinking, pressing sheets of water under me are still contained on all sides by the rough popping lines of standing waves like a high hedge around a field of quicksand. I drive the bow of the kayak into the waves on the far side to break free. Another bucking, spray-drenched, wind-howling ride – like plunging down rapids and waterfalls in a river – and I am propelled back into slow jostling waters and the normality of wind-pushed waves.

After this brush with Charybdis, the current and the wind continue behind me, carrying me down the coast at a good lick. I log the current's force and direction as well as my own efforts by the rough indicators of natural navigation. Watching for ripples of water, sharp 'V's around rocks and buoys. Counting how long it takes to pass flotsam and jetsam drifting past me in the waters. Looking onshore I judge my progress by lining up two points, one behind the other, and seeing how long they take to coincide and then diverge again. The spire on a church tower seems as precise as the needle on a speedometer as it works its way along a row of houses on the hills above its tip, marking them off one at a time, plotting my relentless southward advance.

Another measurement of progress are the tiny shapes of cars, little more than coloured pixels, winding their way along the road along the shoreline at Garron Point. It takes half an hour of grinding paddling to increase their size to postage-stamp size, and the same again to grow them to Corgi toy dimensions. By now I am close enough to see that the road runs right along the shore, leaving little room for landing on the seaward side and no space to camp.

I keep along the coastline, looking for any possible place to spend the night, as dusk falls. The sound of cars roaring by, windscreen wipers and sidelights on in the wet gloom, makes me feel as if I am hitchhiking, walking down the slip road of some highway, with little chance of a pleasant night in store.

On a rocky piece of land poking out to sea, marooned on the waterside of the road, there is a dank car park and several tough- and miserable-looking fishermen casting from the rocks. A few neglected pieces of municipal playground equipment – swings, a sparse climbing frame – add to the look of dereliction. But a bit further on there's a neat white house and garden with a patch of grassy wasteland beside it and a small slip running up onto land. I climb out of the kayak just as a car pulls up at the house and a woman climbs out. I shout across the wall to ask if it is okay to camp here. The woman waves, in a way that seems neither welcoming nor affirmative, and disappears into the house. I keep unpacking. Then a man, powerfully built, emerges from the house. Trying to get everything ashore in the surge, I try another attempt at shouted politeness.

'Hullo, is it okay if I camp over there on that grass?' I holler, arm flung out at the roadside patch.

'No! NO! Don't ...' – the wind snatches away his words but his arm beckons me up to him. I drag the kayak ashore and hobble up on stiff legs, preparing to argue my rights to a patch of public-owned, rubbish-strewn wasteland.

'No!' he repeats. 'Don't camp there – it's all rocks and rubbish. Come in and put your tent up in the garden; bring in the kayak as well ... I'd say you might like a shower, would you? And Pat has the kettle on for tea already.' He paused in this litany of hospitality, '... or would you rather have a drink. Or both?'

Coming out of the shower I find a beer and a pot of waiting tea. From the kitchen Pat asks if I could eat 'something' and introduces me to her husband, Brendan, and a young friend called Judith and her son, Christopher. After days living outside, I feel the flush of indoor warmth that leaves one with a strange mix of lethargy and animation.

Pat presents me with the full Ulster fry, a heart attack on a plate. Fronds of bacon hanging over the edge, rounds of black and white pudding like draughts pieces, portly sausages, two fried eggs and a pile of toast. 'I thought you might be hungry after your paddling all day, and we couldn't have had you sleeping out there on the waste ground,' she hesitated, 'and, well, you being from the south, and with your accent, well there can be odd people along this road sometimes, and we wouldn't have liked to think of you out there.'

Apart from a brief victualling stop in Ballycastle, and my wander round the museum at Dunseverick, and some shouting with the RNLI, I've been talking to myself since I crossed the border. As I eat, Judith tells me of her life – sent to Athlone in the Republic to escape the Troubles and then off to au pair in Vienna – and it is a relief to hear a voice and a story not my own.

The next morning is autumnal, misty and chill. I fire up the Kelly Kettle with a few twigs, make coffee, pull on my damp wetsuit and launch. For the first twenty minutes I just drift with the tide, sipping from my mug, rocking on the breeze, stretching arms and legs, and rotating my shoulders and neck sleepily, before picking up the paddles. Less than three hours later I've done close on twenty miles, passed the busy port of Larne and reached the northern tip of Island Magee, a long, wide isthmus of land.

The wind has built up during the morning, and as the tide turns so I turn shorewards to find shelter in a neat little harbour. I have six hours to pass till the tide favours me again. Six Sunday hours. I leave the kayak and most of my kit on a neatly mown lawn and skirt the sand beach of Browne's Bay, where even the hardiest children are fully dressed, hanging back from the surly waves that slam down on the shore, and squinting their eyes against the sand devils blown up by the wind.

It is good to be walking. A shop, inland a bit, has piles of Sunday papers. There is a cafe a few miles further down the island, the girl behind the counter tells me, though it'd be a bit difficult to find, she thinks. A thin-faced, wide-mouthed young man leans over towards us and offers to drop me off there. He is almost going that way and it won't be a bother to take me. In his car I don't mention the kayak or my trip and he is too polite, or too Northern cautious, to show curiosity at my sandalled feet, stubbled chin, windburnt face and black waterproof kit-bag. Through the window I note an enclave of neat, modern houses with small, obsessively tended gardens. Many fly Red Hand of Ulster flags, one of the north's shibboleths, used on both sides of the sectarian divide but given a context here by being painted with Union flags.

From past practice my own accent has become neutral, faintly mid-Atlantic, poised to sweep southwards to Cork or harden into brittle English, or take off into the protective mimicry of whatever voice seems needed. When I'd hitch-hiked in the North, barely out of my teens, in the 1970s and 1980s, at the height of the Troubles, I'd consciously affected foreign accents and matching personae. On one trip I'd stolen the voice, the life story and mannerisms of a guitar-playing friend from Massachusetts. On another trip that took me back and forth through 'bandit country' along the border with Donegal, I'd drawn on two winters' living in the Netherlands to become a heavily accented Dutch tourist. At the time these had seemed like wise, if cowardly, precautions against serious misunderstanding; certainly wiser than talking in my own accent that mixed BBC English tones with West Cork syntax and vocabulary – an accent that veered between the voice of an SAS officer who'd failed to put in enough study time before going undercover, and that of a rebel-rousing Fenian studying at RADA.

The cafe turns out to be a bright, happy, aromatic place. Coffee and breakfast pass an hour and I settle back with the paper to do the crossword. I can sense curiosity from the couples and families at the small cluster of tables, and from the middle-aged pair toing and froing between the counter, the kitchen and the tables of regulars. I finally break cover going up for another cup of coffee whom I realise that the muggy heat of the cafe is transmuting the marine damp of my clothes into an ozone-y miasma.

'Paddling, is it? Right round Ireland? Good man. That's a big trip, alright.' The owner turns to his pals at the table nearest to the counter. 'Really, he should meet Bill, shouldn't he?' Yes, they agreed, I should meet Bill. He was a great canoer, they were almost sure that he'd canoed right around Ireland himself, he'd been at it for years, anyway, and one time he went for a wee paddle and just kept going and a few hours later he was in Scotland, and he had to come back by ferry.

There was a discussion about where I'd find Bill Freel; apparently he was moving that weekend. Then, just as a majority decision came down in favour of him being in the new house, an elderly woman with a girlish smile and a bright-patterned Mother Hubbard dress came in. This was Bill's wife and he followed a few minutes later. Somewhere in his eighties, he exuded the same positive vigour as Mrs Freel. They were taking a quick break midway with the packing, so there was little time for talk. Or not much. We sat around a table whilst he dispatched rumour and corroborated fact. No, he hadn't paddled around Ireland. He'd been a canoeing instructor for forty years. Paddling to Scotland had been a spur of the moment thing, back in the 1960s, landing on the Mull of Kintyre, without a penny ...

The stories tumbled out of him, and it was only when he pushed himself back to his feet to go and finish the move – 'there's some big bits of furniture we've got to get into a trailer' – that I realised that I'd lost track of whether it was him or a bunch of his paddle protégés who'd skited across to Mull in kayaks on a whim. I did realise that their trip, nearly fifty years ago, would have been far closer to that of the Canoe Boys in its skills and equipment than to mine. One thing I'd been thankful for on this trip was the transformation in kayak design, using new lighter, stronger materials, and the emergence of incredibly efficient weather-proof clothing and safety equipment.

I'd bought my first canoe in the 1960s, a heavy plywood semi-kayak formed of planes and squares and angles rather than curves, and painted in two shades of blue housepaint. Its lines were those of MacGregor's original *Rob Roy*. It cost five Irish pounds at a boat auction and I was the only bidder. At home I launched it on a small pond dammed from a stream down in the woods. A few inexpert, paddle strokes would take me from one bank to the other. Soon bored of this, I recruited two friends to help me carry it over the wall, across the road and into the slightly bigger stream that ran out into the tidal estuary. A few flicks of the paddle blade took me racing seawards on the falling tide, past lead-grey shoals of mullet. The waters flushed under a narrow bridge in what seemed to me then a roaring maelstrom and then down 'The Channel' and into the sea at Harbour View, all of which had been strictly forbidden to me. In shorts and shirts and plimsolls I felt the twin chills of guilt and fear, and the exhilaration of exploration. But I lost my nerve and, unable to paddle the heavy canoe back up against the tide, grounded it in the shallows and began dragging it back the way I'd come, slipping in the mud, fearful of falling and being swept away. Back at the weir separating stream and estuary, its pool emptied by the falling tide, I felt only relief. A passing man was persuaded to help me carry the canoe back across the road, over the wall and to the pond.

Walking back from the cafe I get confused by the labyrinth of lanes and find myself back in the rural housing estate, in what I had imagined a Loyalist enclave. At walking speed I can see heavy dogs tied up in yards, and powerful motorbikes on hard stands. I stop to ask directions from a young man hoovering out a car and affect a neutral accent and vocabulary – when I left the cafe I'd found myself involuntarily adding a *slán* – Irish for 'goodbye' – to my farewells. The man with the car straightens up, hits the off button on the hoover, and begins to explain a mazy route of lanes but then gives up. 'Come on, I'll take you there,' he says. 'Me brother'll enjoy the ride.'

He pops into the house and emerges with a grown man, wearing a beatific smile, leading him by the hand and seating him in the back. On the few miles down the road back to the beach we talk about the weather, and looking back over the seats I exchange big wordless grins with his brother. My thanks, when I get out, are brushed aside. 'Och, you'd only have lost yourself otherwise.'

The tide still hasn't turned and, fully clothed, I lie in a dip in the sand on the beach, the wind-whipping grit above me. A father leads three wetsuited children down to the water's edge, where they shriek and tumble in the surf. Everyone else on the beach is dressed for winter. Closing my eyes I doze for a while. I've become a lunaquatic, so in tune with the moon's pull on the tides that I awake, alert, just as the tide begins to slacken and flow southwards.

The wind and tide together propel me down the coast. The waves have become big, regular pulses, like the line of a strong heartbeat crossing an ECG screen. The land rises up in earthy cliffs and I play my regular in-flight, are-we-there-yet game, trying to pick out places on the sheer faces where it would be possible to land in an emergency, grading them according to desperation. An (A) would be anywhere I'd be able to scramble ashore and get above the waters even if it meant losing the kayak and all my kit. (B)s are narrow ledges and rocky outcrops above the tide line where I'd probably get everything ashore and wait out bad weather even if trapped and uncomfortable. A (C) is where I can pull off a bit of a crash landing but then reach the top of the cliffs or somewhere quite pleasant to camp.

With dusk approaching – the nights really are drawing in now – I am looking for anything a little better than a (C), but the soft contours of the red sandy cliffs, with their tufts of vegetation, have turned to soaring drops, walls and convoluted slabs of black rock. These are the Gobbins, remnants of an old Victorian walkway, and I note the ghosts of steps cut into their faces, and pillars thrusting up from under the waves along their edge. A prominent buttress of rock has a tunnel bored through its width, of a height that would take a man wearing a top hat, say, without him stooping. Across one sheer rockface, just above the high-water mark there are pegs and brackets of rusted, twisted iron.

I find a small storm beach at the end of the Gobbins. The only place flat enough to take the tent is a narrow path beaten through the bracken amongst the rock. As I am cooking in the dark, a figure looms up in the ember-light. I apologize for blocking the path.

'Ah, no worry, the path doesn't go any further than this anyway, not now.' He eyes the kayak laid in the bracken. 'Did you come along the cliffs? Did you see anything of the old Gobbins' walkway, or what little's a left of it? That was a big attraction in its time, when you could walk along the whole three miles of the cliffs, on the edge of the water.'

Opened in 1902, the Gobbins promenade brought together the Victorian passion for engineering challenges and an appreciation for nature's big scenery, just in time for the Edwardians to indulge their passion for bracing walks, sea air and novelty. Then the walkway attracted far more visitors than the Giant's Causeway, advertising itself in justifiably purple prose as running under towering cliffs, through tunnels, over spindly bridges and along platforms cantilevered out from the cliff face. It was a sort of self-propelled, slow, but still thrilling horizontal rollercoaster, with the frisson of getting a gush of salt water exploding up your petticoats or losing your hat to a gust of wind.

'It went to hell in the war, the second war, it didn't get the maintenance it needed, though you could walk bits of it up to, ah, I suppose the 1960s, but you'd be taking your life in your hands, and there's nothing left now of it, just a few steps in the rock and bolts.' I notice that my fire is dying but it seems rude to go back to cooking whilst the man is talking. He spits down onto the rocks over the edge. 'There've been all kinds of plots and plans to restore it, though it would take a few million alright, and they'd have to make the whole thing accessible to wheelchairs and to the blind people ... can you imagine? You saw how it is, you couldn't do that, so it'll never get done.'

CHAPTER 22

Coney Island

I TAKE MY CHANCE ON Belfast Lough next morning, heading straight across in the early sun. There are ferries heading for Scotland, the Isle of Man and Liverpool entering and leaving port. Behind me is the Harland and Wolff shipyard where the *Titanic* had been launched in 1912 and no sooner slid down the slip than it was off to Southampton to pick up passengers.

Across the lough, avoiding the still surprising amount of shipping, I reach the large harbour of Donaghadee, a parallelogram enclosed by high quay walls capped by a toy-town lighthouse. This guards an opening not quite narrow enough to keep out a large sloppy swell, which throws water across a roofed area that must once have offered

Edwardian tea dances, twirled parasols, a brass band, promenades and flirting. Landing on a scrap of sand in one corner of the harbour, I change into clothes, as modestly as a towel in a sharpish wind will allow. The majority of the population, it seems, are disapproving elderly women, each with a meek husband attached to one arm – the catches of those promenade flirtings, decades before, perhaps? They glower with undisguised hostility as I dance around on one leg and expose an ankle here, a knee there, and a fish-belly-white slab of damp arse in a particularly unfortunate combination of gust and totter.

Donaghadee's blue-rinse matrons ensure that there's a competitive market in cafes with cakes, but fewer with a good builder's breakfast. I find one eventually and then, back on the streets, realise that I've overlooked a sizeable sub-population: shaven-headed, muscle-bound men sitting in SUVs. The sons of the blue-rinse women, I presume. I'm killing time waiting for the tide, which has retreated hundred of yards from the edge of the town, but eventually get bored enough to unpack the kayak and haul it across the sands, foot by foot. I am paced by a silent, hulking teenage boy. He doesn't offer to help but rather walks slowly beside me as if he was watching a stranded seal or turtle inching its way back to the sea and curious about the outcome. Only when I'm in and about to paddle off does he say, shyly, 'Goodbye,' and raise a hand in a small, tight, stomach-level wave.

That night I find shelter on a small low-lying island with a pebble beach. I'm moated from the mainland so it's a surprise to be woken by a slobbering but friendly black Labrador joining me for breakfast, and then hailed by a stout man effecting a captain's hat, fisherman's boots and a walking stick. On this low-lying coast, the falling tide had joined my fortress back to the shore.

———•———

Strangford Lough is another great body of water that expels itself on the ebb tide. If Lough Foyle had seemed like a mouth spurting water out, the local name for the entrance to Strangford – Squeeze Gut – suggests something more explosively bowel-like. A sailor had told me of having his yacht stopped dead and thrown into the air by eight knots of out-rushing tide. Not a great place to get caught in the wrong conditions in a kayak, he'd emphasised. So it's a welcome anticlimax to slip across the lough mouth in almost stilled waters.

The coast is peaceful here. Or it is until a distant mosquito whine rises to a sound like a chainsaw as two jet-skis come into view. I always think of jet-skiers as embittered souls, driven to their antisocial hooning by the realisation that they've been fooled into buying a piece of expensive, motorised nonsense, with all the thrills of a ride-on lawnmower.

I escape the noise by diving into a narrow channel just before Ardglass. It opens out into a sun-warmed pool and I hang over the side of the kayak looking down as if into an aquarium, watching gobies and blennies fluttering through the spinneys of seaweed. There's a handy slab of rock and, as a bit of a luxury, I step out to stretch my legs and take a piss, into the water. I've hardly got back into the kayak when there's a huge flurry in the water and a seal is swimming up the channel, nostrils whiffling. She (I'm assuming it's a she) hauls out onto a flat ledge, a few yards from where I'm floating, and arches back her body, head up, eyes closed. Every few seconds she snuffles her nose back into the water for an ecstatic smell, scented I presume by my own pheromones. I'm intrigued by this display, when I catch sight of a big bull seal surging up the channel, blocking off my exit. He's a very big seal, mottle-coloured and heavy-headed, with only a lack of legs differentiating him from an actual land bull. I'm concerned that he sees me as a rival – he doesn't look happy – and I imagine him as one of the Donaghadee shaved-heads. *Oy! You looking at my bird? Yeah! You!* I try to exude genuine innocence. *Oh, her? No, hadn't even noticed ... very attractive I'm sure, but not my type, look, look you're happy together, the two of you, don't want to disturb, now if you'd just ... maybe move over ... and I could squeeze by, perhaps ... leave the two of you alone.*

The bull sinks down into the water. I can see his huge bulk a few feet down. Miss Seal is blowing flirty little bubbles out of her mouth at me. She's also hooked her back flippers up onto a ledge out of the water and is crossing them and uncrossing them. She then slips into the water and wiggles – as much as an animal with the dimensions of a hippopotamus can be said to wiggle – towards the kayak. The bull resurfaces, too, putting the three of us each at one point of a small equilateral triangle. Flattering as the Lynx effect of my urine on the seal cow is proving, surely it must have diluted to nothing by now. *Go to him*, I will the blowsy, slapper seal, as she undulates through the water away from the bull seal and towards me. *Go to him, we've got no future.*

The bull is only a few feet away from the kayak now, rising up high out of the water. The cow is on the other side of me. I can see a hard, glittering in the he-seal's eye ... and suddenly the fear that had gripped me as I contemplated just how much damage an angered and jealous bull seal might do to me as a rival fades away. To be replaced by a far, far worse horror. *Dear Christ, no! NO! NO! Not a threesome.* Seeing a gap in the channel, I make my excuses.

Ardglass was an important trading port in medieval times, the seven blocky tower houses that once stood around its perimeter forming a bar graph showing peaks of early prosperity. There's a marina, too, a litmus test of more modern prosperity and of my own hypocrisy. Though quick to rant against their fungal growth along the coast, I love the luxury of being able to moor the kayak to a pontoon, change on a boardwalk, leave my kit secure behind a gate, fill up my water bottles and often find a shower as well. The kind of things I guess that the average tie-up yachtie likes just as much. I saunter into town. What did I need? A few stores, a chance to check my emails – though that seemed unlikely – a leg-stretch, some distraction, a set of tide tables for this coast and this year, and a meal out.

On the road from the marina to the town centre I pass a small corrugated-iron shed styled as Charles Mullhall's shop. His son, long-haired, prophet-bearded William Mullhall – a dead-ringer for Willie Nelson – presides through a hole in a tottering wall of stuffed display shelves. There are sweets and chocolate bars of all kinds, many I'd never heard of – brandy balls and clove drops – or thought extinct. Small toys, too. And there are handwritten notes around the shop: *Keep your moaning and complaints to yourself*, reads one. More bizarrely, a bank of mismatched televisions, festooned in cables above the door, show CCTV footage from all over the town; I can even see the yellow splash of the kayak at the marina.

'You look like you're in off the water,' William greets me. I wonder if he's seen my arrival and tracked my route to his door, or just read my clothes. 'Do you need to use the internet?' he continues, proferring a laptop. 'There it is, off you go.' He chats away as I fire up the connection. 'There's many a fisherman comes in here on boats from foreign places, and I think it's nice for them to be able to send a message home. It's hard enough out there without having a little bit of warmth and friendliness when they come in ... Tide tables. Hang on, yes I do ... They're just a little photo-copied booklet for the fishermen.'

My few emails aren't nearly as interesting as this man, who, it turns out, is pretty well known for painting portraits of rock stars. He pulls a portfolio book from under the counter and doesn't need to name his subjects – amidst swirls of colour are Bono and Dylan, painted from sketches made backstage at gigs, a concert poster he did for Led Zeppelin in the 1970s, portraits of Van Morrison, Westlife, Springsteen and of his own doppelgänger, Willie Nelson.

I tell him about my encounter with the seals. 'They're very friendly,' he tells me, 'and that's because the fishermen aren't in competition with them. They look after them, feed them scraps, the way it should be ... Now, for yourself and a feed, go to the Chinese restaurant down on the quay, next to the supermarket, so you can shop first, and tell them I sent you. They're lovely people.'

He's right. The East Essence is a welcome haven and the waitress, a willowy, Irish girl, uncomplainingly piles an unlikely combination of steak, prawn crackers and seaweed salad, as well as several glasses of red wine, before a customer who looks a bit like a hobo. Later, full of Chinese food, I paddle back out of the harbour past a group of people on the rocks below the breakwater, all fishing keenly. As I pass them I realise that they are – must be – the total Sino population of Ardglass. A handful of Chinese men, women and children busily pulling out mackerel.

———•———

Heading down the Lecale Peninsula I could have used the lyrics of 'Coney Island', Van Morrison's paean to the joys of a day on just this stretch of coast, as a guide, albeit that I was doing it in reverse. Van had left Downpatrick to head to the sea, and if I'd taken his advice I'd have eaten a couple of jars of mussels and some potted herrings in Ardglass before buying the Sunday papers just before Coney Island. Like Van, I was stopping off at St John's Point, and felt, as he did, that it would be great if it was only like this all the time.

I'm starting to get a measure of this stretch of shoreline, whose slope is so shallow that with the tide out it can be hundreds of yards to get from the water's edge to the high-water mark. Tonight's camp, beyond wasp-striped St John's lighthouse, is a real assault course, back and forth across a long stretch of weed-covered rocks, to a shingle beach. I boil up water for tea. There's plenty of driftwood. A huge amount, in fact, and much of it wells up in the grass behind the tent. I begin to wonder about tides and finger through my new tide tables, but then just fall asleep. I wake a few hours later as wavelets lap a few metres away from my camp and it takes a Herculean effort to shake myself awake and move the camp further inshore, by torchlight. At dawn, I find that the decomposed corpse of a porpoise, its putrefying guts falling in a tangle from a hole in its side, has washed up to exactly where the tent had been.

As I drink strong coffee I watch in the grey half-light a cloud of small birds hawking insects that are drawn to the swinging light of the lighthouse. Wagtails, I think. I'm trying to imagine Brendan Behan standing where I am now. The gregarious and bibulous writer (self-described as 'a drinker with a writing problem') and ardent Republican spent part of the summer of 1950 repainting the lighthouse. There are so many reasons why this must have been a desperate and ill-considered job, two of which are that he would have been working for the British state (who had only recently released him from prison), whilst the nearest place for a drink was a long, long walk up the head to Rossglass or Killough. The lighthouse keeper inevitably thought that Behan's heart wasn't in the job and, in a letter looking for the writer's dismissal, accused him of 'wilfully wasting material, opening paint tins by blows from a hammer, spilling the contents which is now running out of the paint store door' and noted, 'his language is filthy and he is not amenable to any law or order'.

As the morning progresses, my language becomes pretty filthy, too. The wind has turned cold and snapping, kicking up big seas, and drizzle turns the wide expanse of Dundrum Bay into a grey, foaming expanse. I've checked the map to see just how long that walk to the pub really is. As I push off from the shore, I'm given an accurate scale to measure the seas against; a fishing boat is drawing pots up, and as it rears up on the waves a third of its hull at a time clears the water. The wind is hard offshore. This is unnerving. Whatever goes wrong in an offshore wind is not good. But my progress is smoother than the fishing boat's, as like a duck the kayak rides up and down the swells. It is a long haul, though, with the wind and waves strengthening, and by mid-morning I'm struggling to hold my course and reach land.

Reaching land isn't always good in seafaring. Isambard Kingdom Brunel's *SS Great Britain*, a leviathan ship made of wrought iron and the first passenger liner to be driven by a propeller, ended up aground close by here, in Dundrum Bay, in November of 1846. The captain, on his way through the Irish Sea bound for America, had missed the lighthouse on the Isle of Man, mistook St John's Point for the Manx light and ran onto shore at full speed. The ship lay grounded for a full winter before being salvaged. It brought the shipping company down, and the ship itself – which could make New York in just under two weeks regardless of the state of seas or winds – was first demoted to running emigrants to Australia before being drafted as a troopship in the Crimean War and finally abandoned in the Falklands as a coal bunker.

I'm within a few paddle strokes of shore but unable to land safely in these winds. So I inch towards the massive bulk of Slieve Donard, an outpost of the Mourne Mountains, and find it deflects the wind and curls it round, blowing me along. I'm reminded of how one Irish kayaker used to put to sea with an large umbrella – in a following wind it could be put up and used as a sail; onshore it was an instant shelter to lunch under. I wished I had a brolly, if only to use against the rain. And some lunch would be nice, too. But I am making time too swiftly now to stop.

The Mourne Mountains are an abstracted landscape: a hulking mass of browns, umbers, brackens and stone. A single wall has been built over the range, so sheep can graze one side and not the other, leaving a dead straight line between the pasture and rough land, painted as cleanly as a wide brushstroke. It was claimed, by his brother, that C.S. Lewis used much of this landscape as a blueprint for Narnia, remembering its contours, its colours and its otherworldly atmosphere from his boyhood in Belfast. Northern Ireland could well have supplied the name of his allegorical other world, too. The first humans known to have settled in Ireland, 9,000 years ago, left their stone chippings along the Antrim and Down coastlines, in an Irish archaeological age called the Larnian.

Time has been playing tricks again. The first hours across Dundrum Bay had slunk by – and then suddenly, whoosh, and another five hours had gone by and I'm twenty miles downcoast, crossing the mouth of Carlingford Lough. I've left Northern Ireland and am back in the south, though I have to walk the last bit to find a place to camp, as the spring tides have dropped the shore hundreds of yards out from the tideline.

CHAPTER 23

Beware Shallows

I WAKE IN THE MORNING to a howling westerly wind –a near gale – blowing hard off the land. Far lesser winds have pinned me down along the coast, sometimes for days on end, but now, more confident and desperate not to be trapped on this dull shoreline, I decide to launch and creep round the inside of Dundalk Bay, hugging the shoreline, taking no risks.

From where I've slept on the bay's northern headland it's about ten miles straight across, to Dunany Point. The bay is a neat, almost square bite out of the east coast, and I'm tempted to trust my strength to get me over on the short-est route. But the forecast – and my own gut instinct – is for rising winds, still offshore. I try not to dwell on how much time going round three sides of a square rather than straight across a single edge is going to add to the day's paddling ... but twenty miles and five or six hours seems a conservative guess. I buoy myself up by thinking that I'm at least keeping going, rather than sitting in my tent.

It takes three hours to follow the bay's shore inland, the wind blowing hard and steadily into my face. If I stop paddling for more than a few seconds, I can measure my momentum against the shore as the kayak slows almost instantly, then stops dead and within a few minutes is going back the way I've come. The irritant of the wind in my ears, blocking out all noise but its own insistent whining, is bad. As is the constant salt spray blown up into my eyes.

I begin to feel that I am doing hand-to-hand combat with personal and malevolent forces, though truth is this weather is doing major damage even ashore, beating flat the corn still unharvested in this wet summer. I begin to fear that even now, just before the end of August, the autumn's equinoctial gales have arrived already and that I have missed my chance to get round Ireland this year. The sheer frustration of this thought drives me on. I shovel water over and over to reach the head of the bay. I'm optimistic again. I've beaten my way up against the wind and now I just need to head back out along the southern shore with both wind and tide behind me.

It's a bad call. And in the next ten minutes I compound it with a series of errors. The wind has been too strong to get the chart out and look at the topography of the bay, so I've not realised that Dundalk Bay is, like the rest of this coastline, very shallow, drying out to miles offshore. The next mistake is to take advantage of the relative calm so far inland to root around in the bags behind my seat and find food to make a lunch – I relish being whirled along down the bay by wind and tide as I eat. And a really serious mistake: I opt not to hug the southern shore but to allow myself to be pulled out into a rushing, deep channel, exulting at getting a free ride; I'll paddle back closer to the shore when I've finished lunch. I've not yet noticed that I'm already in serious trouble.

But soon I do. With a mouthful of tinned herring and oat biscuit half-chewed, I realise with a heartstopping thud that I've been carried a huge distance down the middle of the bay in no more than twenty minutes and all three shores are now a long, long way off. The wide shallow bay is draining out into the centre channel, increasing the speed of the water even more, revealing sandbars, banks and drifts. I paddle hard to get out of the channel. Digging the paddle down into the murky water I'm shocked to find the blade jarring on solid ground, only a foot below the surface. It seems illogical, being far out at sea – miles offshore – to have reached water that only reaches my knees. It would have been easy to think of this as being safe – as offering me the chance to get out and just walk back to land. But, with the water's going down fast, going aground several miles out here with deteriorating weather is incredibly dangerous. The chance of being able to walk back to land in this great expanse of waters and channels is remote, and if I wait for the tide to come back in and refloat the kayak, it will be dark and I will find myself in breaking surf.

Then a sudden explosion of water near me, bursting through one of the waves, reveals the body of a seal half-crawling and half-swimming towards a narrow but deep tributary leading back to the main channel. I follow it to deeper water.

The seal has led me out of immediate danger. But it's still a desperate scenario. The bay's combination of shallowness and size means that the tide going out is rather like emptying a bath, climaxing with all the waters rushing towards the plughole. The central channel here is already doing this; I'm far from the shelter of the land, and the wind is gusting. I realise with a sudden jolt of fear that I have no chance of angling myself across the bay and hitting the southern headland. I am going to get swept out to sea.

Panic rises up as a literal cocktail of chemicals – the adrenalin of fear, the calming opiate of inevitability, the rush of physical strength. But I tell myself, I am still afloat, and the right way up, and I have my paddles. Maybe I've enough skill to keep paddling and to stay balanced in what has now become a rushing tumult of waves and current. Using a slight lull in the seas, I ease the kayak across the current and spin it around as it seesaws on a wave-top. I begin paddling at an angle back up the bay, hoping to hold my position and ease sideways to land. I carefully monitor my paddle rate. If I am to succeed, I am looking at hours of ceaseless paddling. I try to estimate how much stronger the current might get at the tide's peak, and then how many hours beyond that before it slackens and finally turns. The tide turning is not a good thing against this wind. Once wind and waters go head to head, I won't stand a chance.

On a continuum between the polar points of being safely ashore and being drowned, I am much closer to the latter. I am being blown away from land in a rising wind amongst big waves and, with scant chance of attracting help, in a few more hours it will be darkness; I am already tired; there is every chance that my VHF radio won't broadcast; I have three parachute flares on my front deck and a smoke signal, but in this grey overcast, drizzling weather there is only a slight chance that they'll be seen and, even if seen and a lifeboat launched, only an equally small chance they'll be able to find or reach me.

I keep paddling. Pulling back hard on the blade at each stroke. Turning every calorie of effort into forward motion. Two hours of strong paddling and now I know I'm losing ground. Paddle as I might against the wind and the current, I've been swept far down the centre of the ten-mile-wide bay. I've picked one pair of landmarks after another, monitoring how the lower one stays in relation to the upper one. A white house in line with another house further up the hill, a stand of trees on the shoreline against a notch in the horizon, and each time I've felt despair as, instead of their positions showing me gaining ground, they've measured how fast I am being pulled out to sea.

I concentrate on staying calm, and avoid flailing with the paddles and tiring myself out or overturning. Over and over I wonder if I should try calling up the coastguard on the radio, or fire off my flares, but something – pride, embarrassment, fear, experience – keeps me paddling. The muscles across my shoulders are torn and aching, sharp pains prick my right wrist. My arse, my legs and my feet are all numb from being clenched in the same position for what is now seven hours of paddling. Seven hours, four of which have been on the ebbing tide, mean that the flow must begin to ease soon, which will bring an hour or two of slacker water before the tide turns against the wind, the wind which is still blowing at a force six, and gusting stronger. Once the tide turns against the wind, I won't be pulled back inshore but merely tossed around by big angry waves until I turn over.

My landmark now is a patch of darkened woods under Dunany Point. As I paddle, I have to look over my shoulder to see if I'm still being swept out to sea. The point is still a mile or more and I'm almost straight offshore from its extremity. Very soon, I will be out of the bay and out at sea. It's early evening, and edging into the long dusk. Is it time to send up a flare or three now, or put out an alarm on the VHF? Time to swallow pride, scream for help, hope to sweet Jesus that I can get rescued. But I am haunted by the idea of what happens next – the point when, having sent the flares aloft and jabbed at my radio buttons, I find that neither have worked. Then I might get pulled out by the tide, and pulled back in again. The wind might drop. I might be able to keep paddling to stay afloat, bob around in the Irish Sea until dawn and get spotted by a passing ship; there is a lot of shipping in these waters. Perhaps I'll surprise myself and draw on unsuspected reserves of strength, keep paddling through the darkness. But I don't know that. If I miss the headland, if I'm carried out to sea, I don't know what will happen.

Some part of my brain is doing complex calculations, even as I paddle. Sifting through incoming feedback on tide, current, wind, strength, morale, position, drift. And it's just sent a message up to the other part of my brain, the abstract, flabby bit that's wondering what to do. Keep paddling, says the brainy bit of my brain, because it looks like – I've run the figures through here a few times – yes, it looks like if you can put in a last burst for about – rough calculation, here, but good enough for survival – twenty, maybe thirty, more minutes then you might just tip the last bit of land.

I dig the paddles in. And again. Then I realise that my cautious, analytical brain had been over cautious. The tide has slackened and I've pulled out of the current. Suddenly, quite fast, I am pulling into land, and not at the very tip of Dunany Point, but inland of it. I can look at the shore and actually decide where I'd like to aim for, where I'd like to pull out and camp for the night. The kayak is acting normally. The fight to just get back to land is over, and with it the desire to land. I inch my way round the head.

Fear and courage are strange things, in uneasy balance. The year before, my nerve had broken not with being hospitalised – a relatively small thing – but with the long convalescence, followed by the operation, followed by more weakness, as if mimicking the steps down, down and down into old age, frailty and then death. I had prescribed myself an adventure to rebuild my strength – not my muscle power, but my mental stamina. Coming through Dundalk Bay, despite my stupidities, because of my stupidities, the ability to keep going as long as keeping going was necessary has reconstructed something of my previous innocent optimism and self-belief. Doom and dread are vanquished, at least for now, for this voyage, replaced by an exhilarating self-belief.

Inuit children are taught to laugh at disaster. Get lost in the polar night, lose a glove in minus forty temperatures, plunge through the ice into Arctic water, and death is only hours, minutes or seconds away. Laughing stimulates the mind, fires the synapses, rushes you into action and ideas and doing something. Crying and moaning and worrying floods the brain with depressive opiates, slows you down, makes you accepting of fate, leaves you wallowing in failure. I've got my laughter back.

It is fully dark when I see a pack of seals bobbing around close into a stretch of rocky shoreline approaching Clogher Head. There are islets of rock, channels and a small inlet leading to a tiny steep beach. After nine hours in the kayak my legs are bowed, stiff and sore as I climb out onto a patch of sand about the size of a tablecloth, below a small cliff. My final challenge of the day is to rock-climb with all my bags, and then with the kayak on my shoulder, to reach a ledge that I hope is high enough to avoid the incoming tide. There is nowhere to retreat to if I've got it wrong. And I've got a long list of things wrong today.

I wake to heavy rain but little wind. The tide has come to within a few feet of my camp, pushing small drifts of flotsam up to where the kayak is balanced atop a tripod of rock outcrops. There is an hour to wait for the tide to turn, I need more food, and I'm still cramped from the previous day.

I scramble along the rain-soaked rocks and cross a small beach full of flotsam. Over the months I've noticed how beaches attract particular debris. I'd been on beaches with hundreds of one-litre plastic bottles. On an island off Donegal, one small bay had drifts of fishing net buoys. Others just had branches, or lengths of alkathene piping, or stoppered glass bottles. I'd found seven footballs along the highwater mark of a tiny scrap of sand near Clifden. The tides and the currents and the winds had busied themselves sifting and sorting rubbish by size, weight and type, like an infinite number of nimble-fingered elves, before popping each piece into the appropriate compartment. I fantasise about finding the 'Beach of Ambergris', 'The Cove of Coconuts', or 'The Bay of Really Expensive Things with High Re-sale Value Lost at Sea, and Having Come Ashore Falling under the International Laws of Salvage'.

Instead, my walk to Clogher village takes me along the 'Strand of Rubber Work Gloves'. There are tens of them. All right-handed. I surmise that innumerable fishermen at sea took one off to do something fiddly and the next minute the glove was washed or whirled over the side to make its slow way to join its brethren here.

I turn inland through a higher-than-head-height field of maze and then into a small lane. There is a strange feeling being inland. Blackbirds skirl along the hedgerow, and pigeons flutter out of the trees. There's a heady smell of meadow flowers as the sun comes out and dries off the wet fields. In a mini-supermarket a counter-hand is making fresh-fried breakfast rolls. I sit on the wall outside with two of them to chew through, and a large mug of coffee. In a garden there is a tree, its trunk a macabre totem pole nailed over with plastic figurines drawn from the whole leprechaun tribe – trogs, gonks, Smurfs, Father Christmases, gnomes, Postman Pat looking a bit surprised to have been put in such company, a Barbie doll and a large butterfly.

Back on the water, rounding Clogher Head, I feel close to invincible. Or maybe just happy. The sun has come out and I'm tracking the mile after mile of sand beach that runs from here nearly to Dublin. It's calm and I look in on the holiday homes behind the dunes, and then at long stretches of strand, before reaching the mouth of the Boyne River. There's a familiar reach of sand which reaches back to a memory of an evening some years back, when an unlikely sequence of events carried me here with a woman I had just met in the Horseshoe Bar in Dublin's grand Shelbourne

Hotel. We came out here to birdwatch and lay wrapped in rugs on the sand, sipping from a Thermos of coffee, looking out for little tern. A cordon of rope and a couple of warning signs had marked off a patch of shingle in which the perfectly camouflaged eggs and chicks lay, while the parents came in with wings scissoring and a twittering screech. Now, late in summer, I think I can spot a few adults, or perhaps they are common or sandwich terns; they look very alike, flitting over the waves.

It's another long day's paddle, but with light winds, occasional sun, and a weak current. It's easy to keep going. I think about yesterday's fear, but only as an abstract. I do wonder, however, if more experience would have lessened that fear; if I would have known that the tide was sure to slacken and I would be able to haul myself to land, just as I had finally done. Would I then have had the confidence to save my energy and remain calm? But it feels important that I had retained some level of choice through the ordeal and hadn't gone entirely out of control.

This leads me into thinking about childhood trials. At my madly anarchic Irish school, on the shores of Lough Derg, a group of the boys, ranging in age from nine (me) to full-grown eighteen-year-olds, had gathered round a towering oak tree one evening before supper. An old boat mooring rope had been thrown over a branch high up in the tree and a car tyre tied to its end, five or six feet off the ground and then another long rope tied loosely to that hanging down. A few of the boys tried out the swing, sitting in the tyre and being pulled out in a wide arc with the trailing rope. I was encouraged to take a turn. I saw the two biggest boys picking up the rope. The first few swings were exhilarating. Flying up till I was high off the ground and then swooping

back again and up the other side of the arc. But then I realised with a cold sense of doom what was going to happen.
As I came down the two figures ran forward with the rope,
pulling me far higher, so I pendulumed up and then fell
back to the ground again. They built on my momentum,
sending me higher still the next time.

'Ah, lads don't send him too high, don't hurt him,' a
voice tried out from those watching. 'Don't worry, he *likes*
it! He's always up in trees and climbing things ... all he's
got to do is hold on.' I was terrified. The centrifugal force
on each swing was overpowering and I didn't know if I
could hold on, or how long for. And the tyre was spinning
round now as it flew through the air, and still they kept
pulling on the rope, in a rhythm that took me up amongst
the big branches. As much as I could think, I knew that
either I'd let go and fly off and down into the ground, or
that the rope would break or – the tyre was oscillating now,
flying out sideways and twisting round – I'd crash into
the trunk. The only control I had was holding on, and not
making any noise. I clamped my arms around the rope and
my legs around the tyre and willed time to pass. The bell for
supper, the second bell, the impatient bell, the in-trouble
bell, pealed out from the house. The rope was dropped and
I swung less and less until I came to a stop. So that was
another dread to have and to hold; the madness of the mob;
the something that started as light and amusing getting
dark and out of control.

By dusk I've rounded Skerries, part satellite town for Dublin's
professional-class commuters and part Irish harbour village,

inshore from a scattering of islands. One of these is Colt, where not long ago thirteen Latvian winkle pickers were stranded on a bleak November night, after the boat that had dropped them failed to return. Freezing and distracted, they were rescued by the local lifeboat, alerted by a passer-by who had spotted the Latvians' fire. Despite being so close to a capital city, there's an odd feel of remoteness.

Below Loughshinny another shallow shore runs out to sea, but this one is mazed by rocky channels and underwater kelp forests and canyon gardens. It's a seals' paradise. On the last day of August the grey and common seals that bask here have decided that their autumnal breeding season has arrived, Cows pull out on small podiums of rock, splaying their flippers; the bulls eye them up and roar and belch obscenities at them and at each other. Every now and again there is a gushing explosion in the water and a turmoil like two submarines crashing headlong as two bulls duel. Then quiet, before the vanquisher pops his head up next to the cow.

I'm put in mind of the stories of the selkies – the seal people – and their closeness to humans. Every marine people of the Atlantic coast, and further afield, it seems, have their own myths of sinuous women who change between human and seal. But they're strongest in the Orkneys, the Faroes and on the coast of Ireland. The archetype story has a fisherman finding a seal skin on a beach and hiding it, thereby entrapping the seal-woman who has shrugged it off for a while to sunbathe. The beautiful, exotic-looking woman becomes his wife, though he notes how she is drawn, often singing, to the shoreline, especially on full-moon nights. Invariably one day she finds her skin where he has hidden it and the selkie woman pulls it on to become a seal again and go back to the sea, leaving home, husband and children behind.

From my camp I can see the glow in the sky from Dublin's lights, and the twin flashes of the red lights on the power station chimneys at Ringsend, and the slow meteor lights of planes taking off and landing at Dublin Airport only a few miles away. Out at sea the huge lit-up bulk of a cruise ship passes. I'm a little way up the cliff face, on a rough track that slopes up to the fields above, so am I high enough that the lights I can see very far off might be those of Holyhead in Wales, or is it just tens of fishing boats out in the dark?

The next day I turn over my map of Ireland, again. I have less than a quarter of the distance left to go. It is the first of September. The wind has eased. A glorious day, even if it is still wet and blowy. But these things are relative. I am heading for Dublin.

CHAPTER 24

Not So Draoghaire

COASTING TOWARDS DUBLIN, I'm on familiar ground. This is the coast of Fingal, meaning 'fair stranger', the description the locals gave to the conquering Vikings. They established Dublin as a Norse city and trading post, but had an early base on Lambay Island – Ireland's most easterly point – which rises up like an island country in miniature. I gaze at its peaks, steep cliffs and a settlement nestled on the landward side around a harbour. Lambay is the only inhabited island along the whole two hundred miles of Ireland's east coast, and that it's but a hard row from the capital adds to its allure.

I thread my way into Howth, Dublin's harbour, amid a fleet of Howth 17s, open gaff-rigged sailing boats that add further to their speed and instability by sticking an upside-down triangle of gaff-topsail at the tip of their masts. Howth Yacht Club is one of the oldest and grandest in Ireland, but the secretary is welcoming. Of course I could leave the kayak and my kit for a few days. Just put it out of the way at the back of the dinghy park. And there's a shower over there should you be wanting it ...

I wash, change, pack up things to take into town, stuff everything else into the kayak, close up its hatches and steal across the road. Although Dublin is so familiar, it feels somehow wrong to be walking its streets. I haven't finished the voyage yet. Indeed, though the weather inshore is sunny and the sharp sea wind is merely a light breeze, I'm still unsure that the weather will hold long enough to finish the circumnavigation before the harsh side of autumn snuffs out all hope. It is September 1st – my birthday – and at forty-eight I'm troubled by an odd mix of regret and elation; regret at the lack of any regular home, nor wife or children; elation to be travelling light with good friends to visit and favourite cafes to revisit. The regret is fleeting and lifts as I take the DART train into central Dublin, kit-bag on my shoulder, stubble on my chin, hat on head, every inch the returning sailor.

I get out at Pearse Street, just down from Trinity College. In the 1970s, when I'd first moved to Dublin, I'd lived in a single room next to the station, with a cold-water sink and a gas ring. I'd worked into the winter on a building site, and then got a job as a stagehand at the Abbey Theatre. I was promoted to flyman, a job that entailed sitting in the fly-loft high above the stage, lowering and raising scenery flats, curtains, props and anything else that could be tied onto wires and whisked in and out from above. Often there was nothing to do except open the curtains at the start of the play and close them and roll down the fire curtain at the end. I had a huge armchair and a small reading light and piles of books from the Pearse Street library.

The books were often about epic solo sailing voyages and boat adventures. *Sailing Alone Around the World, The Voyage of the Dove, The Riddle of the Sands, Survive the Savage Seas*. I bought a large, heavy fibreglass kayak out of the classified ads in the *Evening Herald*, trundling it across Dublin on a set of pram wheels found in a skip. It only fitted in my room if angled from one ceiling corner to the opposite corner of the floor. I began to plan a voyage. Cutting bulkheads and mixing up cups of fibreglass to fix them into place. Making storage hatches. Sewing up water-proof bags. Swimming a mile every day in the pool across the Liffey. I handed in my notice at the Abbey and a few days later set off to paddle south through Ireland, heading out of Dublin on the Grand Canal on a trip by rivers and canals that several months later ended up on the beach at Saintes-Maries-de-la-Mer, on the Mediterranean.

This stay in Dublin is short. Two nights. Partying and hanging out companionably with old friends around city centre bars and drinking dens for late-night talk. It is a luxury to wake up late in the morning and not care about the tide, nor about the time, nor the weather. But tides and weather still drive me on. I wake early on the second morning and pack. I am still paddling around Ireland. It isn't over. I must make it before the autumn closes in and the gales start up. Actually, now that I'm so close to success, or so it feels, I tell myself that I'll just keep going into the winter if necessary, taking it day by day, getting out on the water whenever I can. I have no doubt that if I don't complete the trip in this one go, I won't return to finish it in any following year.

Having missed the morning tide I have all day to get back onto the water for the evening flow. A leisurely breakfast, a newspaper, an hour in a bookshop, a wander down to the centre of town and a gawp at the Liffey as it streams under the Ha'penny Bridge, O'Connell Bridge, the Loopline, Talbot and Seán O'Casey bridges and out into Dublin Bay. Several hours fiddling with kit and repacking. Then, like a selkie returning to the sea, I pull on my still-damp rubber long-john, launch down the slip and paddle out of the harbour. I slip between Ireland's Eye, a pointy inshore island, and Howth Head, and round into Dublin Bay. It's early evening now, and off the headland I meet two kayakers returning from a post-work paddle. They report porpoises playing further out in the bay. I'm now in the waters that I watched flowing out to sea under the city bridges.

I have to decide here whether to cut straight across the bay, dodging shipping as I go, or add on miles following the shoreline inland and then crossing almost at the river mouth, where it's safer, before heading back out along the far shore. I can only see one ship, large but far away and heading south of me and out to sea. Given the size of the bay, even if a fleet of large boats really wanted to – were actually trying to – run down a flighty little fella in a tiny kayak in tens of square miles of water, what chance would they have? The odds are similar to an elephant trampling on a specific termite in one expanse of veldt. Or a speeding lorry squashing one particular little scurrying rat. Or

JASPER WINN : PADDLE

me paddling around the Atlantic in a kayak and spotting the one big shark in the ... I give up my list of unlikelihoods at this point and plump for the direct route. The promised porpoises are wheeling up from the depths, jumping between the small waves to distract me. One of them, forgetting its normally shy and retiring demeanour, breaches, throwing itself clear of the water, and finds the experience so exciting that it immediately dances up and dives out into the air again.

All is well with the world. Except for a troubling little dot on the Welsh side of the horizon. Which might have been a buoy that I hadn't previously noticed. Though, if so, it was a buoy that five minutes later has doubled in size. Still it is not much more than a tiny dot on the far reaches of the sea's limit. Then suddenly not half so small as it had seemed ... and looking more ship-like, though obviously so far away that I'm going to be long across the shipping lane before it ... doubles in size in half the time. It's now looking like a tower block that has fallen on its side and is sliding across the ocean at a fair old rate. Towards me.

It's actually the *Swift*. The big fast ferry from Holyhead. Obviously there's no panic – given my earlier logic – but I do know that it can hit close to forty miles an hour, slow for a family car but fast for something the size of a football pitch. Of course, all I have to do is wait until I can see the whites of one of the ferry's sides, and then, if it's the port side, then I'll just speed up south a bit, putting more distance between me and it. And if it's the starboard side, then I'll just back up for a while and let it pass by. But now I notice that the ship doesn't seem to have any sides as such, but is all bow. In fact, my vision is filled with a soaring wall of white-painted aluminium. And then it's past and I can see the wake creaming off as it surges on and into the heart of Dublin. Leaving me rocking in the big curling stern wave sent up in its wake.

●━━━●

I land on Dalkey Island, a rock with rabbit-trimmed grass and a Martello tower, set into the south side of Dublin Bay. It really is autumn now, and all the better for it. The sky is crystal-clear and star-scattered. The night is refreshingly chilly and dead still. The lights glitter along the shore amidst slabs of black; the more lights in one block surrounded by darkness, the bigger the garden. Sparks shoot out of the Kelly Kettle's chimney. And there are still lights moving across the waters. Boats coming into Ireland. Children in Dún Laoghaire, the harbour just around the corner, really do have ferries at the bottoms of their gardens.

Dún Laoghaire is an equivalent to Cobh, down in Cork. The former was Kingstown under British rule, and the latter Queenstown. Perhaps in some kind of payback, both of the Irish names are pronunciation puzzles for visitors. Cobh, pronounced 'cove', is often referred to as 'Cob-Aitch' by locals, simply to confuse the tourists, whilst Dún Laoghaire (pronounced 'Dunleary') inspired Flann O'Brien – writing as his own unpronounceable alias, Myles na gCopaleen – to this 'follow-the-rhymes' limerick:

Said a Sassenach back in Dun Laoghaire
I pay homage to nationalist thaoghaire
But wherever I drobh
I found signposts that strobh
To make touring in Ireland so draoghaire.

James Joyce, too, left traces around here. He was tower-mate of Oliver St John Gogarty in the Martello tower across the water from me on Sandymount Strand, where gentlemen still bathe in the nude before nine in the morning. Joyce left the tower barely a week into his occupancy after a bit of intemperate gun-play by Gogarty, but it was enough time to give him the start of *Ulysses*, in which stately Buck Mulligan stares out from the tower's roof over the 'snot green. The scrotumtightening sea.'

I'm in good spirits, replete with what Joyce called 'morning rashers' – bacon sandwiches (and a mug of coffee) – and paddling through a sea that for once is far from snotty; indeed, is blue and mirror calm. I drift happily along, the drips from every paddle stroke making tiny ripples on the surface. The horizon to the east is like the edge of an infinity pool. Inland, I can see the train from Bray taking early commuters to Dublin on the line known as Brunel's Folly. The engineer, not content with his big ship going aground in Dundrum Bay, had designed a railway line running along the cliff face, over bridges, through tunnels and on embankments that had collapsed more than once and put trains and carriages into the sea. Now it tootles in and out of the hillsides' contours like a Hornby model.

My own commuting is going well. Today's dawn start isn't so early as back in the 'summer', but I am still on the water long before most people have set off to work, and I'm well on the way to Wicklow Head.

In Dublin, I'd met Sean Pierce and Eileen Murphy, both round-Ireland-kayakers, whose trips hadn't been one-off whimsies, but logical steps in long paddling careers. Eileen had filled me in on the coast immediately ahead: flat and sheltered; sand shore for mile after mile, no big cliffs nor

Atlantic swells; no islands throwing the currents awry and not much chance of things getting exciting. I'd be horribly bored, she warned. It sounded just dandy to me.

The ten days of non-stop, long-distance paddling down from Malin, and two nights of big city action, has taken some of the vim and vinegar out of me. I paddle-stroll contentedly down the mile after mile of Leamore Strand: a strip of blue, and then, where the blue waters shallowed a strip of green, and then a wide band of that golden sand. There is a walking path on top of the bank and I am overtaken by cyclists, keep pace with joggers and cruise past solitary figures walking their dogs. Each of these figures appears silhouetted against the skyline, making for a frieze of gentle activity to mirror my own.

I've slipped into Zen reverie. Small details fill all my interest. A hen harrier flap-fluttering over a reed bed. The change in yellows of the sand – banana, kayak, gold, copper, carroty, canary. Terns dipping the water with their beak tips. The sudden bombing splash of a basking fish plunging under my bow. This Indian summer of weather.

I am thinking, too, of the end. Thinking that I might, I really might, make it, whilst at the same time knowing that it's autumn now and bad weather will come soon – a slide into gales and storms. I'm trying to get in as much mileage as I can. Perhaps this is why this stretch of coast isn't dull. I'm using every trick I've learnt over the past three months to get me forward mile by mile. I'm like a bird on a seasonal migration, tuned to movement; sleep and muscles and eating and diversion all subservient to keeping going.

My speed, though, falls off as the tide turns against me and, as a wind springs up from the south and onto my bow,

I can see my pace slowing to that of the dogwalkers. I'm wasting my energies. So I pull up on the beach through a ruffle of light-breaking surf. Two cups of packet soup, rice cakes spread with tomato sauce, a tin of herrings, a handful of plums, oat cakes dipped into honey. I've often wondered at the strange illogicality of keeping the different courses of a meal separate before they go down one's throat, but given such staples you wouldn't want it any other way. Then, with the kayak between me and the wind, I lie down and fall asleep like some basking sea mammal, my slippery skin of rubber drying pleasantly in the sun, twitching one of my flippers every now and again to shake off a fly.

Flann O'Brien, composer of the Dun Laoghaire limerick, is best known for a surreally logical book called *The Third Policeman*. In it he posits the theory of molecular interchange, suggesting that old men who ride bicycles will, through the constant friction between arse and saddle, transmute over time into part-bicycles, whilst their bikes become more human. Proof of this, he claimed, was the way old fellas in Ireland have of leaning up against walls all day, and how a bicycle left outside a pub might just wander away and never be found.

If I added up the hours I'd spent shifting my bottom back and forth in *An Fulmaire*'s bucket seat, then by the same logic I must have become at least part-kayak. And, indeed, coming ashore I tended to lie out immobile until taken to sea again, while the kayak, I sensed, had almost a mind of its own, too, nosing out the strata and pulls of favourable currents, like a horse picking a route across difficult terrain.

I wonder if I stop paddling and let the kayak take charge whether in time we'll just drift back to Cork.

A few hours later, though, having slept out the strongest part of the contrary current, I remount, splash out through the surf and paddle off again towards the lighthouse on Wicklow Head, where I begin picking up a good southerly tide down to Brittas Bay.

It's really noticeable how much less daylight I have each day. By eight I need to start looking for a place to pull in and camp. I amble on, looking at beaches and headlands and strands, and finding none of them quite to my liking, until, almost dark by now, I come upon a crazily steep rescue boat slip. It rises onto a steep headland with a backing of mani-cured lawns and superior but unoccupied holiday houses. There is a golf bunker of thickly matted grass, so I haul all my stuff up to an airy perch and set up camp.

On this stretch of the Irish Sea I'm roughly at the mid-point, where waters flooding in from the north, and up from the Western Approaches in the south, have used up their volume and their energy; tides are less and currents weaker. I've used up a lot of my volume and energy, too; I have become quieter over these past couple of weeks. The voice, the voices, I talked to myself in have become muted, limited to a bit of salty swearing when something surprising and unpleasant happens. And even then, so committed am I now to my forward progress that I synchronise my swearing in time with my paddle stroke so as not to lose breath.

On this coast, in these light offshore breezes, the odours travel further and are as much land-based as marine. Pig farms, hay, silage, crushed flowers, abandoned seabird nests. Some light industry: fertilisers, distilleries, breweries, light machine oil. I've become almost a perfumier, mixing and identifying the molecules. By the time a last tractor burst of diesel dies away behind me, it's close on dusk and I've landed on a small beach of plattery flat stones. There is the gentlest of breezes, a force one, just enough to keep the midges away. I build a fireplace out of the stones, fuel it with driftwood and in the heat of the flames change into dry clothes. Sitting on a couch of my soft kit, I measure out my progress on the map. Holding out the index and little finger on one hand, like a pair of stubby dividers, and pacing them down this flat length of coast, marks off exactly twenty-five miles. That's been the gain from each single day's paddling since leaving Dublin. I've got wary of extrapolating past success into the future, though. Each time this trip has gone well, I've crash-landed, been storm-bound or pinned down by wind.

But the next day looks good, a morning of Mediterranean intensity and azure sky as I set off again, past Cahore Point, paddling parallel to golden beaches and a line of dark pines that could almost be the Riviera of Brigitte Bardot. This long, sun-drenched, super-saturated whiteness of beach seems both familiar and foreign to me. The déjà-vu is maybe an actual 'seen-before', made ghostly only by the stretch of time. We came to Wexford on family holidays before we moved to Ireland to live, so when I was five and six and seven, around the time that the Beatles released *Rubber Soul*, *Revolver* and *Sergeant Pepper*. My memories of the beaches are in the jump-cut edit of a child's memory. A deep hole dug down into the sand filling with water. The red metal blade and wooden handle of a child's spade.

The dull clunk when it struck the small red tin bucket. Cold water, rough towels. The heat of the sun out of the wind. My mother, wearing a headscarf and slacks, reading a book. Biscuits dusted with fine sand. Distant people on the beach. A dog running up, and off again.

But being on the water now I see an oddly deserted world, looking in on the beaches I once looked out from. Schools have gone back and so, in the most summer weather of the summer, there are few people on the sands. A smattering of infants. A black dog running round and around in circles and then off up the beach.

Inland from here are the Wexford Slobs. The word 'slob' – soft mud, but also a flabby person – is from the Irish *slab*. It's one of those Irish words that's slipped into English because it does the job so well. Like *hooley*, for a wild party, and for the crazed actions of hooligans. *Craic* for the fun to be had when partying. 'Galore' from *go leór*, very likely describing the 'sufficiency' of whiskey – itself from *uisce beatha*, 'water of life' – that could well be fuelling the same party. Anyway, there's *slab go leór* here, a sanctuary for ducks, waders and especially white-fronted geese, which arrive in winter in huge numbers from Greenland.

CHAPTER 25

Indian Summer

THE ENTRANCE TO WEXFORD HARBOUR is a real archipelago of sand spits, sand bars and sand islands that grow, shrink and disappear with the ebb and flow of the tide. I arrive at low water, under a burning sun, and it's a faintly surreal scene, a hot flooded desert with huge seals laid out like couched camels. The currents swirl around, the falling tide looking for new, faster ways back to the open sea; but it's not like Dundalk Bay. There's almost no wind, no swell, no danger.

On the spit, Rosslare Point, a few miles into the bay, I spot a sunwashed beach and pull in for a rest. The afternoon flows away, as I doze, half-naked, and then walk the foreshore. It seems a good idea to make camp, even if it is early, and on sand. But, ah what sand – warm and sun-gilded and low-lying. I don't bother with the tent, just lay my sleeping bag in a hollow among the dunes and lie back to stargaze.

Suddenly a rapid succession of flares soar into the air from further along the point. My first thought is that they are fireworks, but then my conscience niggles at me and I thnk how if I was out in the bay and in trouble, blasting all my flares into the air, I'd rather hope that if someone saw them they might do something. So I call 999. A centralised switchboard puts me on to the coastguards. The line is bad and there's the need to spell words out – my name, where I am, that kind of thing. I should use the NATO phonetic alphabet. The Alpha, Bravo, Charlie, Delta one. Except that I can never remember the correct word for each letter. U for Umbrella, but N for what? And Y is? I'm on Rosslare Strand, no, Ross – lare! Oh, hang on, R for ... I want to say R for arse, but it's coming back to me, from those childhood hours with my father in a plane's small cockpit listening to control-tower talk – it's R for Romeo. It doesn't really matter, anyway. Not tonight. They tell me that I'm seeing the Rosslare coastguard training further along the beach, playing with flares and shore rescue kit before going to the pub. I fall asleep composing a 'totally useless phonetic alphabet': A for arbitary, Q for cute, X for extra, K for knitting, ZZZ for snoring.

I am back at sea early the next morning, as the two bulks of ferries depart the ferry terminal; one to France, the other to Wales. Only a few months before, I'd come back from London, on the Fishguard–Rosslare ferry, carrying the paddle I've got in my hand now, and the neoprene longjohn, new then and smelling of rubber, not sweat and salt as now.

Nor slashed at the crotch. From the ferry I'd looked down on the seas, and even though it was May, a warm day, and the basking sharks were massing off the Cork coast, the sea had looked daunting through the heavy glass windows of the ferry's saloon, the waters big and cold and the shore stark and distant.

It feels rather less alien today as I pass a line of offshore windmills cartwheeling very, very slowly in the light breeze. My arms rotate the paddles as mechanically, through the long day, until I land at Kilmore Quay, in the golden light of late afternoon. The shops are still open, and as I walk the supermarket aisles I begin wondering which of my stores might last to the end of the trip. I don't think I need another squeezy bottle of honey. I buy a pound of rice, not two. It's not that I'm so confident, but for four days in a row the weather has been calm and I've done twenty-five miles on the nose each day. At that rate I could be finished within the week.

The forecast is for poor weather again but the actual weather on the quay here is glorious. Some men are shirtless, girls are in short dresses and T-shirts; it's still warm at six as I paddle out, past the Saltee Islands. A local man, Michael Neale, bought the islands in the 1940s and declared himself Prince Michael of the Saltees, complete with throne and coronation. There was talk of erecting a casino, as on a Mohawk reservation in the States, on his principality, but he then got a bit sidetracked by the rabbits, recruiting foxes, ferrets and cats in a vain attempt to wipe them out. On his death he left an edict that all people should be welcome to 'visit and enjoy the islands for unborn generations to come'. Few took him up on his offer.

I end up on a rather less enjoyable island that night – one of the Keeraghs in Ballyteigue Bay. Having left Kilmore late,

I keep paddling after dark, a glorious feeling, rocking as if in a cradle on the wavelets, navigating by sound and the blacker black of the island where it blocks out the lights from shore. I land by torchlight and find an island trashed by nesting birds – a messy ridge of shrubs whitewashed by gull shit, with a narrow band of stones scattered with the corpses of fledglings. Rather fastidiously, I pick the least messy patch of shingle and make camp before being chloroformed into sleep by the stench of rot and guano.

I'd arrived in darkness and I leave in thick fog. It is a long, ten-mile crossing to Hook Head and the forecast is offshore winds rising in strength. Everything is cold and damp as I launch and take compass bearings, paddling off into the eerie, muffling cocoon of the fog. Occasionally it thins enough to give a glimpse of something to back up my compass route – a glimpse of Baginbun Head, the current streaming past a fisherman's buoy, and once a passing Marie Celeste, boom swinging, engine thudding low.

A breeze blows the fog away and Hook Head appears amid wisps of mist and then in dazzling shafts of sunlight, as if stage-lit. The lighthouse on the head is claimed as the oldest in Europe, if not the world. The heavy tower, vaulted within, the base of the present light, with its two bands of black and three of white, was erected in medieval times but monks have been lighting beacon fires here since the fifth century, and for this useful office were left alone by raiding Vikings.

Lighthouses are the symptoms of troubled coastlines, and where Waterford Harbour flushes out between Hook Head and Dunmore East. I'd anticipated troublesome winds, roiling currents and a hard crossing. So the actual ease of slipping across seems deserving of a mid-afternoon breakfast in Dunmore East. Still wetsuit-clad, I walk through the docks, and climb the steep steps up to the town's heart and find a street table in the sun. With a fry-up and coffee, I'm overlooking a world with which all feels right.

There's a group of five ruddy-looking men and women at the next table. They read the semiotics of my clothing and odours. 'You're paddling a-ways, are you?' They are divers. A couple of professionals, three keen amateurs, out here diving on wrecks along the coast.

Wreck-diving on this bit of treacherous, shallow-shoaled coast, they tell me, is a bit like birdwatching on the Slobs: you can't fail for lack of subjects. There are well over a thousand ships on the sea floor in less than a hundred miles of coast. It occurs to me that if the brief century of air travel had produced as many disasters, deaths and capital losses as any hundred years of maritime transport, then flying would have fallen out of favour long ago. The wreck of the *Sea Horse*, alone, in 1816, had meant 360 drowned. The explosion of the *Hindenburg* Zeppelin had killed a mere 35 of the 97 people on board, yet that one incident had brought an end to all serious development of airship travel. But we have been seafarers as a species for far longer than almost any other human activity and we're somehow accepting of the risks.

The divers and I begin talking about risk very quickly. They reckon my trip is tough, not because they know the specific dangers and difficulties but because they know the sea. I counter that, whenever I have dived with tanks, as opposed to snorkelling, I've felt the experience to be so alien that I could never relax fully. They half agree: there is a scatter of anecdote about wrecks and accidents, of going too deep or getting disorientated in caves or poor visibility. But the most thoughtful and experienced of them adds, 'But it's a kind of freedom ... life is very safe now, even in Ireland, and it's less interesting. I see Germans and Dutch here on cycling holidays and I think, you poor feckers, you're twenty years too late. They're just hunted along busy roads by huge SUVs and Jeeps. The only road trip you can do in Ireland today is go to sea. You have to go to the edge now to find adventure.'

He is articulating something that I've always felt about my trip. I've gone to sea, gone around the edge of Ireland, because subconsciously I've realised that the Ireland I want to find – and the Ireland of my childhood – has been pushed away from the heart of things. On an island, those on the run always end up on the shore, or out at sea. I have been on the run, seeking the myths, the simplicity, the people, the dangers, the challenges that I need. Like the divers, I'm a throwback to earlier, simpler and in some ways riskier times.

Off Brownstone Head, in 1834, a young great auk was taken alive. As a species, the 'marine dodo' was massive, hatchet-beaked, flightless, easily captured and good to eat. At one time there had been tens of thousands of great auks, but sailors and coastal communities had already made them rare early in the nineteenth century; so rare that scientists, realising the bird's imminent extinction, commissioned fishermen to kill specimens for their collections. The

Waterford great auk was captured in May and passed from hand to hand, still alive, fed on potatoes, milk and trout, until it died the following September. A Dr Burkitt gave the skin to Trinity College and, demonstrating just how rare the birds already were, was awarded the immense amount of £50 as an annual 'Great Auk Pension' in gratitude. A decade later the great auk was officially declared extinct when the last breeding pair were both killed, on the Icelandic coast, to provide skins 'for science'. The smaller little auk survives still, but rarely visits Ireland. And who can blame them? A midden unearthed in the Tramore dunes, just inland from where I'm heading across Tramore Bay, contained the bones of thousands of great auks taken as food.

The great auk was known to those same scientists who preferred a dead bird in the hand to a live pair at sea as *Pinguinus impennis*, perhaps for its snowy cheek blaze in a black face. The great auk was the original pen-guin ('white head' as in Winn), only to be replaced after extinction when other penguins were discovered in the southern hemisphere. To add a touch of pathos to this sorry story, the great auk was a long-lived bird and, long after it became extinct as a breeding species, individuals must have continued to float alone around the world. The Waterford great auk, even if it had remained free, would probably not have come across another auk in its lifetime.

On Great Newton Head I pick out three tall columns. On the central one, there is a sculpture of some kind which I dip inland to see. It is a large metal statue of a sailor in white britches, blue coat and red ganzey, one arm outflung and pointing out to sea. Later I discover that it was commissioned by Lloyd's of London, after the tragic wreck of the *Sea Horse*, as an indicator to ships that they should keep away from this shallow coast. I can't be the first to have been drawn into the cliff face to receive this message.

The current swirling along the head, under the pointing sailor, has taken me onto the Copper Coast, which today lives up to its name. As the sun disappears over Ireland, it lights up a reflected evening of burnished seas, looking not so much like Ireland as Bali, or Acapulco. And there is even a huge shoal of mackerel turning the wavelets solid and shimmering and bumping against my paddle blades.

The beach I land on is crisp and ticking with pebbles moving against each other. Normal sounds and colours are heightened in this perfect evening. The fire that I light crackles and pops, as the sparks from the salt-soaked shore-wood drift up into the star-filled night.

The next day opens with a perfect Indian summer dawn, the rising sun hitting the beach as I pack and set off. By midday, though, it has reverted to grey autumn drizzle and wind. But I'm still making good progress and even the long, choppy waves out of Dungarvan Harbour barely disturb my paddle strokes. Helvick Head is followed by Mine Head, and a dusk stop on a patch of shingle under a cliff, sheltering my fire from the wind behind a buttress of rock, and falling asleep almost before I'd eaten.

Starting again at dawn the next morning, my automatic routine brings me back to Robert Louis Stevenson's lament about his brain 'turning like fly-wheels'. I fear that this describes my state perfectly as I paddle across Youghal Bay, and then realise, halfway across, that I'm back in County Cork. By some counts I am home. But then again Cork is the biggest county in Ireland, and I'd started off from its far side. I am on familiar territory, though, as I paddle around the next headland and into Ballycotton Bay and an hour later surf a big breaking swell into Ballycotton Harbour and come to rest behind the breakwater.

———•———

There is a menagerie of heavy machinery caged on Ballycotton's quayside: diggers, cranes and trucks, stilled after a day expanding and rebuilding the harbour walls. I pull up on the slip below the lifeboat station and the coxswain, Ian Sheridan, helps me drag the loaded kayak up the slip to the station door – 'It'll be safer here.' He shows me to the shower room, says he is off to put the kettle on and leaves me to scrub and shave.

I emerge into the fascinating workings of a lifeboat station: the immersion suits, helmets, boots, lifejackets, labelled with names, three women amongst them. I find Ian in the operations room; he's been going over the chart and checking out weather forecasts. He reckons I have just sixty miles to get to the end of my trip, and two if not three days of settled weather coming in. We sip from our mugs, looking out across the harbour, in the centre of which sits the Trent class lifeboat. We don't have to talk for long to find people we know in common around the coast. Though he is from Howth himself, this finding of names and a common ground makes me feel that I've arrived back home. We talk about the practicalities of lifeboat rescue. About the gone-wrong drugs drops, the big storms, sick and dying crew members on working boats, and – a regular subject of all the lifeboat crewmen – ungrateful rescuees.

Ian tells me that he knows of crews who, whenever they get a call out for a jet-skier in trouble, call up the police to have them waiting on shore because they've had so much trouble. The jet-skiers treat the lifeboat like the AA. You've just saved their life, and risked your own, and they get mad because their jet-ski's been damaged. Now, he tells me, the problem is kitesurfers blown out to sea. You go to pick them up and there's the sail and all those thin lines, flapping around still in the wind, and we've had lads getting their hands cut to the bone, fingers off even, from the strings. They're like cheese wire – so now it's just cut 'em loose. First thing.

I am getting an idea about the unspoken hierarchy of RNLI rescues. The crews are famously non-judgmental, they provide a service funded by donations, with crew risking their lives on a voluntary basis for all in peril on the seas, even when caused by crass stupidity or overweening arrogance. But how can they not consider professional fishermen and shipping crew caught in storms out at work to be more worthy of rescue than some eejit who's bought a surfboard, a sit-on-top kayak, a jet-ski or a yacht and just set off to sea expecting it to be like land, and then, when they found it wasn't like land at all, expecting to be picked up, along with their expensive playthings? I can see the two worlds. And I know that I've been tightrope walking between them. It would have been so easy for my trip to have gone wrong, for me to have made a mistake – or, rather, a far worse mistake than the many that I had made – and then to have ended up being pulled out of the water. Or to have become a dead body fished out of the water. I feel now how lucky I am to be here after nine hundred miles and more of paddling.

At dark I find a chink in the rocks on a shingle beach, just above high-water mark. There are lines of debris in layers back to the cliff edge. It seems I've found the 'miscellaneous' beach where all the oddities floating on the seas that don't have their specific shoreline end up. Shoe soles, three toothbrushes, tangles of blue string, cod-egg cases, the smallest size of aerosol can and a drift of Bic lighters. There are more than enough twigs for cooking and I bundle extra into a bag for the next few days. There is an atavistic joy in beachcombing, finding the perfect piece of flat, eroded wood to adopt as a chopping board, the right stones to make a hearth for the fire, heavy logs to tie the tent guy ropes to where I've erected it right on the tide line.

CHAPTER 26

Tunnel's End

I F THE AMOUNT OF FLOTSAM is indication that I am on the edge of the ocean again, so is my view to the south-west, along the bottom edge of Ireland, giving me both the last red glow of the sunset and the morning sunrise. There is an Atlantic swell, too, coming up almost to my tent, but giving me the luxury of only having a few steps to drag the loaded kayak to launch it. I've studied the charts and the tide tables and the tidal diamonds by firelight and set my alarm for five in the morning to catch the current that runs westwards. It duly helps me along and, as the tide ebbs, I hit Power Head at the entrance to Cork Harbour.

The city lies at the head of a winding estuary, behind one of Europe's largest natural harbours. For five or six years

I had a house-top flat by the port, looking out over cargo boats coming into the centre of the city to unload timber or take off grain or cattle. One night a killer whale swam up the quays and at two in the morning I stood on a bridge watching its fin slicing the water in circles in the pools of streetlight.

Inside Cork Harbour is Cobh island – Queenstown, as it was then – the *Titanic*'s last port of call. Large ships still head in and out of the harbour, but after Belfast, Dublin and Waterford I've become blasé about these busy sea roads and about the currents that stream in and out of these inshore bodies of water. I straight-line across from Power Head to Roberts Cove, past a flotilla of tugs and harbour boats chugging out to welcome a destroyer.

From Roberts Cove west to Kinsale I am in very famil-iar waters, on a coast that I'd kayaked, climbed, walked and swum. For two summers in the early 1980s I worked at the outdoor centre in Oysterhaven and I find I can still recognise actual rocks slipping past. I tick off the entrances to hidden caves, remember where a peregrine pair had nested and recall pulling tens of mackerel out on just such a calm, sunny September day as this. The memories intensify as I catch sight of the Sovereign Islands. I'd kayaked out and and round their double peaks many a time in a tight-fitting river kayak; once I'd tied on a sleeping bag and water bottle and landed on the rocks, hauled the kayak up onto a ledge and then tried sleep-ing amongst the chorusing babble of shags, gulls and cormorants. That was a mini-pilgrimage, an attempt to experience on those guano-washed rocks the solitude of Ireland's offshore monks. I remember well both the acrid stink that made it hard for me to drift off and the sharp peck on my nose from a curious shag that woke me in the half light of dawn.

I paddle up to the Oysterhaven Centre to say hello to my old friends Oliver and Kate, who still run the place. This is all a bit of a root around my past, a trip down memory estuary. For months I had more or less lived on this beach, teaching people to windsurf, and there are school groups here today, kitted out in wetsuits and buoyancy aids and helmets, chivvied on by an energetic cadre of instructors. Not much has changed. The haul across the strand to the centre is a familiar one, especially when hungry and with damp clothing. If my imaginings about making sea trips have been lit by books read in the Abbey Theatre's fly-loft, it was my months on and in the water in all weathers when I was at Oysterhaven that gave me some sea sense.

I can measure my times here by small remnants of my work, such as the murals of seabirds and dolphins around the cafe walls. I guess, too, that a few of the phrases used by the instructors today, as they talk pupils through the act of uphauling the sails and stepping round the front of the mast and climbing back on board again when they've over-balanced into the water, have been passed by tradition from when Oliver and I first tried to codify the whole experience of what was – twenty-five years ago now – the new sport of windsurfing.

With Oliver and Kate, we settle, once the pleasure of greeting allows, into the comforts of catching up. Oliver, who has recently returned from sailing the Atlantic, knows more than enough of the sea – and about me – to understand what these last three months must have been like. Although they are gratifyingly impressed, I find myself loath to squander this precious shore leave on purely sea matters. Instead, we talk about mutual friends, each name sparking stories and updates, and leading onto other names and other news. Inevitably, they both want to know about Erika and my plans after reaching Reen. I, in turn, want to hear about their two children and their plans for the centre. The trip no longer seems like a discreet entity – to be started, done and finished – and more a part of my ongoing life.

But of course this journey, the circumnavigation, does have a geographic end, at least. And I'm getting very close to it. First, though, there remains the Old Head of Kinsale – a headland that pokes so far into the sea that it creates infamous rips and currents.

Oliver walks me to the shore and watches as I paddle out of Oysterhaven. I'm planning to get to 'this' side of the Old Head, camp for the night, and then round it in the morning. But fuelled by pizza, bean salad and coffee, and carried by favourable currents, I find myself closing on the head with enough evening light to continue. It is calm enough to keep going, or more exciting still to paddle into the eponymous Hole Open Bay and see if I can make my way through the long, dark tunnel that is the 'open hole'.

The Old Head, at its narrowest, has three natural tunnels that cut right through to the other side of the headland. If I go through I'll save the time and distance of going around the head and avoid the rip tides and rough water. But it's a frightening prospect. Paddling from near darkness into a fully dark tunnel several hundred yards long is bad enough, but if a rogue swell pulses through the low-roofed cavern, then I could find myself thrown at and crushed against the rock. Just the thought of drowning in a subterrranean blackness terrifies me but, even putting aside this fear, there's still the problem of which of the three tunnel entrances is the right one to take. They're lined up next to each other, slicing back under the cliff edge, and I know that only one is clear the whole way through and safe. Of the others, I've heard, one becomes a dead end far into the rock, while the other is choked with boulders halfway through. What I can't recall is which tunnel is which. I don't fancy getting halfway into a tunnel and finding myself aground in the dark and having to Braille my way out.

It's coming on for night now and I'm feeling that I have no choice. I have to go through the tunnel or risk losing another day. It all feels a bit mythic, like an ancient trial: the foolish hero takes on the Gods to enter Hades, and the first thing he has to do is choose between three holes in the ground. I'm hoping that perhaps a friendly dolphin will pop up to guide me, preferably one that always tells the truth. But in its absence, I paddle into the one where I can – literally – see light at the end of the tunnel.

The walls glisten and then grow darker until I'm paddling in pitch blackness, save for the dull small patch of light far ahead. The swoosh of water gurgles and belches around and under me and I can hear it echoing off unseen chambers running into the bowels of the headland. The swell lifts me up and down, and slaps back off rock walls and totters the boat. There is a startling surprise when the paddle blade hits something only half solid under me in the water ... thick weed on a rock, I imagine, and hope. But the patch of light is growing and it's obviously big enough for me to go through. Indeed, amply so. It's allowing light back into the tunnel and I can see the glimmer of water on the rock walls, and a light luminescent glow from the water itself. A few more paddle strokes and a helpful surge of water and I pop out like a grinning champagne cork on the western side of the head. I'm through and out and paddling west.

●━━━●

I'm also paddling back even further into my past. This is the coastline where I spent most of my boyhood years. I recognise tiny little cliffs, barely ten metres high, that I froze on when first climbing along the foreshore as a child, and then grew to know as well as a path from repeated use. I recognise, from this unfamiliar angle, the small beach where I found a storm-beaten, dying shag that I carried home dead and then practised my taxidermy on. Now I am passing the ledge where for summer after summer I'd dive into a cold pool, from which a narrow strait led out to the sea. I feel again the 'heart going across me' when, as I swam into the cave at the back of the pool, there had been a sudden explosion and a seal crashed into the water and bolted for the sea, passing me in a cloud of bubbles.

The same ledge was the place where I brought friends when I'd returned home after journeys, carrying rugs and bottles of wine on moonlit nights to watch the silvery path of light across the sea towards the low surf-washed Barrel Rocks far out from the coast. It had become 'my' place for many years. But I hadn't visited it in decades and I was surprised to find how fresh it was in my mind.

I land in Howe Strand, not on the beach, where I can see the last embers of a fire and a group of dark figures in the gloom, but on a small dip in the rocks below a ruined boathouse on the edge of the bay. This had been our family beach, where we'd come after haymaking to net prawns, and swim in the cold waters and to picnic. I pile everything on a tiny patch of grass above the rocks and start making camp, and just as I have the kettle lit and am noting that there is a real September chill in the air, there's a flash of torch, and Tash – whom I'd phoned earlier in the day – comes out along the rocks to welcome me with an apple and berry pie. We sit and drink tea, and talk about that odd time on Mweenish, before I walk her back across the rocks to the beach and onto the road leading to her family house behind the strand.

Heading back to my camp I am surprised to find how after four decades my feet and hands still remember every rockpool and handhold, so that I jump and scramble through the darkness with the confidence and familiarity of someone walking a path to their front door. So many of the places around Ireland that I knew from the past have been barely recognisable when I've landed at them this time around. Some places I'd recognised in the way that I might have recognised past girlfriends who'd grown away from me and reinvented themselves. So it is strange to find that this corner of Ireland that I had known longest has changed least. And that gives me the pleasing illusion that I've not changed so much, either.

I wake to grey before realising that it is gloomy because it is barely dawn rather than bad weather. I'm packing up the last of the kit when Tash comes over the rocks again, with a large Thermos of coffee. As we sip from mugs, a pod of porpoise undulates up and down through the waves and further out we spot dolphins jumping clear of the water. I push off from the small beach to join them.

●━━━●

I cross the entrance to Courtmacsherry Bay and then straight-line past Horse Rock out to the Seven Heads. I can look up the bay to Harbour View, up beyond which is the village of Kilbrittain, and the castle-house where our family had lived. It had been sold after my father's death and I hadn't been there in twenty years. Deep inside the bay, behind the sand dunes of Harbour View, is the stream where, all those years ago, I'd pushed out the heavy plywood kayak and been pulled out by the current. The previous evening I'd thought that maybe I'd paddle into the bay head and up the estuary to the Kilbrittain stream and actually kayak on the waters where I'd spent so many days fishing and rafting and wading and dreaming and bird-watching. I'd paddle back into my childhood. It would be a kind of temporal circumnavigation, as if by travelling right around Ireland, I would bring together my older and younger selves.

But now, out at sea, it feels daft to think of fooling around with time travel, interrupting the focus on getting this trip done. The early morning shipping forecast had been for poor weather coming in, and out at sea the waters are grey and big; loose, sloppy waves are lifting the kayak high and slapping up spray from the bow. I struggle on past Horse Rock – a black chunk of rock that my father told me was named from a ship wrecked with stranded horses on it and which were kept alive by men rowing out bales of hay to them. Then, around the Seven Heads, the wind died and gusted up in turn, making the sea hard and lumpy. Made bold by the thousand miles behind me I cut straight across the bay to Galley Head, taking me far offshore in the big Atlantic swell. When I'd left Castletownshend three months before, turning west, it was Galley Head that I saw far to the east, dropping out of sight behind High and Low Islands, which in turn fell behind Skiddy. If the trip was successful, I'd thought to myself then, with an air of unreality, I'd come up on Galley Head and then High and Low Islands and then Skiddy in reverse order. And now I am off Galley Head and kayaking over a reef of rocks swilled by breaking surf.

A long time ago I'd stopped looking for items of furniture to compare the size of the waves, too. They had become waves the size of waves. Perhaps I'd learnt a little about paddling in the past months. And about fear and dread, too. How did I measure them before? In body parts, perhaps? Sunken heart, breathlessness, headaches, dry mouth and the kicked stomach feeling. Now I have a more accurate external handle on them, and fear is something I react to with some purpose. So today I'm still adrenalin pumped, afraid, going over the reef as the waves rush up under me and tumble the kayak along, but I can use the adrenalin to paddle harder and smarter. If I go over, I can use the fear to roll me back up again. And if I can't roll – I haven't had a chance to practise my rolling on all this trip, so it's probably still a long way from bomb-proof – then I can use the fear to swim to shore. Or do whatever it takes to survive.

I might have paddled to Reen and ended the circumnavigation that afternoon. But with the end in sight I don't want to finish. There is no pressure. Not knowing when I'd arrive, I haven't asked anyone to meet me on the beach, so I'm free to dawdle and to savour the last moments. I cross over to Rabbit Island and make camp on my own little isle, setting up my tent between the two ruined houses on the inland side. Walking to the stony beach, I collect driftwood and look across to High and Low Islands, and then beyond them at the sea rolling out to the horizon.

For supper I cook up the most luxurious of the ingredients left in my stores into a haute cuisine slop. The tin of tuna in *oil*, carried for emergencies since Malin Head! The last three spoons of peanut butter scraped from the jar. All the rice that is left. Two packets of soup stirred in. Three onions chopped up on the board I'd found on the beach beyond Ballycotton. It is a fine example of stew-making, and edible even without whiskey. I sit outside the tent with a mug of tea looking up at the sky and the stars, listening to the waves slapping on the shingle beach.

Later in my tent I listen to the weather forecast, an academic exercise, as pretty much whatever it promises I'll be able to get back to Reen in the morning. Or the afternoon. Or at the very worst in a day or two. The prediction is for rising winds the next day. But for the first time in three months I'm relaxed. Tides and currents and winds and waves only have another hour or two's hold over me before I return to land ways and solar time.

Oddly, I've given no thought as to how my life will proceed when I've got round Ireland. Perhaps in the end it has all happened too quickly. It has taken me two and a half months to paddle the first five hundred miles up the west coast from the Mizen Head to Malin Head, and then only two and a half weeks to cover the other five hundred back from Malin to Mizen. Which was mostly the weather, I tell myself, but also about competence, and commitment. And maybe trips just speed up and get faster and faster as they become more familiar. Or is that just life?

The voyage, now it is almost over, seems clearer to me. There's something about kayaking that I'll always enjoy. The simplicity of it. The ease of carrying a kayak down to a shore and just pushing off. The meditative pace. The adrenalin rush of having one's body, strength and commitment tested to their limits. The consolation of the natural world – the seabirds and dolphins, the landscape and, yes, the weather too. But I didn't have to go a thousand miles to discover all these things. A hundred would have done.

I had started out, though, with an idea that this journey might have a deeper impact; might allow me to feel more connected with Ireland, provide another stamp to my Irishness, as it were. Surprisingly I've found this hasn't been so important. In all those hours peering through the rain trying to get my bearings from the shore, the nights spent sleeping on islands and headlands and beaches, the evenings of talk and music and pubs, I realise that my Irishness isn't questioned. That it runs through my life as a fine but strong strand, strengthened by the threads of all my other experiences. I am Irish by upbringing, by choice and partly by ancestry, but I am a traveller, too. I don't need to own a part of the land, nor even return to Ireland that often. But when I do come back from wherever I go off to on a journey, then, like my coming landfall at Reen, I know that I will be coming home.

The one thing the journey has never been about is records. I smile whenever people asked if I was trying to break a record in paddling the thousand miles around Ireland's coastline. I've surely made the slowest circumnavigation ever – a record of sorts. But I do have a sense of joining a group of initiates. As I've paddled around, I've spent a lot of bad weather time in internet cafes and have rather obsessively researched how many kayakers have gone around Ireland ahead of me. Before I'd set out, I'd reckoned about twenty, but as more and more paddlers come onto my radar I need to double that figure. Still, by contrast, some 448 people have been into space, and close on 1,400 have stood on top of Everest, and in the case of every space voyager, and most of those who have trod Everest's summit, there were back-up teams to put them there. While everyone who's paddled round Ireland has merely pushed off at some point around the circle, paddled themselves forwards for a month or two or – ahem – three, and then climbed out of their little craft back at the point where they started. We could fit the whole reunion party of round-Ireland-paddlers into Dick Mack's in Dingle and still have room for a few musicians and passers-by.

This, as I lie in the cold night air, in silence except for the slap of waves on the rocks and a distant oystercatcher's trilling, seems a pretty good idea.

●——●

The next morning retains a distinct chill and there's not much to jump-start my day: only a handful of oatmeal and a couple of wrinkled apples left to cook up, and enough instant coffee for a couple of cups. But then the sun comes up. So up, indeed, that when I finally push off it is, for the first time on the trip, without my jacket and with bare arms.

There is no need to rush now. I scull away from Rabbit Island, out to sea, to High and Low Islands, where I stop to drift amongst their rocks. I sing a few verses of Elvis Presley's 'Love Me Tender' – a song that had always drawn the more discerning seals of West Cork when Elizabeth and I had paddled out here – and, as if on call, heads pop up all around me. Once again, the seal of approval, I chortle to myself. I am back talking aloud, making terrible puns, and in seal voices again. The bad weather isn't in yet and, as I head across to Castlehaven, ticking off tiny landmarks, I pause to drift for long minutes, feeling the sun on my skin, licking the salt off my lips, hearing the calling of the gulls, watching a comorant pop to the surface and snake back down into the depths again.

Just as I turn into Castlehaven and head inland towards Reen, a fulmar – a late season bird, still flying touch-and-go along the cliffs before heading out to sea for the winter – soars in above me. I've ended up like a seabird, drifting, circling, pushed and pulled by the weathers and by my appetites and the mere energy of being alive. The winds and seas that I've so often cursed have carried me. I'd set off to pit myself against nature and time and instead I've learnt to flow with the rhythms and tempo of the moon, and to move with the tides and the seasons. This is what life entails, really: just keeping going, and enjoying keeping going. Now that I've finished a summer's kayaking, I'll apply this to the next thing – with all the unexpected joys and unforeseen challenges, and nothing to do but keep going. This seems simple. Pleasing, indeed.

As the fulmar passes, I wonder if this same bird had watched me leave back in June and whether we'd greeted each other then as I paddled west, and now was thinking, *Oh, here he comes again.* That was the homecoming I wanted. *Hey! Morning ... how's it going?* The fulmar drifts on, and I drive *An Fulmaire* shorewards and slip back onto league at Reen, there is a crunching of sand and stones under the kayak's bow, and I get out. I've pulled off my simplistic formula for safe seafaring – made one landfall for every time I'd gone out to sea.

Nobody is about. Not even a stranger. I pull all the gear out – most of what I'd started with, the tin whistles amongst the unused ballast that had gone all the way round Ireland for no purpose – and bundle it into bags. Then I hoist *An Fulmaire* up onto Jim's kayak rack and phone Erika's number in Sweden. We talk for a few minutes and then I call a taxi. Within an hour I'll be having a late breakfast in Skibbereen.

Waiting for the taxi in my shore clothes, in my walking-away-to-land shoes, my eyes linger contentedly on the dried seedheads in the grass, and the grains of sand. On the far shore a little egret stalks along the muddy bank, a dazzling flash of white.

●━━━●

When the taxi arrives, bumping over the stones and ruts to the end of the spit, I load my several big bags into the boot, and climb into the passenger seat.

'You were out canoeing, were you? Was it the Baltimore side or Glandore you left from?'

'No, I left from the spit at Reen, from just where you picked me up.'

The amount of kit and my weathered face, stubble and aroma of the sea don't seem to trouble the driver's curiosity. 'Ah, you were just out rowing around for the morning, were you, out around the bays and the islands for a bit? A little round-trip, and back for lunch?'

I nod.

'Well, God knows, you picked the right day for it. Sure, if you'd been out canoeing any other time this bloody summer, you'd have been drowned with the rain or blown to America by the wind. But that's a fine bit of sunshine now.'

Acknowledgments

Paddling alone around Ireland is a solitary task – but one which would have been a whole lot tougher without so much generous advice, hospitality, encouragement and companionship. I'm hugely grateful to all of those below who, in all kinds of ways, kept me going.

The paddlers first: Jim Kennedy, champion endurance kayaker and Zen-calm guide of Atlantic Sea Kayaking in West Cork, who advised me on both the trip and the kayak; Mick O'Meara, round-Ireland paddler, who gave first-hand advice on tides and currents; Sam Crowley, who paddled with me among the basking sharks; and Elizabeth Pisani, who set out with me the first time.

Friends en route were vital: Tash Pike provided coffee, crosswords, cake and company at several points; Melanie De Blank sent one of her famed 'Dundee cakes for expeditions'; Kate, Paul, Alex and my wonderful god-daughter, Holly Cawte, nearly derailed the trip with hospitality on Sheep's Head; Rory Allan almost tempted me to stop at Ballymaloe House; and Oliver and Kate, at the Oysterhaven Centre, welcomed me back into familiar waters. Above all, Erika Willners was a constant companion on the voyage through letters, texts and thoughts, then had to relive it all again whilst I wrote the book's first draft in Åre, Sweden. Her encouragement and belief got me through.

Impossible not to mention pubs and music, too. I have fond memories of sessions with Josephine, Nancy, Mark, Tríona, Mila, Andy and Rob, Mick and the rest of Glór, and Franziska and Elizabeth in Dick Mack's in Dingle; Kings in Clifden; the Crossroads on Malin Head; and of course the Jolly Roger on Sherkin. And for welcome meals, beds and showers, thanks to: the Rainbow Hostel in Dingle; Rodney and Margaret's Sandrock Hostel on Malin Head; Allain and Liz English in Brown's Bay; Seamas and Ann Caulfield at Belderg; and Brendan, Pat and Sheila on Garron Point. Thanks also to the crew of the *Kaparda*.

Taff and Mick of Clifden Lifeboat, Manus, Patrick and Pat at Malin Coastguard, and Ian Sheridan at Ballycotton RNLI station must all have feared that I was only a flare away from putting our relationship onto a professional basis, but were big-hearted enough to give me coastal and weather information and wave me on my way.

Writing *Paddle* was an even more peripatetic activity than kayaking around Ireland. Many, many thanks to David Flower, and Marina, for the use of their house in Sanlúcar de Guadiana, where in two long stays the bulk of *Paddle* was written. David's input as a critic was also much appreciated, not least because in the 1980s he and I paddled the length of the Danube River. Thanks also, in Sanlúcar, to Robert Black and the Journeymen for musical distractions, and to Robin and Sue. For generous hospitality in Dublin, thanks to David Korowicz and Jonathan Korowicz; in London to Sophie Campbell, a friend since the 'night of shooting stars in Iran'; in Oxfordshire to Arabee and James Campbell; in Devon to Isobel Barnes – and Alick and Sally Barnes. Thanks also to Margaret and Patrick Kelly on Lambay Island, where I wrote the second draft, and Chris and Ana Stewart in Andalusia, who lent me their farm to finish the book.

My sister, Minta Winn, provided a place to write for long periods, allowing me to show my nephew Rupert the joys and rewards of a freelance writer's life; he's decided to do engineering. My mother, Betty Winn, probably thought she'd misheard me when I said 'paddle' and assumed I'd meant 'saddle' as the theme for my trip. All her experiences of and on the sea with my father were uncomfortable, and often dangerous, yet at no point did she suggest that kayaking around Ireland was daft.

I have been as lucky in my publishers and editors, as I was unlucky with the summer's weather for the voyage. Not only did Nat Jansz and Mark Ellingham think *Paddle* worth commissioning, but they then used tact, enthusiasm and firmness to get me to bring the book from first draft through to finished manuscript, whilst remaining good friends. And lastly, the book has benefited hugely from Nikky Twyman's proofreading. Thanks all.